Corporate Sustainability Management

Businesses around the world are increasingly turning to an exciting new branch of management known as corporate sustainability management (CSM) to help them better understand and manage their non-financial performance. Indeed, what we are witnessing is nothing less than the birth of a new management function.

The main pillar of CSM is the triple bottom line (TBL), which has been successful as an organizing principle but a disappointment in practice. This is largely due to the absence of 'sustainability context' in related measurement, management and reporting efforts, when, for example, the monitoring of a company's use of freshwater resources fails to take the size of related supplies into account.

This book is the first to introduce a systematic means of including context in sustainability management and doing effective CSM. After making the case for why context matters, the book explains how to do context-based CSM by providing a stepwise, cyclical blueprint for how to practice CSM in any organization. This includes a template for context-based metrics compatible with the Global Reporting Initiative (GRI), as well as specific examples of metrics for each of the triple bottom lines.

Practical examples of best practices are presented throughout, while addressing such challenging issues as how organizations can measure performance against context-based standards in cases where consensus for such standards does not yet exist. Appendices include tools for developing and applying context-based metrics, as well as case studies taken from the practice of context-based CSM at two companies in the United States.

This guide is the essential tool for business and organizational leaders in all sectors committed to improving their sustainability performance, with a particular emphasis on measurement, management and reporting.

Mark W. McElroy, PhD, is Founder and Executive Director at the Center for Sustainable Organizations, Vermont, USA and creator of the Social Footprint Method.

Jo M.L. van Engelen, MSc, PhD, is Chaired Professor of Integrated Sustainable Solutions, Delft University of Technology, The Netherlands.

About the Cover

The cover illustration is taken from *Sylvicultura Oeconomica* (Von Carlowitz, 1713), in which the concepts of *sustainability* and *sustainability management* were first introduced. The scene depicts a procedure for cutting down seed trees whose lower trunks have become so hard, they are impervious to saws and axes and must be taken down from an elevated level.

Mark W. McElroy, PhD

Mark W. McElroy is an accomplished researcher, developer, consultant and trainer in the area of tools, methods and metrics for measuring, managing and reporting the sustainability performance of organizations. He is the founder and Executive Director at the Center for Sustainable Organizations in Thetford Center, Vermont, and a leading advocate and practitioner of context-based sustainability. Dr. McElroy is also the creator of the *Social Footprint Method*, a context-based system for measuring and reporting the social sustainability performance of organizations. He is a veteran of management consulting, including time spent at Price Waterhouse, KPMG Peat Marwick and Deloitte Consulting where he led the Center for Sustainability Performance in Boston, Massachusetts.

© 2011 Images Plus Photography

Jo M.L. van Engelen, MSc, PhD

Jo van Engelen is an experienced scientist and has held top-level management positions at several companies throughout his career. He has been a full professor since 1991 at the University of Groningen (where he also is a research fellow), and since 2010 has been at Delft University of Technology serving as chair of Integrated Sustainable Solutions. In his academic career, he has authored/co-authored five books and more than 140 scientific papers, and presented more than 200 leading lectures around the world. In his business career, he has served full terms on two Executive Boards in an international context and served or serves on more than 10 supervisory boards (including for publicly-traded companies).

Photo by Sjaak Ramakers

Corporate Sustainability Management

The Art and Science of Managing Non-financial Performance

Mark W. McElroy and Jo M.L. van Engelen

publishing for a sustainable future
LONDON AND NEW YORK

First published 2012
by Earthscan
2 Park Square, Milton Park, Abingdon, Oxon OX14 4RN

Simultaneously published in the USA and Canada
by Earthscan
711 Third Avenue, New York, NY 10017

Earthscan is an imprint of the Taylor & Francis Group, an informa business

British Library Cataloguing in Publication Data
A catalogue record for this book is available from the British Library

Library of Congress Cataloging in Publication Data
McElroy, Mark W.
    Corporate sustainability management : the art and science of managing
non-financial performance / Mark W. McElroy and Jo van Engelen.
        p. cm.
    Includes bibliographical references and index.
    1. Management–Environmental aspects. 2. Corporations–Environmental
aspects. 3. Social responsibility of business. I. Engelen, Jo van. II. Title.
    HD30.255.M365 2011
    658.4'083–dc22
                                2011013841

ISBN: 978-1-84407-911-7 (hbk)
ISBN: 978-0-203-12181-8 (ebk)

Typeset in Bembo
by Taylor & Francis Books

WITHDRAWN
UTSA LIBRARIES

Printed and bound in the United States of America
by Edwards Brothers, Inc, Lillington, NC

Contents

List of Tables and Figures   vii
List of Acronyms   ix
Foreword by Mathis Wackernagel   x
Acknowledgements   xii

Introduction   1

Setting the context   1
Project background   3
Chapter summaries   4

1   Context-based sustainability   8

A brief history of context   8
The relevance of capital theory   18
Daly's rules   27
The triple bottom line   29
A modern-day theory of practice for CSM   31
Sustainability context   39
Summary: context-based sustainability   43

**2   Key issues and practice implications of context-based
sustainability**   46

How CBS interacts with core business processes and cycles   46
How CBS relates to measurement and reporting   55
GRI and the prevalence of context-free sustainability   75
Summary: key issues and practice implications of CBS   82

3 How to do CSM 90

Introduction 90
A case study in CBS: Cabot Creamery Cooperative 92
A methodology for practitioners – the CSM cycle 94
Practicing the cycle 99
Stakeholder engagement 138
Summary: how to do CSM 140

4 Summary and conclusions 145

General summary of context-based sustainability (CBS) 145
Mini-cases of CBS in action 150
General conclusions 152
Looking ahead 157
Some closing words 166

Appendix A: Cabot Creamery Cooperative's approach to sustainability 169

Appendix B: Areas of Impact Checklist 176

Appendix C: Formulating duties and obligations at Cabot Creamery Cooperative 182

Appendix D: Corporate Water Gauge® 205

Appendix E: 2007 Water Sustainability Report at the Cabot Creamery 214

Glossary 220
References 226
Index 231

List of Tables and Figures

Tables

2.1	Examples of social sub-bottom lines	58
2.2	The four bottom lines and their capitals	58
2.3	The capital/stakeholder basis of performance	60
3.1	Social bottom line template	113
3.2	Economic bottom line template	113
3.3	Environmental bottom line template	114
3.4	Some sustainability standards at Cabot	115
3.5	Some sustainability metrics at Cabot	116
3.6	Formulating sustainability quotients at Cabot	118
3.7	Some binary and analog metrics at Cabot	119
3.8	Computing sustainability bottom lines	134
4.1A	Mini-cases of CBS in action	150
4.1B	Mini-cases of CBS in action	151

Figures

1.1	Vital capitals and human well-being	36
1.2	The logic of determining context	39
2.1	Context-based sustainability metrics	66
2.2	Sustainability performance scales	67
3.1	Scope of CSM program at Cabot	94
3.2	Organizational impacts on vital capitals	96
3.3	The (double-loop) CSM cycle	98
3.4	Context-based sustainability metrics	117
3.5	Context-based environmental metrics	120

3.6	Context-based social and economic metrics	121
3.7	Sustainability performance scales	132
3.8	The (double-loop) CSM cycle (enhanced)	138
A.1	The four bottom lines and their capitals	171
C.1	WRE profiles of industrial CO_2 emissions	200
C.2	WRE profiles of CO_2 concentrations	201
E.1	Results of water analysis at Cabot plant (2007)	218
E.2	Winooski River Subbasin	219

List of Acronyms

AA1000AS	AA1000 Assurance Standard 2008
CBM	Context-based metric
CBS	Context-based sustainability
CO2	Carbon dioxide
CSM	Corporate sustainability management
CSR	Corporate social responsibility
CWG	Corporate Water Gauge®
D/O	Duties and obligations (owed to stakeholders by organizations to have impacts on vital capitals of importance to their well-being)
ET	Evapotranspiration
GAAP	Generally Accepted Accounting Principles
GDP	Gross Domestic Product
GHG	Greenhouse gas
GIS	Geographic information system
GRI	Global Reporting Initiative
HUC	Hydrologic Unit Code (a USGS term)
IIRC	International Integrated Reporting Committee
LCA	Life Cycle Assessment
MDG	(United Nations) Millennium Development Goals
NGO	Non-governmental organization
PCE	Per capita equivalent (a nuanced per capita unit of measurement)
TBL	Triple bottom line
ULE ISR 880	Underwriters Laboratories Environment Interim Sustainability Requirements 880 (draft standard)
USGS	United States Geological Survey
WBCSD	World Business Council for Sustainable Development

Foreword

Mathis Wackernagel

Fifteen years ago, my colleague William Rees and I published a book together entitled *Our Ecological Footprint* (1996), in which we proposed a methodology for tracking humanity's demands on Earth. Many had an intuition that humanity had exceeded the planet's biocapacity – but no systematic accounting method existed to actually track human demands against nature's regenerative supply. In presenting that argument, we tried to make it clear that the sustainability of human activity needs to be viewed in the context of ecological limits. Thus, ours was a *context-based* approach to understanding sustainability, with context mainly taking the form of limitations in natural capital. To live within such limitations is a necessary condition for sustainability, we argued; to live beyond them is certainly not.

Of course the foundations for our book – conceptually, that is – were in wide circulation long before Bill Rees and I came together. For instance, during the heyday of the classical Greek philosophers, they discussed the implications of ecological limitations imposed by nature. And carrying capacity has been an established concept in biology for at least a century. What Bill Rees and I managed to do back then – and have refined since – was to codify the application of ecological context into a procedure for measuring and reporting the ecological performance of human systems in the context of biological limits.

Mark McElroy and Jo van Engelen are proposing in this book a way to track performance in a number of domains, beyond ecological resources. Mark dedicated his PhD work to this question and called the approach he first developed the *Social Footprint Method* (McElroy, 2008). In what he and Jo now broadly refer to as *context-based sustainability*, the approach has a number of parallels to the Ecological Footprint. Specifically, it addresses sustainability performance in terms of several shared principles:

(a) it is context-based,
(b) it recognizes the vital role of capital formation and maintenance,

(c) it links performance with 'interests' of valuable goods and services yielded from capital stocks, and

(d) it is applicable at the level of individual organizations.

The difference is that they address a broad base of issues, not just one particular one, as is done in specific, but hence narrower, accounting frameworks, such as GDP, Ecological Footprint or GHG inventories, that build on one commensurable measurement unit.

Next comes the issue of allocating impacts on vital capital stocks to individual organizations. For many capital stocks on which human demands draw, it is not self-evident how they can be apportioned to individual organizations. This makes comparisons tricky. But we need to start somewhere, even in the absence of a social consensus, and that's why Mark and Jo start with self-selected standards at a local level. It is important to step into action and try out what works. Only pilot projects and trial and error will help us to progress. And without putting performance measures in a context of targets, thresholds or limits, they do not mean much.

Indeed, consider the alternative – present-day 'best practices' that often lack absolute reference points. A large part of, if not all, sustainability measurement, management and reporting in most corporate reports is without context, and therefore defies interpretation. How far are we off track? Where do we want to go? Is a little better good enough? Are we serious about where we want to go, or are we just engaging in symbolic action?

What holds us back from setting great goals and targets? What is the gain from ignoring real limits? In 2002 Paul Hawken and I tried to invite the business reporting community to embrace 'limits-based' indicators – particularly in the energy and resource domain. Back then we failed to inspire the business community with what we proposed. But still, I got invited back in the spring of 2010 to address the bi-annual conference of the Global Reporting Initiative held in Amsterdam. I recycled the 'limits-based' idea, built it into my delivery, and was delighted to see a far stronger resonance in the business world.

But such 'limits-based' measures do not exist yet. This is why I much welcome Mark and Jo's practical exploration in putting sustainability measurement, with all its dimensions, into a clear context. Whether or not the specifics of their approach will be widely embraced remains to be seen. That's not the point. Rather, if sustainability performance tracking is to become informative and meaningful, we need to build this knowledge base – we need courageous trial and error, because the alternative is failure.

Acknowledgements

There are many people with whom we have collaborated in recent years to develop the ideas contained in this book, most notably consisting of a group of scholars in the United States and the Netherlands. Of particular importance have been the collaborations between ourselves and Joseph M. Firestone (Center for the Open Enterprise), Steven A. Cavaleri (Central Connecticut State University), Benoit Cushman-Roisin (Dartmouth College), René J. Jorna (University of Groningen), Derk Jan Kiewiet (formerly of the University of Groningen and now at APG), Niels Faber (University of Groningen), and two doctoral students at the University of Groningen, Henk Hadders and Kristian Peters. Also involved was Csilla Buiting-Csikos (TU Delft), whose administrative assistance in making the final push for this book possible was indispensable. We thank all of these individuals for their contributions to our work, and we look forward to many more years of collaboration with each of them.

To the extent that the content of this book is an evolution of Mark McElroy's PhD thesis in 2008, he wishes to thank, again, all those who were involved in that effort. This includes most of the individuals already mentioned above, and also Rudy Rabbinge and Ton Schoot Uiterkamp, both of the University of Groningen. There were also a number of other scholars throughout the world involved in the review and validity testing of the *Social Footprint Method*. Those individuals were Rob Gray (University of St. Andrews), Bert de Vries (Utrecht University), Alan AtKisson (AtKisson Group) and Markus Milne (University of Canterbury). We thank them one and all.

Next come our friends at Cabot Creamery Cooperative, without whose trust in our ideas and dedication to context-based sustainability (CBS) this book would not have been possible. As early adopters of CBS, the good people of Cabot made it possible for us to record a case study of activity there that has been underway for more than three years now, and which quite possibly constitutes the most comprehensive and cutting-edge application of CBS by any single organization thus far.

Deeply involved in that effort have been Dr. Richard Stammer, President, Roberta MacDonald, SVP Marketing, Jim Pratt, SVP Operations, Jed Davis, Director of Sustainability, and many others. We are deeply grateful for their pioneering spirit and for their agreement to allow us to use our experiences at Cabot as a case study for this book.

Also featured in this book is a case taken from work one of us (McElroy) performed at Ben & Jerry's, a company well known for its social activism over the years, and quite possibly the company with the longest history of publishing annual sustainability reports in the world, now going on twenty-two years and counting. Starting in 2006, Ben & Jerry's worked with McElroy to pilot (and pioneer) a context-based metric for measuring climate-change mitigation efforts, a measurement model that makes it possible to measure emissions against a standard for restoring CO_2 concentrations in the atmosphere to a safe and stabilized level of 350 parts per million (ppm). Central to that effort were Rob Michalak (Global Director of Social Mission), Andy Barker (Social Mission Specialist) and Andrea Asch (Manager of Natural Resources). We thank them, as well, for their own pioneering spirit and for their willingness to let us use our experiences there as a further illustration of CBS in this book.

Of additional importance to our work was the contribution made by Deloitte Consulting, whose involvement in and support for our efforts at Cabot Creamery in Vermont (our primary case study) were key to the results we describe on the pages that follow. Thanks, in particular, go to Chris Park and Deloitte's Center for Sustainability Performance, both located in Boston, Massachusetts.

We would also like to thank Eric Lowitt, a former colleague of McElroy's at Deloitte Consulting, for his ideas and input in the formulation of our thinking. His specific ideas on the need for radical change in the concept of value in business are important, to be sure. We look forward to seeing more of them in print some time soon.

Our thanks also go out to Bill Baue, a freelance journalist in the United States who was the first to notice, appreciate and write about our work on context-based sustainability in 2006, and who has been following (and *continuing* to write about) our progress ever since. If and when CBS becomes mainstream in corporate sustainability management, it will be due in no small part to Bill's own efforts to call attention to its importance and to the extent to which it has been lacking in business. We thank him for that.

Next comes our gratitude to Margaret Robinson, a freelance German-to-English translator in Vermont who helped us to better understand the seminal writings of Hans Carl von Carlowitz, whose 1713 book arguably contains the first published appearance of the word *sustainable* in a business or management context (i.e., forest management).

We are also grateful for assistance received from Heather Carlos of Acer GeoAnalytics in Vermont. Heather's geographical information system (GIS) talents were instrumental in the water sustainability studies we did at Cabot. She is a co-developer of the Corporate Water Gauge® (described in Appendix D), a context-based water sustainability metric, the results of which when first used at Cabot are shown in Appendix E.

Our thanks also go out to Svend-Erik Filby of Svend Design in New Hampshire for his assistance in helping us with several of our graphics. Svend has been involved with us from the start and we look forward to working with him again in the future.

So, too, are we grateful for assistance received from the good folks at Taylor & Francis, our publisher, for their help and support in making this book possible. Thanks, in particular, go to Robert Langham, Gudrun Freese, Andrew Watts and Michael Jones.

Finally, we wish to thank our wives Amy (McElroy) and Yvonne (van Engelen) for their unending support of our work. Book writing often leaves time for little else, making the life of an author's spouse rather lonely at times. Henceforth, we will try to keep it to a minimum!

Mark W. McElroy (Thetford Center, Vermont)

Jo M.L. van Engelen (Rolde, the Netherlands)

INTRODUCTION

Setting the context

This is a book about the advent of a new management discipline, its origins, the trouble it's in, and how to save it. The management discipline we speak of, of course, is corporate sustainability management, or CSM; and the trouble it's in involves nothing less that its own credibility and prospects for survival. Indeed, as we will show on the pages that follow, CSM has thus far failed to accomplish the one thing it was intended to do, which is make it possible for organizations to measure, manage and report their sustainability performance in a rigorous way. In fact, CSM in its present form does nothing of the kind – literally – despite common representations to the contrary. On the pages that follow, we will explain exactly how it is that CSM fails to do so, and what can be done about it.

CSM, of course, in its modern form is not an entirely new field, and is at least twenty-some years old – not including its *pre*-modern form, that is, which goes back at least three hundred years (see, in particular, Von Carlowitz, 1713). We know this because at least one company – Ben & Jerry's in Vermont, where one of us lives – has been issuing corporate social responsibility, or sustainability, reports since the late 1980s. Others may have been doing so as well, but it is also the case that common frameworks for how to even think about the subject (e.g., the so-called triple bottom line; Elkington, 1997) and standards for reporting, such as the Global Reporting Initiative, or GRI (first deployed in 2000), are much more recent in their appearance.

Earlier theoretical and academic treatments of the subject can certainly be found (see, for example, Friedman, 1970 and Davis and Blomstrom, 1975), but reporting and standards for reporting, per se, are not that old. Nonetheless, given the modern intellectual history of the subject – at least forty years old – and the fact that corporate sustainability management functions have been in place in some companies for at least twenty years, one would have thought that the discipline would be much further along than it is in terms of having acknowledged its shortcomings and taken steps to resolve them. In fact, it has not.

What, then, is the trouble we speak of? The trouble we speak of is that mainstream sustainability reports – which are supposed to report on the sustainability performance of organizations – rarely if ever actually do so, and in the process reveal a serious conceptual flaw in CSM as a whole, or at least a willingness to put up with it (we're not sure which is worse). The flaw we are talking about is the absence of what in sustainability theory and practice is known as *context* – or *sustainability context*, as GRI puts it.

Context in sustainability, or in CSM, has a particular meaning, not to be confused with broader or looser interpretations of the term. In so many words, what it refers to is the background state of vital social and environmental resources in the world, and what an organization's impacts on them ought to be (or not to be) in order to be sustainable. If a vitally important water resource, for example, is already over-taxed and nearly depleted, knowledge of that is important to include when measuring and reporting the sustainability of an organization's use of it. Indeed, the same level of use might be sustainable on the one hand or not sustainable on the other, depending on what the status of the resource is to begin with.

Thus, the status of social and environmental conditions in the world matters, insofar as an organization's efforts to measure, manage and report its sustainability performance are concerned. Context, that is, is fundamental to CSM, so much so that CSM can't be done without it. Why, then, is it so regularly and conspicuously missing from contemporary practice? And how can we take CSM seriously as long as it is?

Imagine, by analogy, a management discipline for measuring and reporting the financial (or profitability) performance of organizations that systematically failed to take costs into account. Profitability measurement and reporting under such a system would be solely a function of revenues (as if costs didn't exist, when in fact they do) and would be reported on *income statements*, accordingly.

Apart from the difference between financial and non-financial measurement and reporting, the analogy we have drawn here is quite literal. Mainstream practices and standards for measuring and reporting the sustainability performance of organizations, that is, quite literally fail to achieve the one thing they set out to do, which is make it possible to understand the true or actual sustainability performance of the organizations that use them, thanks to their exclusion of the social and environmental equivalents of costs. Such factors may be non-monetary in form, but they are no less vital to the accounting task at hand.

If it is, in fact, the case – and we think it is – that the absence of context in the mainstream practice of CSM makes it impossible for organizations to measure and report, much less manage, the sustainability of their operations, then it is entirely possible, if not probable, that the vast majority of organizations on Earth have no real idea of whether or not their operations are sustainable. And given the extent to which organizations – businesses, in particular – are quite possibly the dominant human institution on Earth, with the greatest social and environmental impacts the world has ever seen, the fact that the most basic internal measurement system for monitoring and reporting the sustainability of their operations is fundamentally flawed should be of great concern to us all. Indeed, how can we possibly expect organizations to manage the social and environmental sustainability of their operations when their own internal dashboards, as it were, are deeply defective? And how, under these circumstances, can we expect the conduct of human affairs, more broadly, to be sustainable given the prominent role that businesses and other organizations play in modern civilization? To be sure, we can't.

What this means, we're afraid, is that even as the number of organizations around the world actively involved in measuring, managing and reporting their sustainability performance is growing every year, their *actual* sustainability performance – despite claims to the contrary in their reports – may, in fact, be worsening, unbeknownst even to themselves; for without the inclusion of context in related accounting and management efforts, no one can possibly know what the true sustainability performance of an organization is, much less whether it is improving, worsening or what have you.

This, we believe, is an utterly untenable situation that should not be tolerated, especially given the plainly visible social and environmental stresses around us, many of which are attributable to commerce. In a very real sense, human well-being from this point forward hangs in the balance insofar as whether or not context is properly attended to in CSM, which at the present time it is not. In short, the need for context in CSM is urgent!

The good news is that (a) we are not the only ones who have identified the absence of context in CSM, although we may be the most vocal critics of it, and (b) principles, procedures and methods for injecting context into CSM, where it belongs, now exist, including in the book you are holding. We also take great comfort from knowing that the leading international standard for corporate sustainability measurement and reporting, GRI, strongly advocates for the inclusion of context in related efforts. That said, however, GRI fails to provide sufficient guidance on how to do so, and regularly endorses superior ratings for GRI reporters (and their reports) that don't include context.

We will have a great deal more to say about this throughout the book, as well as about how to perform context-based CSM. That, of course, is the main purpose of the book: to provide a methodology for performing context-based CSM, or *context-based sustainability*, as we will refer to it from this point forward.

Project background

As co-authors of this book, the two of us first met at a symposium held in the Netherlands in June 2004, jointly organized by the Dutch National Initiative for Sustainable Development (NIDO) and the Dutch Association of Inventors. Each of us, and our respective colleagues (see Acknowledgements section and the discussion below), had already for several years by then been focusing on the connections between knowledge, innovation and sustainability. In 2005, a core group consisting of ourselves (McElroy from the Center for Sustainable Organizations and Van Engelen from the University of Groningen), René Jorna (University of Groningen), Derk Jan Kiewiet (University of Groningen), Joseph Firestone (Center for the Open Enterprise), Steve Cavaleri (Central Connecticut State University), Benoit Cushman-Roisin (Dartmouth College) and Henk Hadders (University of Groningen) gathered in May at Dartmouth College in New Hampshire to more or less begin the process of collaborating more closely on what we all felt was a promising new theory of sustainability that could have profound practice implications – which indeed it has.

Of central importance to our view was, and still is, that (a) effective action of any kind in life requires access to information about the world that is timely and accurate, and (b) such information has, in fact, been largely missing from the general practice of CSM in business, a serious shortcoming that must be addressed if sustainability, or CSM, is to have any chance of success.

Out of the collaboration cited above – including work performed both before and after the May 2005 gathering at Dartmouth – came several works of great importance to the thinking set forth in this book (see, for example, McElroy, 1997; McElroy, 2000; McElroy, 2002; Firestone and McElroy, 2003; McElroy, 2003; Jorna et al., 2004; Cavaleri and Seivert, 2005; Faber et al., 2005; Firestone and McElroy, 2005; Faber, 2006; Jorna, 2006; McElroy et al., 2006; McElroy et al., 2007; Cavaleri et al., 2011).

Of particular relevance was the doctoral dissertation produced by one of us at the University of Groningen (McElroy, 2008), in which the concept of context-based sustainability as described and advocated in this book was formally developed, along with the *Social Footprint Method*, a context-based approach for measuring the social sustainability performance of organizations. Working closely with McElroy at the time were Van Engelen, Jorna and Kiewiet, all from the University of Groningen.

This book, in turn, was motivated by a desire on the part of the authors to take what was a scholarly, academic and scientifically vetted concept and express it in a more practical and business-friendly form, so as to make the significance and substance of context-based sustainability more accessible to CSM practitioners. Not only is it our hope and intent, then, that the methodology we are proposing here will be embraced by businesses and other organizations; we also hope that standards-setting bodies, such as GRI and others, will at least consider what we have said as a possible starting point – if not a ready-made solution – for establishing context-based guidelines of their own. Indeed, we would be very pleased if they did and would happily support them.

Chapter summaries

In Chapter 1 we begin by providing a summary of the intellectual history of CSM, or of sustainability the concept, more broadly. Our intent is to show that sustainability is not a new idea, and that its appearance in the literature as a formal school of management practice goes back at least three hundred years to the writings of one Hans Carl von Carlowitz (1713), a Saxon mining administrator who more or less singlehandedly invented the practice of sustainable forestry. On the basis of that case and many others that follow below, we will show that the inclusion of context in sustainability theory and practice is not a new idea, just a sorely neglected one.

Next we will show in Chapter 1 that the modern form of CSM we have before us today is arguably the result of the convergence of two otherwise separate intellectual streams of thought that came together some time in the mid- to late twentieth century. One stream we will refer to as the *context* stream (i.e., utilized by sustainability theorists over the years, like Von Carlowitz, who all relied on the concept of context in their writings on sustainability to make their points), and the other is the *capital* stream. The capital stream mainly appears in the writings of economists, who eventually expanded the application of the term from its narrow economic sense to encompass vital (capital) resources of all kinds, including natural capital, a term that has regularly appeared in the sustainability and environmental literatures for years now. Sustainability theory and practice in its modern form, then, is the product of the convergence of the context and capital streams, the implications of which for the practice of contemporary CSM are profoundly important.

In Chapter 2, having laid the intellectual foundations of context-based sustainability (CBS) in Chapter 1, we go on to apply our thinking to the treatment of several key issues of frequent debate and interest in CSM today. Here we will distinguish between issues involving (a) how CBS ties into, or interacts with, other mainstream management practices in use – strategy-related practices, in particular – and (b) how CBS relates to measurement and reporting as compared with other, more conventional CSM practices also in use today. The intent of this chapter, then, is to demonstrate the context-based approach in action, at least in terms of how it can be used to address several of today's key issues in CSM. By so doing, it is our hope that the reader will develop a more intuitive understanding of CBS, and thereby better comprehend its significance and practice implications for CSM.

Of greatest importance, perhaps, in our discussion of key issues in CSM and how it relates to other established business practices is the extent to which the context-based approach we are advocating here is, in a sense, nothing more than a new application of an old (and still predominant) management theory – long used in the financial domain – to the sustainability or non-financial domain. Here we will argue that just as conventional management involves the care and feeding of monetary capital on behalf of shareholders, so, too, does non-financial, or sustainability, management involve the care and feeding of (other) capitals on behalf of (other) stakeholders. After all, stakeholders include more than just shareholders, if only because the effects of an organization's activities affect more than just the well-being of its shareholders. The other capitals involved here are natural capital, human capital, social capital and constructed (or built) capital; and the stakeholders are whomever they might be (a criterion for which we provide in Chapter 3).

Chapter 2 also includes an in-depth critique of GRI, or more narrowly of the extent to which GRI advocates for the inclusion of context in CSM, on the one hand, but fails to define and enforce it on the other. Here we will take the language currently contained in the GRI standard on the principle of *sustainability context* and critique it, line by line. Along the way, we will offer our own thoughts on what the text means, and also how, in principle, to act upon it from our own point of view. In general, we will take the position that the principle of *sustainability context* in GRI is laudable, if not vital; that it should be interpreted in terms of the context- and capital-based concepts we describe in Chapter 1; and that the methodology provided in this book is at least one viable way of operationalizing GRI's call for it (context) as a basic principle for sustainability measurement and reporting.

In Chapter 3 we lay out the methodology associated with context-based sustainability in great detail. The purpose of the chapter is, in fact, to provide CSM practitioners with a step-by-step procedure for performing CSM in a way that takes context fully and properly into account. Included is a comprehensive case study from a company in the U.S. – a dairy food producer known as Cabot Creamery Cooperative, or Agri-Mark, Inc. – in which the methodology we describe has been used, including a procedure we recommend for developing context-based metrics. All of this is discussed against the backdrop of an overarching, six-step methodology for CSM that we refer to as, simply, the *CSM cycle*, a general methodology for CSM that can be used to understand, operationalize and perform CSM in an organization.

Chapter 3 also includes more discussion of the important role that stakeholders play in CBS. Indeed, the very substance and boundaries of a CSM program, we argue, are determined by – or *should* be determined by – an understanding of who the organization's stakeholders are, and what its duties and obligations are to each of them to have non-financial impacts of one kind or another in order to ensure their well-being. As in the case of the intellectual streams of context and capital theory discussed in Chapter 1, here, too, we have found a kindred and well-established body of thought and literature that has a crucial role to play in CSM: *stakeholder theory*. Shareholders, we will claim, are not the only stakeholders to whom an organization owes a duty of performance; they are only a subset of a much broader range of constituents (stakeholders) whose needs and interests can and should inform and legitimize the design of a CSM program in any organization.

In Chapter 4 we provide a general summary of our thinking as otherwise put forward in Chapters 1 through 3, but we also include some thoughts as to where CSM should go from here. Five areas of interest, in particular, are discussed: standards, accounting, assurance, organizations and the capital markets. In each case, context as a principle is regrettably still missing from contemporary practice, although in some cases (e.g., the GRI standard) it is at least acknowledged.

Of most importance, though, to the continued development of CSM and to the context-based approach we are proposing is the need for further development on the accounting front. Why? Because accounting, in principle, logically precedes everything else. Standards for measurement and reporting, for example, must be reflective of general principles for what needs to be measured, how it should be measured, and what it means when it is. Assurance practices, too, must be based on prior agreements for what measurement and reporting should consist of, and whether or not reports are true to accounting principles. And all of that, in turn, must be properly operationalized in organizational and capital market settings.

It is because of that that we wish to have our own thinking, as put forward in this book, viewed as a contribution to the management discipline of sustainability accounting, and not just CSM. Indeed, what we have tried to do here is explain what it means for an organization's activities to be sustainable or not, in a way that translates into a system of metrics and indicators for non-financial performance accounting. Context, it turns out, is indispensable in CSM, and without it there can be no truly meaningful sustainability accounting; no meaningful sustainability measurement; no meaningful sustainability management; no meaningful sustainability reporting; and no meaningful sustainability assurance. And without any of that, there can be no *sustainability* in the conduct of human affairs, for how can we expect ourselves to be sustainable in our own behaviors if we are blind to their effects? Context, we believe, provides us with just the light we need.

1

CONTEXT-BASED SUSTAINABILITY

A brief history of context

The central claim of this book is that sustainability measurement, management and reporting must be context-based in order to be meaningful. All aspects of corporate sustainability management (CSM), that is, must be performed with explicit reference to, and in light of, actual social and/or environmental conditions in the world in order to be effective. The sustainability of water use, for example, cannot be determined without reference to the size and sufficiency of available water supplies; nor can the sustainability of an organization's social impacts be determined without reference to the general well-being of its stakeholders.

In this chapter we will unpack and explore this idea further, culminating in a summary of exactly what we mean by context-based sustainability, or CBS. But first we want to make it clear just how long the idea of including context in sustainability management has been around by highlighting its appearance in the literature over the past three hundred years. As we will show, context in sustainability is not a new idea, just a currently neglected one.

Hans Carl von Carlowitz

The concept of sustainability arguably first appeared in 1713 in the writings of one Hans Carl von Carlowitz (Von Carlowitz, 1713), a Saxon tax accountant and mining administrator who more or less invented the practice of sustainable forestry. In the early eighteenth century, the mining industry in Europe was in a state of crisis, not because of any shortages in ore or in mines per se, but because of the scarcity of lumber required for smelting. Whole forests were disappearing through clear cutting, leading to soaring prices, bankruptcies and the collapse of the mining sector in certain areas. In response, Von Carlowitz argued that the forestry industry should alter its practices such that the rate of logging does not exceed the rate at which trees grow; in so doing, he singlehandedly ushered in the principle of sustainability to management, the relevance and importance of which have been growing ever since.

Indeed, Von Carlowitz's writings arguably constituted the first formulation of what would later become known as the *triple bottom line* (Elkington, 1997). Edinger and Kaul (2003, p. 5) put it this way:

> One year before he died, [Von] Carlowitz published his book *Sylvicultura Oeconomica* (The Economics of Forestry). He outlined the triad principles of sustainability (ecology, economy and social aspects) and, like the modern eco-logical economists ... subordinated human economic activity to natural restraints. Von Carlowitz believed that trade and commerce had to serve the society and treat nature in a careful and considerate way. Also, he saw economic activity as responsible for future generations.

Throughout the entirety of his 1713 text, Von Carlowitz used the word *sustainability* only once – or *sustainable* or *sustained*, in fact, since he used the term in its descriptive form as an adjective (*nachhaltende*), not as a noun. He did so while advocating for the adoption of sustainable forestry practices as follows:[1]

> Therefore the highest level of art, science, industry and institutions in this country will have to make every effort to achieve conservation and cultivation of wood for continuous and sustained utilization, because it is an indispensable matter, without which a country cannot continue in its *esse*.
>
> *(Von Carlowitz, 1713, pp. 105–06)*

In making his argument, Von Carlowitz relied on context – sustainability context – to give his proposals meaning. The particular type of context he relied on was the stock of forests and the rate at which trees grow, an environmental condition or fact that should determine, he argued, the maximum rate at which humans should harvest trees. Context in sustainability management, then, is always reflective of one or more social and/or environmental conditions in the world, which in turn give rise to thresholds or *standards of performance* that tell us what our impacts should or should not be in order for our behaviors to be sustainable (i.e., so as to preserve stocks of vital resources important to human well-being). In Von Carlowitz's case, the context of interest was an environmental kind – the finite supply of trees and their actual rate of growth – and his management proposals were expressed in precisely those terms: *the rate of tree logging should not exceed the rate at which trees actually grow or reproduce*. It would not have been enough simply to say that humans should be logging less; rather, the question was *by how much less*. The actual rate of tree growth supplied the answer.

Thomas R. Malthus

In 1798, eighty-five years after Von Carlowitz's seminal work on sustainability, another auspicious moment in the history of sustainability context took place, this time in the writings of Thomas R. Malthus and his infamous *An Essay on the Principle of Population* (Malthus, 1998[1798]). The essence of Malthus's *Essay* was his claim that the rate of human population growth would eventually exceed the rate of food production, since the former grows geometrically and the latter arithmetically. Thus, he argued, population will sooner or later outstrip the food supply on Earth, with widespread famine and misery to follow. Here, in his own words, is how Malthus put it (Malthus, 1998[1798], p. 14):

> Population, when unchecked, increases in a geometrical ratio. Subsistence increases only in an arithmetical ratio. A slight acquaintance with numbers will shew [*sic*] the immensity of the first power in comparison of the second.
>
> By that law of our nature which makes food necessary to the life of man, the effects of these two unequal powers must be kept equal.
>
> This implies a strong and constantly operating check on population from the difficulty of subsistence. This difficulty must fall some where; and must necessarily be severely felt by a large portion of mankind.

Whereas for Von Carlowitz the relevant context that should govern or constrain human behavior was the rate at which trees grow, for Malthus it was the rate at which food is produced. Thus, in both cases, we have a pair of rates being compared with one another. In the case of Von Carlowitz, it was the rate of logging compared with the rate of tree growth; for Malthus, it was the rate of human reproduction compared with the rate of food growth. Stated in more general terms, both cases involved comparisons between some type of human behavior (mining and reproduction) and the capacity of an environmental resource (trees and food, respectively) to support it (the behavior) on a continuing if not indefinite basis.

Generally speaking, if human activity puts the quality and/or sufficiency of a supporting (if not vital) resource at risk relative to levels required for human well-being, the behavior can be said to be unsustainable, thanks entirely to what its impact on the supporting resource is. Here it should be clear that both Von Carlowitz and Malthus were ultimately appealing to the principle of human well-being – and the need or desire to ensure it – as the basis of their thinking. Placing resources required for human well-being at risk, they seemed to be saying, is unsustainable precisely because it puts human well-being at risk.

The main goal of sustainability management must therefore be to ensure that the quality and/or sufficiency of vital resources in the world are always maintained at levels required to ensure human well-being. Thus, explicit knowledge of such levels – or at least well-reasoned *claims* about them – is essential for sustainability measurement, management and reporting, and that is precisely the kind of context that must be embedded in everything we do as sustainability managers in business. Effective sustainability management simply cannot be done without it.

John Stuart Mill

Next in our journey through the intellectual history of sustainability (and context) comes John Stuart Mill. Exactly fifty years after Malthus published his *Essay*, Mill published a work entitled *Principles of Political Economy with Some of Their Applications to Social Philosophy*, in which he included his concept of the *stationary state* (Mill, 1923 [1848], Book 4, Chapter 6). Mill contrasted the stationary state with the prevailing *progressive state*, the latter being a reference to the growth-oriented, resource-based economy, and the former comprising a fundamentally different, if not utopian, alternative. In contemplating his vision of a stationary state, Mill asked (p. 746):

> Towards what ultimate point is society tending by its industrial progress? When the progress ceases, in what condition are we to expect that it will leave mankind?

Mill answered his own question by envisioning a world in which all finite resources are harnessed, controlled or consumed by the (conventional, growth-oriented) progressive state, a prospect entirely possible in a world with limited resources – that is, our world. He was clearly troubled by this (pp. 750–51):

> Nor is there much satisfaction in contemplating the world with nothing left to the spontaneous activity of nature; with every rood of land brought into cultivation, which is capable of growing food for human beings; every flowery waste or natural pasture ploughed up, all quadrupeds or birds which are not domesticated for man's use exterminated as his rivals for food, every hedgerow or superfluous tree rooted out, and scarcely a place left where a wild shrub or flower could grow without being eradicated as a weed in the name of agriculture. If the earth must lose that great portion of its pleasantness which it owes to things that the unlimited increase of wealth and population would extirpate from it, for the mere purpose of enabling it to support a larger, but not a better or a happier population, I sincerely hope, for the sake of posterity, that they will be content to be stationary, long before necessity compels them to it.

Here, as in the case of Von Carlowitz and Malthus, we see Mill raising the specter of human suffering and misery as the consequence of a failure to take context – what he calls 'necessity' – explicitly into account, this time with respect to the general conduct of human economic affairs in all of its dimensions. The alternative vision he offers is that of the stationary state, an economic system in which the level of human demands placed on vital resources in the world more or less conforms to their continuous availability, and vice versa. In so many words, he seems to be saying: *manage our numbers and activities in the world, or else the world will manage them for us!*

Meadows et al.

From Mill in 1848 we jump to the twentieth century in 1972, when Donella Meadows, Dennis Meadows, Jorgen Randers and William Behrens III published their highly acclaimed book *The Limits to Growth* (Meadows et al., 1972). Their purpose in publishing *Limits*, in their words, was as follows (pp. x–xi):

The intent of the project is to examine the complex of problems troubling men of all nations: poverty in the midst of plenty; degradation of the environment; loss of faith in institutions; uncontrolled urban spread; insecurity of employment; alienation of youth; rejection of traditional values; and inflation and other monetary and economic disruptions. These seemingly divergent parts of the world 'problematique,' as The Club of Rome calls it, have three characteristics in common: they occur to some degree in all societies; they contain technical, social, economic, and political elements; and, most important of all, they interact.

The particular methodology used by Meadows et al. in their work involved the deployment of system dynamics tools (Forrester, 1961, 1969, 1971) and the development of a model of human activity called the *World* model, in which sustainability context was firmly ensconced. This context took the form of many premises and assumptions about ecological constraints in the world, prevailing social conditions, consumption patterns, population growth, etc. that the authors relied on for their analysis. The model, in turn, was used to determine whether or not various possible futures of human activity on Earth would be viable given certain predicted and hypothetical social and ecological constraints. In effect, what they did was to measure and report, albeit on a prospective and exploratory basis, the *sustainability performance of humanity*, with sustainability context (i.e., then-current and future conditions in the world) taken fully into account. Indeed, the very 'limits' referred to in the title of their book were – and are – instances of context, confronting humanity in terms of the finite environment on Earth, and by the equally finite scope and dimensions of social services and institutions in the world available to address human needs. Five specific types of context were of particular concern to them (p. xi):

> The team examined the five basic factors that determine, and therefore ultimately limit, growth on this planet – population, agricultural production, natural resources, industrial production, and pollution.

Here we see how context came explicitly into play for the *Limits* team. In order to assess the sustainability performance of humanity on a global basis, existing and future conditions in the world were factored into the analysis. The long-term viability of human behaviors on the planet (given trends in evidence at the time) would have to be assessed relative to agricultural production – a tip of the hat to Malthus – natural resource constraints and so forth. Background population conditions, too, would have to be considered, since existing levels at the time already placed certain demands on society and the environment, thereby constraining the capacity of social and environmental systems to accommodate future (and growing) human needs.

The conclusions reached by Meadows et al. were as follows (p. 29):

> Our conclusions are:

1. If the present growth trends in world population, industrialization, pollution, food production, and resource depletion continue unchanged, the limits to growth on

this planet will be reached sometime within the next one hundred years. The most probable result will be a sudden and uncontrollable decline in both population and industrial capacity.

2. It is possible to alter these growth trends and to establish a condition of ecological and economic stability that is sustainable far into the future. The state of global equilibrium [note the similarity here to Mill's notion of the 'stationary state'] could be designed so that the basic material needs of each person on Earth are satisfied and each person has an equal opportunity to realize his individual human potential [notice here, as well, the elliptical reference to human well-being as a criterion for sustainability].

3. If the world's people decide to strive for this second outcome rather than the first, the sooner they begin working to attain it, the greater will be their chances of success.

Regardless of how one may feel about the *Limits* team's analysis and conclusions, it should be clear that their assessment of the sustainability of human activity in the world could not have been rendered without explicit consideration of human, social, economic, environmental and material conditions in the world, no matter how hypothetical. Indeed, it is quite literally impossible to draw any meaningful conclusions about the sustainability of human activities – at any level of analysis, global or otherwise – without taking such conditions systematically into account. As we will see, this is true for businesses and other kinds of organizations as well.[2]

World Council of Churches

Only two years after *The Limits to Growth* was published, there appeared what may be the earliest expression of sustainability principles in modern terms from a very surprising, if not unlikely, source: the concept of a 'sustainable society' as put forward at an ecumenical study conference on 'Science and Technology for Human Development', held by the World Council of Churches in 1974. There the concept was defined as follows (World Council of Churches, 1974, as quoted in Dresner [2002, p. 29]):

> First, social sustainability cannot be obtained without an equitable distribution of what is in scarce supply or without common opportunity to participate in social decisions. Second, a robust global society will not be sustainable unless the need for food is at any time well below the global capacity to supply it and unless the emission of pollutants are well below the capacity of the ecosystems to absorb them. Third, the new social organization will be sustainable as long as the use of non-renewable resources does not out-run the increase in resources made available through technological innovation. Finally, a sustainable society requires a level of human activities which is not adversely influenced by the never-ending large and frequent variations in global climate.

This remarkable, yet relatively unknown and prescient, manifesto arguably preceded and upstaged every leading sustainability theory and practice from the mid-twentieth century to modern times. Not only is it ecological in focus; it is also socially grounded as well. In effect, then, it preceded Elkington's (1997) notion of multiple bottom lines (a much better-known model for multi-dimensional sustainability), while also taking context fully into account in ways that are still applicable today. Climate, too, was addressed long before the subject became mainstream.

Like Von Carlowitz, Malthus, Mill, and Meadows et al. before it, the World Council of Churches spoke of sustainability in terms that were inseparable from real social and environmental conditions in the world. They spoke in particular of 'what is in scarce supply' and the 'opportunity to participate in social decisions', thereby invoking the facts of ecological resource conditions and socio-political institutions (another kind of resource) in assessing the sustainability of society. Moreover, a society could not be sustainable, they argued, unless its need for food 'is at any time well below the global capacity to supply it'. Pollutants, too, must be 'well below the capacity of the ecosystems to absorb them'. All of this constitutes direct reference to the quality and/ or sufficiency of vital resources in the world relative to levels required to ensure human well-being. These and other similar ideas would later show up in the impressive writings of the well-known ecological economist Herman Daly, as we will shortly see.

The Brundtland Report

No historical survey of sustainability theory and practice – context-based or otherwise – would be complete without at least paying lip service to the Brundtland Commission's treatment of sustainability – or, more precisely, *sustainable development* – which was so famously defined as follows (WCED, 1987, p. 8):

> development which meets the needs of the present without compromising the ability of future generations to meet their own needs.

Apart from the appealing brevity of this particular articulation of sustainability, it is hard to understand why it has become so popular a mantra for the sustainability movement. Indeed, by itself, it hardly provides us with an executable model for measuring, managing or reporting sustainability performance. In fairness to the Commission, however, the report in which the now famous slogan appears was quite conscious of social and environmental conditions in the world and was demonstrably context-based in terms of how we are using the term here. Consider the following passage in which the Commission critiques the growth doctrine, or mentality, vis-à-vis environmental constraints (a type of sustainability context), very much in line with the Meadows et al. team fifteen years earlier (WCED, 1987, p. 45):

> Growth [as an economic doctrine] has no set limits in terms of population or resource use beyond which lies ecological disaster. Different limits hold for the use of energy, materials, water, land. Many of these will manifest themselves in the form of rising costs and diminishing returns, rather than in the form of any sudden loss of a resource base. The accumulation of knowledge and the

development of technology can enhance the carrying capacity of the resource base. But ultimate limits there are, and sustainability requires that long before these are reached, the world must ensure equitable access to the constrained resource and reorient technological efforts to relieve the pressure.

Apart from the clear reference to environmental context in the statement above (i.e., to ecological limits), we see the Commission invoking another theme most often associated with its trademark orientation to sustainability – fairness, equity and justice. Of particular note here is the appeal to *inter-generational* equity embodied in its oft-quoted definition, in which it makes reference to 'the ability of future generations to meet their own needs' as something that the then living generation should bear in mind as it manages and assesses its own sustainability performance.

This, however, in our view is an unnecessary complication and only confuses the matter. Why not simply focus on attending to the needs of the present generation in a sustainable way, such that the present generation's performance on any given day is always sustainable? Indeed, would not strictly sustainable performance in the present help to ensure, if not largely guarantee, sustainability in the future, since no present behavior would ever diminish or fail to maintain vital resources at levels required to ensure human well-being, albeit for a current population? We think so.

Indeed, it is precisely unsustainable behavior in the present that puts human well-being in the future at risk. And it is the deliberate incorporation of context in sustainability measurement, management and reporting that makes it possible to determine whether or not present-day behaviors – or *any*-day behaviors, for that matter – are sustainable in the first place. By always taking context properly into account in the present, the needs of the future will automatically be met, for they and we will always be living within our means and ensuring the means to live on a real-time basis.

Gray, Bebbington and Milne

When we turn to the world of present-day authors, academics and practitioners in the field of sustainability, we see that the issue of context is gradually taking hold, but not at the pace or extent to which it must if sustainability is to be achieved. To the extent that organizations, for example, are practicing context-free styles of sustainability measurement, management and reporting – *which they are* – the effects of such habits have made, and will continue to make, it impossible for them to understand: (1) what their actual sustainability performance is, (2) whether or not their sustainability strategies and interventions are working, and (3) how big the gaps are, if any, between their current and target levels of performance. Worse yet is the fact that with so much uninformed and arguably unsustainable behavior going on at the local enterprise level, sustainability performance at the global societal level, too, is more or less out of control. We are quite literally flying blind on both fronts.

Several other authors have reached the same conclusion, albeit with a much stronger dose of pessimism than will be found here. Most notably, Gray and Bebbington (2007) describe the situation as follows (pp. 386–87):

> Within those reports identified as 'sustainability reports' … even those that are 'in conformance with' the Global Reporting Initiative *Sustainability Reporting Guidelines* provide only the most superficial data on the extent of the organization's sustainability or otherwise. Indeed, sustainability is much more likely to be entirely ignored; it is rare to see any corporation address it all. No reasonable person could make any sensible judgement on the basis of an organization's reporting in their 'Sustainability Reports' on whether or not the organization was [sustainable or] un-sustainable.

The authors go on to comment on the view that third-party monitoring and attestation can bring legitimacy to sustainability measurement and reporting as follows (p. 387):

> The more formal role of 'audit' – which is also a voluntary undertaking in this field – has also shown itself unable to challenge its (voluntary) clients. Research has shown that the attestation or assurance statements which attach to these reports are, at best, useless and, at worst, highly misleading. They certainly do not tell us that the 'sustainability report' that they are assuring [tells us anything] about sustainability … Accountability over sustainability it certainly is not … As things currently stand, we believe we must treat the current crop of 'sustainability reports' with the profoundest mistrust as one of the most dangerous trends working *against* any possibility of a sustainable future.

If what Gray and Bebbington say is true – and it demonstrably is – it is hard to interpret the situation as amounting to anything less than a crisis in corporate sustainability management (CSM) – or in business as a whole, for that matter. It is a crisis because as long as mainstream sustainability measurement and reporting tools are being used *as if* they are addressing sustainability – when, in fact, they are not – the probability will exist that the actual sustainability performance of organizations will never be known, even as their impacts in the world potentially worsen (i.e., in the form of increasing social and environmental harms, or in the failure to produce *goods* or benefits at required levels) – all under the watchful eyes of independent auditors, no less. Indeed, Gray and Milne (2002, p. 68), for their part, lay the blame on mainstream accounting methods as likely contributors:

> It is bound to be contestable whether we are currently at, below or beyond the point of sustainability. Our reading of the evidence, however, is that our current systems of economic, financial and social organisation are moving us in the wrong direction – that is, our current systems are making us less sustainable.
>
> Threats to sustainability are legion, and all of them are contestable. Is it population, land use, pollution, consumption or economic growth that is the principal enemy of sustainability? In all probability, it is a combination of these and other factors.
>
> One thing seems clear, however, and that is that current trends of industrialisation, production and consumption are amongst the most likely suspects.

Accounting, as a primary mechanism encouraging these patterns, is closely implicated in these apparent moves away from sustainability.

Perhaps the most damning, if not most succinct (and germane to our thesis), condemnation of mainstream sustainability practice is made by Gray and Milne (2004), as they invoke the central theme of this book – that context is necessary for meaningful measurement and reporting, yet still missing (p. 72):

> Current forms of [sustainability] reporting can verge on the meaningless as they are both too simple and devoid of context.

It is our contention that it is precisely the absence of context in mainstream sustainability measurement and reporting that makes it impossible to tell whether or not an organization's performance is sustainable – in any sort of literal sense. But that is what sustainability reports are supposed to do – tell us whether or not an organization's performance was sustainable, and yet they don't. This is very much akin to what financial reporting would be like if income statements were routinely prepared without any mention of costs. As hard as it may be to believe, though, this is exactly what passes for best practice in today's world of CSM.

Stiglitz, Sen and Fitoussi

Perhaps the most recent notable reference to the importance of context in CSM can be found in a report prepared by the Commission on the Measurement of Economic Performance and Social Progress, founded in 2008 by French president Sarkozy to study current measures of economic performance, and in particular the adequacy of those involving GDP (Gross Domestic Product) for measuring human/social well-being. The Commission was also asked to examine other contemporary and emerging measures of economic, environmental and social sustainability. Heading up the Commission were Joseph Stiglitz, Amartya Sen and Jean-Paul Fitoussi. In 2009, they issued their report (Stiglitz et al., 2009) in which the following statement was made (p. 12):

> Another key message, and unifying theme of the report, is that the time is ripe for our measurement system to shift emphasis from measuring economic production to measuring people's well-being. And measures of well-being should be put in a context of sustainability.

As in the case of their predecessors, Stiglitz, Sen and Fitoussi made the all-important link between sustainability and well-being, while calling attention to a 'context of sustainability' as the lens though which the impacts of human economic and development activity should be measured. The time is ripe, as they put it, for bringing context into measurement, because classical measures of production fail to take sustainability and the complexity of society, the environment and human well-being explicitly into account. At a time when social and environmental conditions in the world are arguably worsening – thanks, in part, to the modern economy and to a growing human population with unprecedented levels of consumption – we simply cannot afford to wait any longer to reform the metrics we use to measure and report the sustainability of business and of the economy in general.

Closely related to this (and to our thesis) is the extent to which Stiglitz et al. relied upon a *resource-based* view of sustainability performance, according to which the sustainability of human activity in the world is seen as a function of what its impacts are on vital resources required for human well-being. The particular kinds of resources involved, as we will shortly discuss below, are *capital* resources. The authors explain this concept as follows (p. 11):

> Current well-being has to do with both economic resources, such as income, and with non-economic aspects of people's life (what they do and what they can do, how they feel, and the natural environment they live in). Whether these levels of well-being can be sustained over time depends on whether stocks of capital that matter for our lives (natural, physical, human, social) are passed on to future generations.

They further expounded on the capital basis of sustainability as follows (p. 265):

> [O]n a complicated subject where many misunderstandings can take place, it is good practice to first start by elaborating a common language or a common general framework. The one that we have tried to emphasize is the so-called 'stock-based' or 'capital-based' or 'wealth-based' approaches to sustainability. The argument is that, ultimately, the sustainability issue is about how much stocks of resources we leave to future periods or future generations.

These key themes – human well-being and the sufficiency of vital capitals to ensure it – are utterly central to the conception of CBS we are advocating here. Moreover, it should be clear from the above that we are not alone in our thinking on this, and that the contemporary understanding of the subject as reflected in the writings of Stiglitz et al. and many others has a long and venerable history to it (further discussed in the next section). Nonetheless, it is an interpretation of sustainability that has not yet quite wound its way into the corporate world. But indeed it must, if sustainability measurement, management and reporting are to be meaningful in business.

The relevance of capital theory

Even as the idea of context as a basis for measuring, managing and reporting sustainability was evolving from the early eighteenth century to modern times, so were the ideas of capital and income – in the narrow economic sense, or what we shall refer to as *capital theory* – also evolving. Eventually, however, it would be capital theory, more broadly applied, that would give context – in the sustainability sense – the finer point it required in order to be operational. Sustainability context, that is, would come to be seen as a mixture of capital stocks and flows, the presence of which at certain levels is vital for human well-being. Thus, context – an otherwise vague and ambiguous term – would eventually take on a very specific meaning for sustainability theorists and practitioners, the origin of which was clearly grounded in capital theory and economics.

Of central importance to the CBS perspective put forward in this book, then, has been the gradual embracing of capital theory by leading sustainability theorists, from the early twentieth century to today. Indeed, a strong case can be made, we think, that sustainability, the social science or management discipline, is a descendant of economics, at least in terms of its reliance upon capital theory as a conceptual foundation, and the degree to which so many of its early thinkers were in fact economists – and still are – not to mention *political* economists and sociologists. In this section of Chapter 1 we would like to provide yet another historical summary of what has come before us, this time with respect to the evolution of capital theory and its clear and inexorable convergence with sustainability theory, the latter of which had also been evolving on a path of its own, as we have already outlined above.

Before jumping into capital theory and its convergence with sustainability, however, a brief word on the manner in which concepts like *capital* can evolve – in very fortuitous and legitimate ways – would be in order. Listen to how Ostrom and Ahn address this issue in their very fine book *Foundations of Social Capital* (2003, p. xxv):

> [W]e call attention to the way the concept of capital itself is transformed when human capital is considered. The concept of human capital is today widely accepted; see Becker (1993[1964]), for example. In the earlier stage of its development, the use of capital referring to knowledge and skills embedded in humans was heavily criticized.
>
> Exactly the same thing is happening now with regard to use of the concept of capital in 'social capital'. One does not wish to arbitrarily modify such a foundational concept as 'capital'. It is also counterproductive, however, to assume that the concept of capital has a fixed set of innate meanings. As knowledge grows, the denotation and connotation of a core scientific concept may change in a direction that is not purely whimsical. Conceptual development may well be productive in helping scholars understand more phenomena using a core set of conceptual tools.

We will have more to say about our own use of the term *capital* later on in this chapter. Now, however, it is time to briefly trace the evolution of *capital-based thinking* as a core concept in sustainability theory and practice, starting with Irving Fisher in 1906.

Irving Fisher

We begin with the writings of the American economist Irving Fisher, who in the early twentieth century was focused on the fundamental differences between capital and income. In 1906, he wrote as follows (Fisher, 2003[1906], p. 52):

> A *stock of wealth* existing at an *instant* of time is called *capital*. A *flow of services* through a *period* of time is called *income*.

Explicit reference to Fisher's ideas would later show up in the writings of Herman Daly, Robert Costanza and many other modern-day sustainability theorists, including ourselves, whose commitment to capital theory as a basis of sustainability practice is unshakable. Of particular importance in Fisher's contributions to both economics and sustainability is the all-important distinction he made between stocks (of capital) and flows (of income, or of goods or services), the combination of which is important for human well-being. While the concept of stocks and flows certainly did not originate with Fisher, his careful application of the idea to economics set the stage, as it were, for the broader application of capital theory to sustainability in the years that followed. As we shall see, the concept of capital stocks and flows, the dynamics between them, and their vital importance for human well-being would resurface repeatedly in the economics literature, especially in that part of it that would later converge with sustainability theory, per se.

Of additional importance in Fisher's writings, although to a lesser degree, was the manner in which he recognized non-traditional forms of capital (e.g., human capital) as no less legitimate forms of capital in the conceptual sense of things (i.e., as stocks that produce flows of valuable goods and/or services). This idea would later blossom into the more fully elaborated, multi-capital model we rely on so heavily today (further discussed below). Indeed, that, in combination with the stock–flow concept, the dynamics involved, and the importance of it all to human well-being, constitute perhaps the most basic and important conceptual foundations of modern-day sustainability theory and practice.

John Hicks (early)

From Fisher in 1906 we jump to 1939, to the writings of another influential economist, John Hicks, whose similar focus on the capital/income distinction was important not just to economics but to sustainability theory as well. In the passage that follows below, in which Hicks expounds on the concept of income (i.e., flows from capital), we see shades of things to come in terms of economic ideas that would later come home to roost in sustainability theory and practice (Hicks, 1939, p. 172):

> The purpose of income calculations in practical affairs is to give people an indication of the amount which they can consume without impoverishing themselves. Following out this idea, it would seem that we ought to define a

man's income as the maximum value which he can consume during a week, and still expect to be as well off at the end of the week as he was at the beginning. Thus, when a person saves, he plans to be better off in the future; when he lives beyond his income, he plans to be worse off. Remembering that the practical purpose of income is to serve as a guide for prudent conduct, I think it fairly clear that this is what the central meaning [of income] must be.

The parallels here between capital stocks and flows in the economic sense and, say, stocks of natural resources and the ecosystem services they provide in the sustainability sense are quite clear. Stocks and flows of *natural capital* are limited. Thus, in order to be 'better off', as Hicks would put it, we must live within our means and not beyond them.

Kenneth Boulding

Kenneth Boulding, another economist, was among the first in his field, if not *the* first, to make the definitive connection between capital theory and sustainability (although he didn't use that word) in a way that still informs us today. In 1949, Boulding wrote as follows (pp. 79–80):

> I shall argue that it is the capital stock from which we derive satisfactions, not from the additions to it (production) or the subtractions from it (consumption): that consumption, far from being a desideratum, is a deplorable property of the capital stock which necessitates the equally deplorable activities of production: and that the objective of economic policy should not be to maximize consumption or production, but rather to minimise it, i.e., to enable us to maintain our capital stock with as little consumption or production as possible. It is not the increase of consumption which makes us rich, but the increase in capital, and any invention which enables us to enjoy a given stock with a smaller amount of consumption and production, out-go or income, is so much gain.

In the same article from which the quotation above is taken, Boulding names no fewer than four non-traditional or non-economic forms of capital that he feels are subject to the principles he describes: human capital, cultural capital, intellectual capital and geological capital. It is the last capital (geological) that is perhaps the predecessor to what today we refer to as natural capital. On that topic, Boulding had the following to say (1949, p. 82):

> In the case of commodities, however, the problem is complicated by the existence of what may be called 'geological capital'; the stores of coal, oil, minerals, metal, ores, etc., which have been accumulated in the earth over the long process of geological time.
>
> We may be squandering our geological capital of ores, fuels, and soils, that it has taken the whole of geological time to accumulate, on such frivolities as war

and a high standard of life at a rate which bodes ill for much permanent future for the human race.

Here we see in graphic terms an economist in 1949 applying the otherwise purely economic terms of capital and income to the environment in ways that clearly not just evoke, but explicitly raise, sustainability themes and concerns. If it is possible to point to a specific moment in time when the convergence between economics (capital theory, in particular) and sustainability took place, this is probably it: 1949, in the form of Boulding's article.

Despite the fact that Boulding had already more or less bridged the economics–sustainability divide by 1949, he is perhaps best known in this regard for an essay he wrote in 1966 entitled 'The economics of the coming spaceship earth' (Boulding, 1966). In that essay, he wrote as follows (pp. 9–10):

> The essential measure of the success of the economy is not production and consumption at all, but the nature, extent, quality, and complexity of the total capital stock, including in this the state of human bodies and minds included in the system. In the spaceman economy [Boulding's term for the increasingly ecologically constrained economy], what we are primarily concerned with is stock maintenance, and any technological change which results in the maintenance of a given total stock with a lessened throughput (that is, less production and consumption) is clearly a gain. This idea that both production and consumption are bad things rather than good things is very strange to economists, who have been obsessed with the income-flow concepts to the exclusion, almost, of capital-stock concepts.

Commenting on Boulding's writings, Pearce (1988, pp. 70–71) had the following to say:

> The idea that human welfare flows from the stock of capital, widely construed, rather than the flow of services from it (income or throughput), owes its origins to Kenneth Boulding (1966). But Boulding's conception embraced all capital including the stock of knowledge and 'spiritual capital'.

Other than the fact that Boulding had already published his thinking along these lines as early as 1949 (i.e., long before 1966), we agree with Pearce's assessment. Indeed, Boulding was demonstrably the first economist/sustainability theorist to (a) apply both the language and the principles of stocks and flows to sustainability issues, and (b) intentionally expand the scope of capitals to include more than just narrow economic, or even natural, ones. Indeed, the capital theory we and many others rely on today as a basis for sustainability theory and practice can be traced to Boulding's words in 1949 and 1966, the effects of which were clearly seminal and prophetic.

John Hicks (late)

From Boulding in 1949 and 1966, we circle back to John Hicks, who in 1974 in an influential article entitled 'Capital controversies: ancient and modern' (1974, p. 308) drew the now-familiar connections between capital stocks and income flows as follows:

> [T]he capital of an economy is its stock of real goods, with power of producing further goods (or utilities) in the future – the stock of such goods existing in the economy at a moment in time.

Here we see echoes not only of Hicks' own earlier writings in 1939, but also of those before him by Fisher in 1906. Of additional significance in what Hicks wrote was the focus on the productive nature of capital, which according to capital theory, of course, is one of its defining characteristics. Capital, that is, is a productive thing, not a passive one, in that it can actually generate flows of valuable goods and/or services. This idea, that there are capitals in the world that can actively produce flows of valuable goods and services, is perhaps the most important thing to understand about contemporary sustainability theory and practice, including the notion that such flows are vital for human well-being, and that capital, therefore, is also vital and must be preserved, produced and/or maintained in order for human well-being to prevail. The choice of whether or not to do so, then, is a key determinant of the sustainability performance of organizations.

Herman Daly

Not too long after Boulding and Hicks came Herman Daly, another economist and well-known co-founder of *Ecological Economics*, who in the same language of stocks and flows had this to say about what a steady-state economy (i.e., a sustainable one) might look like (Daly, 1977, p. 17):

> Thus we may succinctly define a *steady-state economy* (hereafter abbreviated SSE) as *an economy with constant stocks of people and artifacts, maintained at some desired, sufficient levels by low rates of maintenance 'throughput'*, that is, by the lowest feasible flows of matter and energy from the first stage of production (depletion of low-entropy materials from the environment) to the last stage of consumption (pollution of the environment with high-entropy wastes and exotic materials). It should be continually remembered that SSE is a *physical* concept. If something is nonphysical, then perhaps it can grow forever. If something can grow forever, then certainly it is nonphysical.

Here again we see the familiar language of stocks and flows being applied to sustainability subject matter, this time by a former World Bank economist and major contributor to the sustainability literature – a living testament to the convergence of economics and sustainability, if ever there was one. Daly would go on to make many more contributions to sustainability, as we will shortly see.

Pearce and Turner

Next we want to acknowledge the writings of Pearce and Turner, who in 1990 added to the growing chorus of thinkers who were clearly settling on the idea that sustainability is capital-based, and that in order for the conduct of human affairs to be sustainable – its *economic* affairs, in particular – natural capital stocks, at the very least, must not be allowed to decline in size or sufficiency. They expressed this idea as follows (Pearce and Turner, 1990, p. 52):

> Our discussion so far has suggested that sustainability can be analysed in terms of a requirement to maintain the natural capital stock. This requirement ensures that we observe the 'bounds' set by the functioning of the natural environment in its role of support system for the economy.

Pearce and Turner's use of the term 'bounds' can be seen as foreshadowing the manner in which we and others have since argued that sustainability performance is a function of impacts on vital capitals relative to specific limits or thresholds for what such impacts ought to be, or must be, in order for behaviors to be sustainable. Pearce and Turner, however, were primarily concerned with the bounds of natural capital only. As we will show in Chapter 3, in particular, the concept of bounds or thresholds is applicable to all forms of capital, not just natural capital, the fact of which is crucial for CSM.

Paul Ekins

Following Pearce and Turner came Paul Ekins in 1992, when he published an article entitled 'A four-capital model of wealth creation' (Ekins, 1992). There he took the position that there are four vital capitals required for economic well-being: *environmental capital, human capital, physically produced capital* and *social/organizational capital* (p. 149). These classifications of capital have arguably held steady to this day in terms of how sustainability theorists view the vital capitals required for human well-being. Indeed, the typology of capitals we ourselves rely on in this book, while expressed in slightly different terms in some cases, is largely identical to Ekins', as are the capital frameworks used by many others.

Robert Costanza and Herman Daly

Also in 1992 – a busy year for sustainability theorists – came Costanza and Daly, who, like Boulding in 1949 and 1966, really planted the sustainability flag, so to speak, in the territory known as capital theory. That year they wrote as follows (Costanza and Daly, 1992, p. 38):

Since 'capital' is traditionally defined as produced (manufactured) means of production, the term 'natural capital' needs explanation. It is based on a more functional definition of capital as 'a stock that yields a flow of valuable goods and services into the future'. What is functionally important is a relation of a stock yielding a flow – whether the stock is manufactured or natural is in this view a distinction between kinds of capital and not a defining characteristic of capital itself.

In this book we use the terms *capital* and *vital capitals* in a fashion largely consistent with the definition given above, and would only very slightly modify it as follows:

Vital capital is a stock of anything that yields a flow of valuable goods or services important to human well-being.

Our use of the term *vital* to modify *capital* is intended to designate those forms of capitals (and their flows) that are essential to maintaining basic levels of human well-being, as opposed to capitals or flows that might exceed or are irrelevant to such needs. In any case, the sense in which we use the term *capital* is clearly consistent with the way in which many leading theorists and scholars in sustainability now routinely use the term. Moreover, our addition of the phrase 'of anything' to the Costanza/Daly formulation (in line with Porritt, 2005, p. 112) is intended to help secure a permanent place for the inclusion of non-material – or non-natural – capitals in the capital basis of sustainability theory, as others before us, such as Boulding and Ekins, have also attempted to do.

William Rees and Mathis Wackernagel

Next in the convergence of capital theory and sustainability came the Ecological Footprint Method (Rees, 1992; Wackernagel and Rees, 1996) in which natural capital, in particular, was the main focus of interest. About that the authors had the following things to say (Wackernagel and Rees, 1996, p. 35):

Natural capital refers to any stock of natural assets that yields a flow of valuable goods and services into the future. For example, a forest, a fish stock or an aquifer can provide a harvest or flow that is potentially sustainable year after year. The forest or fish stock is 'natural capital' and the sustainable harvest is 'natural income.' Natural capital also provides such services as waste assimilation, erosion and flood control, and protection from ultraviolet radiation. (Thus, the ozone layer is a form of natural capital.) These life support services are also counted as natural income.

The Ecological Footprint Method holds a special place in our own thinking because it is perhaps the first and most explicit attempt to convert capital theory into context-based sustainability measurement and reporting. How so? Mainly in the way it took actual capital conditions on the ground, so to speak – albeit natural capital only – explicitly into account while measuring human impacts against them. This would later turn out to be an important source of inspiration for our own attempts to broaden the approach so as to include vital capitals of all kinds, and also to apply it at the level of individual organizations in a much more rigorous way (i.e., the subject of this book, or what can be thought of as *sustainability accounting*).

John Elkington and the triple bottom line

Following Wackernagel and Rees, more or less, came John Elkington, whose intro-duction of the phrase *triple bottom line* into the lexicon of sustainability earned him a permanent place in the sustainability hall of fame, if only because of the sticking power of his metaphor. There should be no confusion, however, about the extent to which Elkington relied on capital theory as the basis for his thinking; indeed, he did so to a very great extent. In Chapter 4 of his 1997 classic *Cannibals with Forks – The Triple Bottom Line of 21st Century Business*, Elkington clearly lays out the capital basis of his thinking for each of the three bottom lines in terms of (1) economic capital (for the economic bottom line), (2) natural capital (for the environmental bottom line), and (3) social capital (for the social bottom line). As a prelude to all of that, Elkington makes the following statement (p. 72):

> But sustainable capitalism will need more than just environment-friendly technologies and, however important these may be, markets which actively promote dematerialization. We will also need to address radically new views of what is meant by social equity, environmental justice and business ethics. This will require a much better understanding not only of financial and physical forms of capital, but also of natural, human, and social capital.

We will have more to say about the connections between Elkington's thinking and our own approach to CSM in a separate section on the triple bottom line below.

Jonathon Porritt

Leaving the twentieth century now and stepping into the present one, we find another very influential thinker, Jonathon Porritt, whose 2005 book *Capitalism as if the World Mattered* constitutes an overt commitment to capital theory by a leading sustainability theorist. In a chapter entitled 'The five capitals framework' in which Porritt builds on the work done by others before him, including Ekins and his four-capitals model, Porritt defines capital as 'a stock of anything that has the capacity to generate a flow of benefits which are valued by humans' (Porritt, 2005, p. 112), a definition after which our own version (given above) has been patterned, and which along with our own thinking has been influenced by many others.

The specific capitals Porritt identifies in his book are as follows (p. 113):

- Natural Capital
- Human Capital
- Social Capital
- Manufactured Capital [what we call *constructed* capital, and what others call *built* capital]
- Financial Capital.

Only the first four non-financial capitals are of interest to us in CSM, of course, since financial capital is otherwise the subject of financial management, not non-financial management. That said, it should be clear that financial or monetary capital is also required to help preserve and/or create non-financial vital capitals, and that financial capital, too, is therefore needed in order to ensure human well-being. We understand that. Our point here is to simply say that while we already have measurement models and metrics for recording impacts on financial or monetary capital that are context-based, no such (context-based) solutions for recording the *non*-financial impacts of business are yet in widespread use. Our purpose in this book is to propose one.

Daly's rules

Turning back to Herman Daly, whose individual writings on sustainability theory and practice have been especially influential, he was among the first to codify the practice implications of the capital-based approach in a way that could be harnessed for implementation at a social, and even organizational, level. More specifically, three principles of sustainability for managing impacts on natural capital, in particular, were developed by Daly, which together are sometimes referred to as *Daly's rules*. Daly explains his rules in an article written in 1990, entitled 'Toward some operational principles of sustainable development', as follows (Daly, 1990, pp. 2 and 4):

> For the management of renewable resources there are two obvious principles of sustainable development. First that harvest rates should equal [or not exceed] regeneration rates (sustained yield). Second that waste emission rates should equal [or not exceed] the natural assimilative capacities of the ecosystems into which the wastes are emitted. Regenerative and assimilative capacities must be treated as natural capital, and failure to maintain these capacities must be treated as capital consumption, and therefore not sustainable.
>
> There remains the category of nonrenewable resources which strictly speaking cannot be maintained intact short of nonuse ... Yet it is possible to exploit nonrenewables in a quasi-sustainable manner by limiting their rate of depletion to the rate of creation of renewable substitutes.
>
> The quasi-sustainable use of nonrenewables requires that any investment in the exploitation of a nonrenewable resource must be paired with a

compensating investment in a renewable substitute (e.g., oil extraction paired with tree planting for wood alcohol).

Meadows et al. (1992), for their part, openly embraced Daly's principles and summarized them as follows (p. 209):

> In order to be physically sustainable [a] society's material and energy throughputs would have to meet economist Herman Daly's three conditions:
> 1. Its rates of use of renewable resources do not exceed their rates of regeneration;
> 2. Its rates of use of nonrenewable resources do not exceed the rate at which sustainable renewable resources are developed;
> 3. Its rates of pollution emission do not exceed the assimilative capacity of the environment.

Here we wish to make two general observations regarding Daly's principles, or rules, that are important to our thesis. The first is that his principles deal exclusively with the ecological impacts of human activities on natural capital. There is no standard of performance or criterion for social or economic sustainability in his formulation. Instead, his principles are expressed in terms of impacts on natural capital only, and there is no reason to believe he had anything else in mind (see our discussion of rules for impacts on anthro capital in Chapter 2).

Our second point is to simply observe that Daly's formulation is a highly quantitative and almost operational one. Not only does he provide mathematical conditions or criteria for sustainability, but he implicitly tells us how to operationalize a corresponding measurement and reporting scheme. To assess the ecological sustainability of a human social system, he seems to be saying, one need only measure and compare the related rates of renewable resource use, non-renewable resource use and waste emissions with the corresponding rates of renewable resource regeneration, renewable resource development and waste assimilation, respectively.

It should also be clear that the Ecological Footprint Method (EFM) discussed above is, for all intents and purposes, an implementation of Daly's rules. Both bodies of work are based on the view that natural resources, living organisms and ecosystem services (i.e., natural capital) are limited, and that the human use of and/or impact on such resources cannot be open-ended without putting their existence and human well-being at risk. Both bodies of work also share the same limitations, consisting mainly of (a) their confinement to environmental sustainability issues as opposed to sustainability more broadly defined, and (b) their rare appearance or use in organizational or business settings. It is a very rare thing indeed to see the EFM applied at the level of an organization in ways that are true to the context-based roots that lie behind it. Instead, it is most often used in connection with country-level or regional analyses. But that, of course, is part of what has motivated the writing of this book – context is just as critical to understanding the sustainability of a company as it is to understanding the sustainability of a country. The measurement principles applied on both fronts, too, must be the same.

The triple bottom line

Next in our investigation of the origins and meaning of CBS is the very well-known concept, or organizing principle, of the triple bottom line (TBL). By most accounts, the TBL phrase itself was first coined by John Elkington in his book *Cannibals with Forks – The Triple Bottom Line of 21st Century Business* (Elkington, 1997). Elkington explained his meaning of the term as follows (p. 70):

> Today we think in terms of a 'triple bottom line,' focusing on economic prosperity, environmental quality, and – the element which business had preferred to overlook – social justice.

While it may be true that Elkington first coined the TBL phrase itself, it should also be clear from the historical survey of sustainability concepts above that the idea of non-financial impacts of three kinds and the need for businesses to bear them in mind has been in the air, so to speak, since as early as the beginning of the eighteenth century. Again, Edinger and Kaul's references to the writings of Hans Carl von Carlowitz (Von Carlowitz, 1713) come quickly to mind here, given the evidence they found of Von Carlowitz's concern with 'the triad principles of sustainability (ecology, economy and social aspects)' (Edinger and Kaul, 2003, p. 5).

Functionally, the concept of the triple bottom line is an organizing principle for sustainability that happens also to involve the use of a metaphor – in other words, the relatively new non-financial performance idea expressed in more familiar financial terms. Most important, however, is the fact that the TBL is an organizing principle for non-financial (or sustainability) measurement, management and reporting. It is an organizing principle in the sense that it tells us, roughly, what the subject includes and how it should be structured. Specifically, it tells us that organizational performance is not just a matter of profits and losses; there are non-financial dimensions of performance to be accounted for as well. Indeed, it tells us that there are three of them: social performance, environmental performance and economic performance, where *economic* performance is distinguished from *financial* performance (further discussed below).

Perhaps the best and most significant illustration of the TBL in practice can be found in the Global Reporting Initiative (2011), the leading international (de facto) standard for corporate sustainability measurement and reporting. GRI's third-generation or G3.1 standard, as it's known, is explicitly organized around the triple bottom line, with indicators identified for sustainability and reporting purposes falling into four categories that include the following three: *Economic*, *Environmental* and *Social*. The fourth category, *Strategy and Profile*, is more descriptive of the organization, whereas the other three categories are intended to describe performance, per se.

The TBL brings two things of interest to us in our thinking:

1. We, too, subscribe to the TBL as an organizing principle for sustainability measurement, management and reporting, albeit with some important differences (further discussed below). In other words, it helps us to simplify an otherwise complex world in a rational and compelling way.
2. We, like Elkington, focus explicitly on capitals as a basis for thinking about sustainability performance, and for how to measure, manage and report it; what's more, the capitals of interest to us map neatly into the three areas of impact identified in the triple bottom line: natural capital into the environmental bottom line, and human, social and constructed capitals into both the social and economic bottom lines (further discussed in Chapters 2 and 3).

Despite the common underpinnings of CBS and the TBL, all implementations of the TBL have thus far been context-free. Indeed, while some people (very few) have called for the inclusion of context in TBL reporting (including GRI), there are no commonly accepted, much less published, guidelines for how to do so. This is a serious problem, since one can hardly subscribe to points 1 and 2 above without having a methodology for how to operationalize and practice the kind of capital-based TBL theory they entail. After all, if the impact of an organization's activities on various non-financial capitals must be taken into account when assessing its sustainability performance – as Elkington and others have argued – then such capitals must play an explicit role in related tools, methods and metrics. Elkington, however, provided no guidance for how to do so, nor has GRI to a sufficient degree.[3] And yet sustainability performance cannot be meaningfully measured and/or reported, much less managed, without it.

For all intents and purposes, then, the capital-based, TBL orientation to sustainability (i.e., the dominant school of thought in the field) has never really been fully operationalized, and is practically begging for guidance on how to finish the job by including context in practice. Indeed, what the field of CSM desperately needs right now is a body of context-based TBL theory and practice, which of course is what we claim to be offering in this book.

In our embrace of the TBL model as an organizing principle for sustainability, we actually depart from Elkington and many others who hold to it in two important ways:

1. We do not subscribe to the view that the economic bottom line is synonymous with the financial bottom line. As Jennings put it (Jennings, 2004, p. 157):

> So, while the economic component of the triple bottom line is often assumed to be synonymous with financial performance, in fact, there are significant differences between the two. In its simplest form, finance is about the provision of money when and where required for consumption or for investment in commerce. As such, it concerns the market valuation of transactions that pass through a company's books. Economics, on the other hand, is the means by

which society uses human and natural resources in the pursuit of human welfare. As a result, economics extends beyond the boundaries of a single organization and is inextricably linked to both the environmental and social elements of sustainable development.

What this means, then, is that there are actually four major bottom lines to contend with, not three. It is not *people–planet–profit*, as the now common TBL refrain would have us believe. This is decidedly misleading and leaves out altogether the important economic impacts an organization can have (positive and negative) in society at large, in ways that have nothing to do with their own financial bottom lines. We will have more to say about the practice implications of this view in Chapter 2.

2. We do not subscribe to a strict TBL interpretation in the sense that there are only three non-financial or sustainability bottom lines: social, environmental and economic. Rather, we take the position that there are many more such bottom lines, each of which, however, can indeed be categorized in one or more of the three major groupings (i.e., bottom lines can be composed of sub-bottom lines). An organization's social bottom line performance, for example, might consist of impacts on employee well-being, community well-being and customer well-being in ways that involve impacts on different forms of capital. Since dissimilar capitals are not interchangeable or substitutable for one another, one cannot simply add them up together in order to arrive at a blended sum (further discussed in Chapter 3). Thus, each might require its own bottom line – or sub-bottom line – thereby leading to the possibility of having many more than just three.

For all of its virtues and attractive qualities, the triple bottom line has been little more than a metaphor since it was first conceived in 1997. What has been missing has been a methodology for operationalizing it. In order to have that, however, some agreement on basic or first principles is required. We now turn our attention to exactly that.

A modern-day theory of practice for CSM

In Chapter 3 we will provide a highly detailed methodology for operationalizing the triple bottom line, or CSM more broadly. That methodology, in turn, will be an implementation of CBS, which itself is predicated on a number of basic principles we have already mentioned, but which require further explanation. Of most importance to CBS are three concepts, in particular, which together provide CBS with the theoretical basis it needs in order to be effective and to be truly *context-based*. Those three concepts are (1) human well-being, (2) vital capitals and (3) carrying capacity. In this next section of Chapter 1, then, we will take each of these three concepts and explain what it is, and how it contributes to the development of an operationalized form of the triple bottom line.

Human well-being

The overall approach to sustainability measurement, management and reporting put forward in this book is founded upon the view that sustainability performance is a function of impacts on vital capitals – or vital capital resources – relative to what such impacts need to be in order to ensure human well-being. This is sometimes called the capital-based or capital theory approach to sustainability (see, for example, Stern, 1997; Ruta and Hamilton, 2007; Stiglitz et al., 2009). Under the capital-based view, the sustainability of an organization's operations can be determined by first establishing standards of performance for what its impacts on vital capitals ought to be in order to ensure human (or stakeholder) well-being – which can sometimes require *no* impact, such as not poisoning a neighbor's well – and by then measuring its actual impacts against them.

Stated in more precise terms, the approach to sustainability we are advocating here is one that holds organizations accountable to a test of measuring their impacts on resources of vital importance to their own stakeholders' well-being. Thus, inherent in the capital-based approach is a central role for stakeholder consideration, and the idea that organizations have certain duties and obligations to act with the well-being of their stakeholders in mind. While this has always been the case in terms of financial performance (i.e., the norm that organizations should always try to maximize profits on behalf of their *shareholders*), it has only recently become the case for non-financial or non-monetary performance as well.

What we are arguing for, then, is a broader interpretation of organizational performance, according to which *performance* consists of *both* financial and non-financial outcomes. In addition to existing models for measuring, managing and reporting financial performance – which we accept – our purpose here, therefore, is to propose a new (and similarly context-based) solution for measuring, managing and reporting non-financial performance. This, too, is one reason why we make the sharp distinction between the financial and economic bottom lines, as earlier discussed, since we do not want to confuse the two or muddy the waters in terms of which methodology should be used for each. That said, we fully recognize the role that financial or monetary capital can play in helping to achieve sustainable, non-financial performance – we simply want to focus on only the non-financial side of performance in such cases, not the financial one.

Despite the distinction we can make here between sustainability in the financial sense and sustainability in the non-financial sense, sustainability as a social science or management discipline in either case is ultimately grounded in the concept of human well-being. The reason anyone cares about sustainability at all, that is, is because *un*sustainability in the conduct of human affairs puts human well-being at risk, usually by diminishing or failing to produce and/or maintain vital capital resources at levels required to meet basic human needs. Thus, the impacts of unsustainable behaviors on human well-being are usually indirect – we only directly impact vital capitals, that is, the effects of which are then indirectly felt by people who depend on them (the capitals) in order to meet their needs.

Despite the importance of *human well-being* as a conceptual foundation in the approach to CSM put forward in this book, we will not be advocating for a particular thesis or interpretation of that idea here. Indeed, there are many different and competing points of view as to what constitutes human well-being and how to measure it. Instead, we have opted to take the position that whether or not a particular human activity (e.g., a manufacturing operation) is sustainable is ultimately a function of the degree to which the effects of such activity on vital capitals in the world are what they ought to be in order to ensure stakeholder well-being. From a methodological standpoint, then, it is up to individual sustainability managers, not us, to determine how best to define stakeholder well-being, or which interpretation of it to employ, and also to determine what the corresponding levels of vital resources must be in order to ensure it.

With that in mind, it may be helpful to provide the reader with a summary of resources that can be used to investigate the literature on well-being, and the many different, if not competing, points of view about how to conceive of and express it. McGillivray and Clarke provide very useful background and a collection of related articles on human well-being in their book *Understanding Human Well-Being* (2006), in which they first call attention to the ambiguity of the term (p. 3):

> Human well-being, however, is an ambiguous concept. It lacks a universally acceptable definition and has numerous, often competing, interpretations … Further, terms such as quality of life, welfare, well-living, living standards, utility, life satisfaction, prosperity, needs fulfillment, development, empowerment, capability expansion, human development, poverty, human poverty, and, more recently, happiness are often used interchangeably with well-being without explicit discussion as to their distinctiveness.

The authors go on to make the very important point that despite differences in how various scholars define well-being, most agree that it cannot be directly measured, and that indicators (or indirect measures), therefore, are required to monitor and keep abreast of it. While most such indicators in the past were of an economic sort, many contemporary indices have broadened to include non-economic aspects of human life, including capabilities, agency and functionings (see, for example, Maslow, 1971; Sen, 1984, 1999, 2006; Nussbaum, 1988, 1992, 2000; Doyal and Gough, 1991; Max-Neef, 1991; and Narayan et al., 2000). Importantly, the authors further point out that issues 'such as gender and sustainability have also become increasingly integrated within human well-being analysis' (McGillivray and Clarke, 2006, p. 4).

Dasgupta (2001), however, observes that income 'continues to be regarded as the "quintessential" well-being indicator' (p. 53). Indeed, many analysts tend to equate human welfare with material wealth. Accordingly, various economic metrics such as Gross National Product (GNP), Gross Domestic Product (GDP) or income per capita are frequently used to assess and report the general well-being of people in national settings. As McGillivray and Clarke point out, however, 'the limitations of income-based (or consumption-based) measures of human well-being are well known, including limitations around equity, environment and [their] own construction' (2006, p. 4).

In response to the perceived limitations of such uni-dimensional indicators, another class of *composite* indicators has emerged over the years, including the UNDP's Human Development Index (HDI), the UN's Millennium Development Goals (MDGs), the UN's Commission on Sustainable Development (CSD) indicators, the World Bank's World Development Indicators (WDIs) and many others. Some sources have even gone so far as to combine aspects of multiple indices into meta-indices. Cherchye and Kuosmanen (2006), for example, combine aspects of 14 well-known indices into a single, synthesized sustainability index.

Separate and apart from the kind of *objective* indicators discussed above, there has recently emerged an entirely new and different class of *subjective* schemes (McGillivray and Clarke, 2006, pp. 4–5). Such subjective schemes tend to focus on happiness as the principal indicator of well-being, including consideration of 'cognitive judgements of life satisfaction and effective evaluations of emotions and moods' (McGillivray and Clarke, 2006, p. 4; see also Diener, 1984; Argyle, 1987; Diener and Larsen, 1993; and Eid and Diener, 2003). One particularly extensive index, or database, of subjective happiness, the World Happiness Database (Veenhoven, 2004), contains 2,300 surveys from 112 countries, dating from as far back as 1946 to the present day.

Again, we provide the brief summary of human well-being indices above for background purposes only, and not because we intend to study them further or choose from among them. Our preference, instead, is to remain neutral on the subject, since it is our intention to provide a measurement solution, or methodology, for determining the sustainability performance of organizations that can be used with any one of them.

Vital capitals

Earlier we defined vital capitals as stocks of resources that produce flows of valuable goods and services essential to achieving and maintaining basic levels of human well-being. In this section we want to build on the claim that vital capitals are important to human well-being, and also be more specific about the particular forms of capital we have in mind.

As noted earlier, the essence of capital theory is that there are resources in the world, known as capitals, which are productive in the sense that they generate flows of valuable goods and services important to human well-being. Natural capital, for example, consists of natural or ecological resources in the world that generate material flows of nutritional and life-sustaining resources (e.g., food and water for human sustenance, and physical materials for housing and other needs), living organisms, and non-material flows of ecosystem services (e.g., photosynthesis, water filtration, climate regulation, plant pollination, decomposition of wastes, and even spiritual, aesthetic and recreational enrichment).

While natural capital may be the only type of capital of interest to ecological economists or practitioners of the Ecological Footprint Method, it is not the only form of capital of interest to corporate sustainability managers, or to sustainability theorists and practitioners interested in sustainability in its broader form. Indeed, there are three other types of vital capital to consider, all of which pertain to sustainability in the non-environmental or non-ecological sense of the term. The three additional capitals are as follows:

Human capital: Human capital consists of *individual* knowledge, skills, experience, health and ethical entitlements that enhance the potential for effective individual action and human well-being.

Social capital: Social capital consists of *shared* knowledge and organizational resources (e.g., formal or informal networks of people committed to achieving common goals) that enhance the potential for effective individual and collective action and human well-being.

Constructed capital: Constructed capital (or built capital) consists of *material objects and/or physical systems or infrastructures* created by humans. It is the material world of human artifacts in which human knowledge is also embedded, and which humans use in order to take effective action.

These non-natural forms of capital are very much like natural capital in the sense that they produce flows of valuable goods and services required for human well-being; they differ from natural capital, though, in the sense that they are exclusively human-made – natural capital is not. In other words, they are anthropogenic. For this reason, we refer to them collectively as *anthro capital*.

As the definitions above imply, capital is very instrumental in form; that is, it is not only productive, but the flows of beneficial goods and services it produces are consumed and utilized by humans in ways that allow them to take effective action in order to ensure their own well-being. Thus, the capital-based theory of sustainability holds to a view of the world in which four kinds of capitals and related flows can be found, the latter of which (the flows) humans depend on and consume in order to take effective action in the service of their own well-being (see Figure 1.1 for a schematic view of the dynamics we describe here). Of course, the volumes of flows may not always be sufficient to meet the levels of demand placed upon them, in which case human well-being can suffer.

On the other hand, because anthro capitals, for their part, are anthropogenic, we can almost always make more of them if and when they are in short supply, given the will and the resources required to do so. We can do this by learning, for example, and thereby increase the stock of human capital available to us as individuals; we can do this by creating more schools, hospitals, or judicial or law enforcement agencies, and thereby increase our stocks of social capital; or we can create more roads, utilities, public transportation systems, buildings, tools and technologies, and thereby increase our supply of constructed capital. All of this and more we can do with anthro capital, but not with natural capital. Why not? Because natural capital is not anthropogenic; rather, it is natural in origin and limited in supply. To the extent that we use it, we must do so with care and with attention paid to whether or not the resources we are

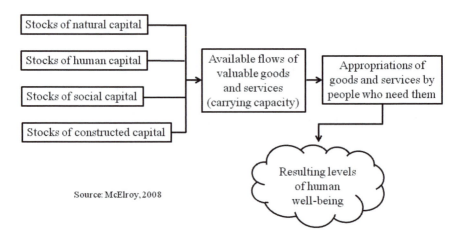

Source: McElroy, 2008

FIGURE 1.1 Vital capitals and human well-being.

using are renewable, non-renewable or in sufficient supply to meet the needs of a rapidly growing human population on Earth.

Insofar as the quality or sufficiency of vital capitals is concerned relative to levels required for human well-being, there are many things in the world that can affect them (the capitals and their sufficiency). One such thing is commerce, and the effects organizations (businesses) can have that function within it. Organizations can have enormous impacts on the quality of natural capital, for example, including negative ones, as recent events in the Gulf of Mexico made clear. Similarly, organizations can have very positive effects on the quality of human well-being, as the life-enhancing effects of educational and healthcare institutions also make clear.

The main point here is that organizations can and do have impacts on the quality and sufficiency of vital capitals in the world, and it is precisely the nature and extent of those impacts that determine whether or not their operations are sustainable. Exactly how to operationalize related measurement, management and reporting will be the subject of Chapter 3. For now, suffice it to say that it is the quality and sufficiency of vital capitals in the world, relative to standards for what impacts on them ought to be (in order to ensure human well-being), that constitute the particular kind of context of interest to us in context-based sustainability. All of this can be quantified in ways that make non-financial bottom line management much more than a metaphor, the quantitative expression of which involves a concept that we and many others refer to as the *carrying capacity* of capitals.

Carrying capacity

Above we made the claim that the sustainability performance of an organization is a function of what its impacts on vital capitals are, compared with what such impacts ought or need to be in order to ensure human well-being. Impacts that conform to *normative* levels or *standards of performance* grounded in basic levels of human well-being can be said to be sustainable; impacts that do not can be said to be unsustainable.

In this regard, we have specifically made reference to the *quality and sufficiency* of vital capitals as the key consideration in determining whether or not an organization's impacts are sustainable. Implicit in our logic, then, is a prior determination of some kind as to how much capital is required to ensure human well-being as a basis for determining what an organization's impacts should or should not be. What, then, is it that determines whether or not a volume or quantity of capital is of a sufficient quality or supply to ensure human well-being? The answer, we suggest, is its *carrying capacity* relative to the needs of a population that depends on it. This gives rise to the following definition of sustainability, upon which we will rely from this point forward:

> *Sustainability is the subject of a social science or management discipline that measures and/or manages the impacts of human activities on the carrying capacities of vital capitals in the world, relative to standards or norms for what such capacities need to be in order to ensure human well-being.*[4]

If, as we have suggested, capital can be defined as a stock of anything that yields a flow of valuable goods or services to people who need it in order to ensure their well-being (see again Figure 1.1), it is the quality or size of the flows, in particular, that determines whether or not a stock of capital from which they come is sufficient, or big enough. This measure of the quality or sufficiency of flows from capital can be expressed in terms of the size of a human population they (the flows) are capable of supporting and/or the volume of demand they can meet. The number of beds in a hospital, for example, is a measure of its carrying capacity to provide healthcare services; the number of students a school can handle is a measure of its carrying capacity to provide educational services; and the number of people a water resource can support without exceeding the rate at which its flows are regenerated is, in turn, a measure of its carrying capacity to meet the freshwater needs of a community.

Carrying capacity is therefore a measure of the size and sufficiency of valuable goods and services that flow from vital capitals, the relevance of which to sustainability measurement and reporting is fundamental. Indeed, when we set out to measure and report the sustainability of an organization's impacts on vital capitals (i.e., to assess the sustainability of its activities), it is the organization's impacts on the carrying capacities of *flows* from vital capitals, in particular, that we are talking about. In fact, if it is *not* the organization's impacts on the carrying capacities of flows from vital capitals we are talking about, then we are not talking about sustainability at all – something else, perhaps, but not sustainability.

Here it should be clear that the use of carrying capacity as a concept is certainly not new to sustainability, or at least not to some aspects of it. Most of us, for example, perhaps first encountered the term in our readings on ecology, where the concept of carrying capacity is frequently defined as 'the maximum population size that can be supported indefinitely by an environment' (Begon et al., 1996, p. 955). In the sustainability literature, however, the term is sometimes used in an inverted sense

(Rees, 1992, 2003; Wackernagel and Rees, 1996). Instead of referring to the population size that an environment can support, we can specify an environment size that a population must have. Thus, we can speak of carrying capacity as a requirement, and not just a de facto state of affairs.

This inverted sense of the term is especially important in the sustainability context, because it (a) helps us to quantify the disparities, if any, between human impacts on the natural environment and the capacity of the environment to withstand them, and (b) also helps us to quantify the levels of *anthro* capital that must be produced and/or maintained in order to ensure human well-being.

As a concept, then, the carrying capacity of capital provides us with precisely the kind of construct we need in order to do a proper job of measuring and reporting sustainability performance. And we are certainly not alone in thinking so:

> Carrying capacity may be the most versatile and widely popularized concept in environmental politics today. Like sustainability – which it predates and in many ways anticipates – carrying capacity can be applied to almost any human–environment interaction, at any scale, and it has the additional advantage of conveying a sense of calculability and precision – something that sustainability thus far lacks.
>
> *(Sayre, 2008, p. 120)*

To be clear, the specific approach to sustainability measurement, management and reporting put forward in this book relies very heavily upon the direct application of the concept of carrying capacity to vital capitals in the world. The methodology we advocate in Chapter 3 will therefore focus, in large part, on how organizations can and should measure, manage and report their impacts on the carrying capacities of vital capitals, relative to what such impacts must be in order for their activities or operations to be sustainable. It is precisely the state of such vital capitals, then, in terms of both their existing or required size and the quality and sufficiency of the flows they produce (or must produce) in order to ensure human well-being, that constitutes the *context* of such importance to us in context-based sustainability. Absent the carrying capacity of vital capitals to work with as a concept, there could be no context-based sustainability, much less *sustainability management* in any sort of literal or meaningful sense at all.

In sum, then, what all natural and anthro capitals have in common is that they produce flows of valuable goods and services that people rely on for their well-being. People quite literally consume these flows as resource inputs in their attempts to take effective action in order to ensure their own well-being. All of these flows, therefore, can be measured and expressed in terms of the number of people or the magnitude of human needs they can support. In cases where the available supply of valuable goods and services from capital flows is insufficient to meet such needs, human well-being is liable to suffer. That, in turn, is exactly what makes human activities or inactivities (i.e., actions or inactions) unsustainable under most interpretations of sustainability, including the context-based one to which we subscribe here. In other words, any action or inaction that results in the diminishment of vital capitals below required levels, or in the failure to produce and/or maintain them at levels required to ensure human well-being, can be said to be unsustainable. Carrying capacity, in turn, is the specific property or unit of measurement we can use in making such determinations.

Sustainability context

Having laid the conceptual foundations for CBS by looking at the history of context, the centrality of capital theory to sustainability, the relevance of human well-being, and the meaning of vital capitals and their carrying capacities, it is now time to provide a working definition for *sustainability context* in terms of how we will be using the idea from this point forward. For the purposes of CSM, then, the logic of defining or determining context in sustainability measurement, management and reporting can be described as a three-step procedure as follows:

1. **Carrying Capacities of Capitals**: First we identify the vital capitals (stocks) and their carrying capacities (flows) an organization is having impact on in ways that can affect stakeholder well-being, as well as capitals it *should* be having impact on in order to *ensure* stakeholder well-being.
2. **Responsible Populations**: Next we determine who the responsible populations are for ensuring the quality and sufficiency of such stocks and flows.
3. **Organizational Allocations**: And last, based on the first and second steps above, we allocate proportionate shares of available stocks and flows (in the case of natural capital) and/or burden shares for producing and/or maintaining them (in the case of anthro capital) to individual organizations.

Whether or not an organization's activities and impacts in the world are sustainable cannot be determined without reference to each of the three steps summarized above as a basis for determining context (see also Figure 1.2). In Chapter 3, we will illustrate

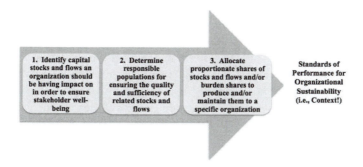

| 1. Identify capital stocks and flows an organization should be having impact on in order to ensure stakeholder well-being | 2. Determine responsible populations for ensuring the quality and sufficiency of related stocks and flows | 3. Allocate proportionate shares of stocks and flows and/or burden shares to produce and/or maintain them to a specific organization | Standards of Performance for Organizational Sustainability (i.e., Context!) |

FIGURE 1.2 The logic of determining context.

the application of this framework in more detail; now, however, we will simply explain it, starting with the first step in the determination of context: *Carrying Capacities of Capitals.*

Once an organization's impacts on a vital capital of some kind have been established as germane to a CSM program (i.e., either as a result of impacts it is already having on the capital, or because of an impact it ought to be having by dint of the relationship it has with a stakeholder group), the nature and status of the capital stocks and flows involved must be determined. The use of water resources, for example, must be assessed in light of available supplies (i.e., what their carrying capacity is), and whether or not they are sufficient in quantity and quality to ensure human well-being. Listen to how Gleick et al. from the Pacific Institute make the same point in their critique of mainstream (and context-free) sustainability reporting (2009, p. 36):

> **Lack of context in water reporting is a problem.** Most [corporate sustainability] reports provide some water data, but they do not provide context to these numbers ... Water performance – such as water use or wastewater discharge volume and load – and its impact on local environment and communities vary greatly according to the type of business and the water landscape where their facilities operate. Without the information on company- or industry-specific water challenges and associated water policies and management objectives, the readers of these reports can not fully understand or interpret the performance data presented.

Once an organization has determined who its stakeholders are and which capitals it either is or should be having impact on as a consequence of its relationship with them (further discussed in Chapter 3), the status of the specific capitals involved must be determined relative to levels of related flows required to ensure their well-being. A manufacturer that uses water resources in a community where it does business, for example, has at least a de facto relationship with all other members of the same community who rely on the same resources.

In order for its water use to be sustainable, then, the company involved must take steps to ensure that its use of local water resources does not deprive its neighbors of their own fair and proportionate shares, and that there is, in fact, enough water to go around. Thus, what must be determined as a first step in defining context is (a) what the relevant vital capital is that an organization either is already affecting or should be affecting (i.e., one of several, perhaps, required to ensure stakeholder well-being), (b) whether it is a form of natural capital or anthro capital, (c) what the overall size or volume of its stocks and flows are (or need to be), and (d) what the corresponding magnitude of demand is (expressed in terms of carrying capacity).

The second step in the determination of context – the *Responsible Populations* step – deals with the issue of who (or what party, group or population) is responsible for ensuring the quality or sufficiency of the flows of vital capital(s) identified in the first step (i.e., responsible for preserving, producing and/or maintaining the quality or sufficiency of the carrying capacities involved). In other words, is the organization solely responsible for ensuring such capitals and flows, or is it only one of many parties who share the same responsibility? In considering this question, it is first important to understand that the responsibility for ensuring the quality and sufficiency of vital capitals and their flows can take two forms: one form in which the responsibility is to constrain the organization's own use of related resources (e.g., water), and another form in which the responsibility is to produce and/or maintain a minimum level of available resources (e.g., product safety control as a component of its own operations). The first case involves impacts on natural capital, the second case on anthro capital.

Turning to cases where the vital capital of interest identified in step 1 is a form of natural capital (e.g., water), the implication is that the flows of valuable goods or services involved will lead to a *not-to-exceed* standard of performance to which the responsible population should orient itself, accordingly. Why? Because natural capital (and the flows that it produces) is only available in fixed amounts, which cannot be increased at will. The use or consumption of its flows, therefore, must be shared, budgeted and allocated in some way to the parties involved, so as to meet everyone's needs without exceeding total available supplies.

In cases where the vital capital of interest identified in step 1 is a form of anthro capital, the implication reverses, such that the flows of valuable goods or services involved must be continuously produced and/or maintained, thereby leading to a *not-to-fall-below* standard of performance to which the responsible population should orient itself, accordingly. Why? Because whereas natural capitals cannot be increased in volume or size, anthro capitals can. Parties responsible for the quality or sufficiency of anthro capital, that is, almost always have the option of producing more of it in order to meet their stakeholders' needs no matter what the demand. Thus, standards of performance for impacts on anthro capitals should be expressed in terms of minimums, not maximums.

Having determined whether or not the vital capital identified in step 1 is a natural capital or an anthro capital, step 2 then continues by determining who (or what group or population) is responsible for either (a) constraining its use of the capital involved (in the case of natural capital), or (b) producing and/or maintaining it (in the case of anthro capital). Why? Because in order to proceed to step 3, where we determine what an organization's own fair or proportionate share is, or ought to be, to have impact of some kind on a vital capital, the overall population responsible for managing the related stocks and flows must first be determined. The population served by (and that otherwise has impacts on) a given water resource, for example, would be the responsible population for preserving that resource, as opposed to only one organization that happens to use it. A manufacturer, by contrast, would typically be the only party responsible for maintaining the quality and sufficiency of its own product safety function, a type of internal anthro capital that stakeholders (customers, in particular) rely on for their own well-being.

The determination of the responsible population for preserving, producing and/or maintaining a vital capital therefore tells us whether or not the organization is solely responsible for the capital, or alternatively shares the responsibility with others. In cases where the responsibility is a shared one, the size of the population involved can be used to determine what the organization's own fair (or proportionate) share of the shared responsibility is, since the size of a proportionate share in such cases cannot be determined without reference to the overall size of the population involved. This takes us to step 3.

Once the responsible population for managing a capital has been identified, the third and final step in the determination of context – the *Organizational Allocations* step – deals with the issue of what the individual organization's specific allocation should be, of either a natural resource flow (i.e., a share of available natural resources) or an anthro capital flow (i.e., a share of the burden to produce and/or maintain vital human, social and constructed capitals). A company that does business in developing countries under extraordinarily favorable labor, tax and environmental conditions, for example, might feel compelled or duty-bound to contribute to the improvement of social conditions, but not exclusively so. In that case, the number of other companies involved in the same circumstances (i.e., as revealed by the *Responsible Populations* element above) coupled with a norm or an ethic for how such a general social burden ought to be shared or allocated to individual organizations could come into play – thereby leading to a calculated allocation or share of the burden to produce and/or maintain anthro capital that is context-based. Once this has occurred – be it for an anthro capital or a natural one – a normative, if not scientific, sustainability standard of performance will have been established.

Here it should be clear that the resulting allocation of either a natural resource flow or a burden to produce and/or maintain an anthro capital flow is, under our methodology, a voluntary and purely self-selected one – at least until such time as context-based reporting with shared principles for setting standards becomes the norm, or the subject of a standard itself. Until then, the allocations resulting from our method need only satisfy an organization's own sense of fairness, justice and proportionality, while also being open to inspection and criticism by others – especially stakeholders – as *more fair*, *more just* and *more proportionate* propositions are developed over time. In the meantime, neither consensus nor standards for any of this are required, only a willingness to hold oneself open and accountable to the allocation choices that have been made, recognizing all the while that it is better to have debatable standards of performance than no standards at all – a claim we will make more than once in this book. Meaningful sustainability measurement and reporting simply cannot occur without first determining what the allocations of duties or obligations should be to have impacts on capitals of vital importance to stakeholder well-being. This is the essence of context-based sustainability.

It is the *Organizational Allocations* element of context, then, that is perhaps the most defining characteristic of the context-based approach put forward in this book, since it makes it possible to define non-financial social and environmental standards of performance at the organizational level, given the actual state of vital capitals in the world, stakeholder demands for them, and an organization's proportionate share of responsibility for preserving, producing and/or maintaining them. Indeed, no other method we know of does this, not even the Ecological Footprint Method; although the latter does take the first two elements (or steps) of context determination into account, it does not the third.

Summary: context-based sustainability

In this chapter we have attempted to reveal the intellectual history of sustainability theory and practice, mainly in terms of context and the role it has played – and should continue to play – in mainstream thinking, and also capital theory, without which there would be no meaningful sustainability theory or practice to point to. It has also been our intent, of course, to define what *we* mean by context and how we intend to use it from this point forward. In sum, then, our key points have been as follows:

- The earliest known reference to context – not to mention the first use of the word *sustainability* in a management publication – took place in the writings of a Saxon mining administrator, Hans Carl von Carlowitz, in 1713, as he was developing principles for sustainable forestry.
- Following Von Carlowitz came a long procession of other thinkers whose writings also either (a) reflected the use of context in sustainability discourse, albeit under some different names, or (b) lamented the absence of it in places where it really ought to be – such as in sustainability measurement and reporting.
- This trend culminated, as it were, in 1997 with the launch of the Global Reporting Initiative (GRI), the leading international standard, or set of guidelines, for corporate sustainability measurement and reporting. According to GRI, any attempt to properly assess or report the sustainability performance of an organization should be done with *sustainability context* taken fully into account.
- Notwithstanding the boost provided to context by GRI as a key principle for sustainability reporting, the precise meaning of it and how to, in fact, use and include it in practice has been missing from the literature, including the GRI standard itself.
- It is our contention, in response, that the technical meaning of context can be found in *capital theory* (i.e., in the economics literature), and in the role it has already played in the development of sustainability theory in the hands of both economists and sustainability theorists alike. With that in mind, we then turned our attention to the evolution of capital theory in economics, and to the convergence of it with sustainability concepts, per se, in the mid-twentieth century – especially in the writings of Kenneth Boulding (1949 and 1966).
- Out of the convergence of capital theory and sustainability came two things of great importance to modern-day CSM. The first was the extent to which the concept of capital stocks and flows (and their necessity for human well-being) can be applied to understanding and managing the sustainability of human behaviors and their impacts on critical resources in the world. The sustainability of human activity, that is, can be seen as a function of what its impacts on vital capitals are,

since the flows of valuable goods and services provided by capitals are essential for human well-being. We further argued that the quality or sufficiency of such flows can be measured in terms of their *carrying capacities*, a term more often seen in the ecological literature, perhaps, where natural capital is involved, but which is also applicable to vital capitals of any other kind.

The second contribution of capital theory to sustainability was the recognition that there are, in fact, many different types of capital, and that human well-being is dependent on capital not just in the narrow commercial or economic sense of the term, but also in the broader sense (i.e., in a sense that includes non-monetary and even intangible forms of capital, such as knowledge, relationships and ethical entitlements). Capital, that is, is a stock of anything that yields a flow of valuable goods or services required for human well-being.

- We then went on to discuss an especially noteworthy implementation of capital theory to sustainability concepts in the form of *Daly's rules*, which provide detailed principles for determining whether or not human impacts on *natural capital* are sustainable. Daly's rules would later be reflected in the Ecological Footprint Method, which was perhaps the first formal implementation of context-based sustainability in the form of a quantitative measurement and reporting system.

- Another important application of capital theory we discussed was John Elkington's development of the *triple bottom line* (TBL). Perhaps best described as an organizing principle for sustainability management, the TBL essentially stood for the idea that an organization's impacts on vital capitals in the world can be accounted for in three broad categories (the environment, society and the economy), implying, in turn, that human impacts on vital capitals should be measured, managed and reported accordingly. That said, the TBL has never really been fully operationalized in the form of a methodology – until now, that is.

- We then turned our attention to the application of the key ideas to CSM summarized above, by specifying three core principles for modern-day practice. The first two, *human well-being* and *vital capitals*, come directly out of capital theory in the ways we have described. The third, *carrying capacity*, is at least implied by capital theory (i.e., as a conceptual tool for measuring the size of flows) and can be used for determining whether or not the flows from a vital capital are sufficient for purposes of ensuring human well-being.

- Armed with the intellectual history and key principles identified above, we finally turned our attention to the business of providing a core definition of context – or sustainability context – the content of which we plan to use from this point forward. Context, from an organizational perspective, we argued, consists of three things:

1. **Carrying Capacities of Capitals**: First we identify the vital capitals (stocks) and their carrying capacities (flows) an organization is having impact on in ways that can affect stakeholder well-being, as well as capitals it *should* be having impact on in order to *ensure* stakeholder well-being.

2. **Responsible Populations**: Next we determine who the responsible populations are for ensuring the quality and sufficiency of such stocks and flows.
3. **Organizational Allocations**: And last, based on the first and second steps
   above, we allocate proportionate shares of available stocks and flows (in the
   case of natural capital) and/or burden shares for producing and/or maintaining
   them (in the case of anthro capital) to individual organizations.

In order to effectively measure, manage and report the sustainability performance of
an organization, then, these three elements of context must be determined and taken
into account. In other words, once an organization has identified the relevant areas of
impact its CSM function should be focusing on, the definition of context in each case
must be determined in terms of the elements we have provided (i.e., as a basis for
assessing and/or managing its sustainability performance). Specific examples of this
procedure will be provided in Chapter 3.

Now, however, it is time to consider what some of the key issues and practice
implications of CBS are, the substance of which we take up in Chapter 2.

Notes

1. English translation of Von Carlowitz (1713) provided by Margaret Robinson in Vermont.
2. Donella Meadows would later go on to publish a monograph on the subject of sustainability
   indicators (Meadows, 1998) that in many ways foreshadowed our own work. In particular, she, like us, was strongly influenced by Herman Daly's writings and the capital-
   based theory of sustainability. Our approach differs from hers, however, by the extent to
   which we (a) define sustainability metrics only in terms of *actual* versus *normative* impacts
   on vital capitals, with the latter conforming to how we define *sustainability context*, (b)
   provide a general specification for sustainability metrics with two subtypes: one for
   impacts on natural capital and another for impacts on anthropogenic capitals, (c) rely on
   stakeholder theory for making materiality and boundary decisions, and (d) provide a
   solution for use at the organizational level.
3. Here we acknowledge that GRI has, in fact, provided some guidance on how to
   incorporate context in sustainability reports, especially in the new Technical Protocol
   (TP) included with the latest version of the GRI Guidelines issued on March 23, 2011
   (i.e., the G3.1 version). Of particular importance in the new Protocol are statements to the
   effect that (a) performance should be expressed in the context of relevant locations (e.g., water
   use should be expressed in terms of available supplies at specific locations), and (b) performance
   should also be expressed 'in relation to other actors' (GRI, 2011, TP section, p. 6). We
   agree with these directives but would observe that GRI still falls well short of providing
   specific guidance on how to follow through with them, especially in terms of how to
   construct metrics in order to operationalize context-based measurement and reporting
   (see Chapter 3 for our own very detailed guidance on how to do this). Worse yet is the
   fact that the metrics and indicators that GRI *does* specify in other parts of the same G3.1
   document are utterly context-free and thereby fail to take sustainability context properly
   into account, much less fulfill the measurement and reporting guidelines cited above.
4. We take the position, as well, that human well-being depends, at least in part, upon
   non-human well-being, and that the health and stability of other species in the world matter
   to humans, in the sense that human well-being is contingent upon the health and well-being
   of other species – including, therefore, upon the status and quality of biodiversity and
   ecosystem services. From this point forward, then, whenever we use the phrase *human
   well-being*, it should be understood that we mean to include non-human well-being too,
   in our use of the term, without having to say as much each time – the one entails the other.

2

KEY ISSUES AND PRACTICE IMPLICATIONS OF CONTEXT-BASED SUSTAINABILITY

In Chapter 1, we chronicled the intellectual history and evolution of context-based sustainability, leading up to present-day thinking about the importance of context to CSM, and the still unfortunate fact of its absence from mainstream practice. In this chapter we want to do several things in follow-up. First, we want to highlight and discuss the manner in which context-based sustainability (CBS) relates to common management processes and cycles found in most organizations. Then we want to focus more narrowly on the issue of what the practice implications of CBS are, insofar as measurement and reporting are concerned. And last, we want to devote some special attention to the manner in which the world's leading international standard for corporate sustainability measurement and reporting – the Global Reporting Initiative, or GRI – addresses the issue of context in its scope, and how CBS compares with it.

All of these topics constitute key issues and practice implications raised and/or addressed by CBS as we see them. The selection of the issues we have opted to cover, therefore, was based on our own recent experiences in the field, and is by no means a comprehensive one.

How CBS interacts with core business processes and cycles

In this first part of Chapter 2, we want to address the issue of how CBS relates to conventional strategy formulation and management processes found in most organizations. Of particular interest to us in this regard is the relationship that should exist between CSM and the business strategy of an organization – when viewed through a CBS lens, that is – and also whether there is, or even needs to be, a business case for sustainability. Here, then, are two specific issues or questions we intend to address:

1. Should sustainability strategy align with business strategy?
2. Is there a business case for sustainability?

Should sustainability strategy align with business strategy?

It is customary practice in business to subordinate corporate programs and initiatives, no matter what they are, to business strategy in some way or another. Few would dispute this – first we acknowledge strategy, then we determine how best to support it with whatever program or initiative we happen to be dealing with. One articulation of this approach, where sustainability is concerned, can be found in the writings of Michael Porter and Mark Kramer (Porter and Kramer, 2006). Here is how they explain the connections between CSM and strategy from their perspective (p. 85):

> A corporate social agenda looks beyond community expectations to opportunities to achieve social and economic benefits simultaneously. It moves from mitigating harm to finding ways to reinforce corporate strategy by advancing social conditions.

In this book we take a slightly different position. It is our contention that the social agenda of an organization should be a function of who its stakeholders are, and the duties and obligations it has to each of them to have impact (or not) on vital capitals of importance to their well-being. The position expressed by Porter and Kramer, by contrast, is no less stakeholder-based; it just happens to grant priority status to one stakeholder group above all others – *shareholders*.

Sometimes referred to as the doctrine of *shareholder primacy*, this policy of relegating non-shareholder stakeholders to the status of second-class citizens is to all intents and purposes codified in law in many parts of the world, including most notably in the majority of U.S. states. Bakan (2004, p. 35) explains the situation as follows:

> Corporations are created by law and imbued with purpose by law. Law dictates what their directors and managers can do, and what they must do. And, at least in the United States and other industrialized countries, the corporation, as created by law, most closely resembles Milton Friedman's ideal model of the institution: it compels executives to prioritize the interests of their companies and shareholders above all others and forbids them from being socially responsible – at least genuinely so.

Greenfield (2006), for his part, contends that the shareholder primacy doctrine is fundamentally specious to begin with, not because of its failure to take non-shareholder interests into account, but because of the shaky foundations on which its central assertion sits (i.e., that tending exclusively to shareholder interests is good for society). He explains this as follows (p. 22):

> [Advocates of shareholder primacy never fully] explain why they believe shareholder primacy is best for society. Their jump from the welfare of corporations to the welfare of society is only a slightly more sophisticated way of saying 'what is good for General Motors is good for America' and is adduced

by way of simple assertion ... This is simply the trickle-down theory superimposed onto corporate law: what is good for shareholders is good for corporations, and what is good for corporations is good for society.

If this connection existed, the shareholder bandwagon would be attractive indeed. The problem is that advocates for shareholder primacy do not purport to say how the connection occurs or test whether the connection is true. In fact, the real reasons for shareholder supremacy have absolutely nothing to do with any testable assertions that we are better off as a society. The most contractarians really say is that we are better off as an *economy*.

Greenfield also questions the assumption that shareholder primacy is even good for organizations that embrace it (pp. 25–26):

> The argument is contestable in the far more fundamental sense that serving shareholder interests may not actually maximize the value of the firm, even in economic terms. Because of shareholders' limited liability and broadly diversified investment portfolios, they are largely indifferent to the well-being of any given corporation in which they own stock. Most shareholders these days do not even know all the companies whose stock they own. Instead, what shareholders care about is not the fortunes of any particular company but the overall return on their mutual fund, pension fund, or stock portfolio.
>
> Diversified shareholders want the management of any particular company to make decisions that maximize the expected value of the results, even if the results are also highly variable. They will prefer decisions that might have a high payoff but risk bankruptcy over safer decisions that provide lower returns but have less risk of pushing the firm into liquidation.

Striking a chord with the stakeholder primacy view we ourselves are advocating (i.e., as contrasted with the shareholder primacy view), Greenfield concludes as follows (p. 26):

> Since shareholders are largely indifferent to the possibility of any single firm failing, managers who make decisions according to what is good for the shareholders will bring about the failure of their companies more often than managers who make decisions based on what is good for a broader mix of stakeholders.

Of course we agree with Greenfield here, but we would go even further in terms of explaining how to go about the business of taking the interests of multiple stakeholder groups into account. First, we identify the stakeholder groups with whom an organization has relationships and whose interests are thereby affected by its operations; then we specify the impacts the organization is duty-bound to have on vital capital resources of importance to their well-being. The resulting list of duties and obligations can be viewed as standards of non-financial performance, against which an organization's actual behaviors and outcomes can be measured. In so many words, that is the essence of the approach to CSM we offer in this book.

It is not the capital-based view of management, then, that we object to (i.e., the one that lies behind the shareholder primacy doctrine); indeed, we are using it ourselves as a basis for non-financial management and CSM. Rather, it is the exclusive application of capital theory to shareholders and monetary capital (in a purely monistic sense), instead of its broader application to *all* stakeholders and *all* capitals of relevance to an organization (in a more pluralistic sense). The fact is that organizations have more than one stakeholder group to whom duties and obligations are owed, and more than one capital to contend with. Corporate statutes that effectively deny these truths are not particularly helpful, and are begging for reform. The sustainability of the modern economy depends on it.

In the face of criticism from the likes of Greenfield, Bakan and many others, the dominance of shareholder primacy in the U.S. and elsewhere has, in fact, been coming under increasing attack, as social and environmental conditions around the world worsen, and calls for higher corporate accountability grow ever louder. One such call has come from a fairly new non-profit in the U.S., B Lab, which has been leading the way to more or less eradicate the exclusive hold shareholder primacy has on corporations in America. Its solution has been to create a new kind of corporation known as a *B Corporation*, where B stands for Benefit, and to lobby state legislatures around the U.S. to allow such corporations to exist without having to abide by the shareholder primacy doctrine.

In April of 2010, Maryland became the first U.S. state to enact legislation creating B Corporations. Vermont followed in May and, at the time of writing, seven other states were in the process of considering similar legislation. A press release that followed the signing of Maryland's legislation into law read as follows:

> 'Milton Friedman would have loved this,' said Andrew Kassoy, co-founder of B Lab, the non-profit that drafted the model legislation with William H. Clark, Jr., partner in the Corporate & Securities Practice Group of Drinker Biddle and Reath. 'For the first time, we have a market-based solution supporting investors and entrepreneurs who want to make money and make a difference,' Kassoy added.
>
> The new law addresses a long time concern among entrepreneurs who need to raise growth capital but fear losing control of the social or environmental mission of their business. These entrepreneurs and other shareholders of Benefit Corporations now have additional rights to hold directors accountable for failure to create a material positive impact on society or to consider the impact of decisions on employees, community, and the environment. From a company's point of view, the new law empowers directors of Benefit Corporations to consider employees, community and the environment in addition to shareholder value when they make operating and liquidity decisions. And, it offers them legal protection for those considerations.

'Today marks an inflection point in the evolution of capitalism,' said B Lab co-founder Jay Coen Gilbert. 'With public trust in business at an all-time low, this represents the first systemic response to the underlying problems that created the financial crisis – protecting companies from the pressures of short-termism while creating benefit for shareholders and society over the long-haul.'

(B Lab, 2010)

To the extent that the advent of B Corporations makes it possible for a company to legitimately pursue social and environmental initiatives without having to justify them in terms of shareholder primacy, corporate sustainability strategies no longer need to be tightly coupled to strategy in the conventional, subservient sense. Nor do corporate strategies, for that matter, need to be expressed in profit-making terms alone. Instead, corporate strategy should be thought of as being inclusive of the pursuit of *both* monetary and non-monetary goals, the origins of which can be found in the relationships organizations have with *many* stakeholder groups – not just one – and the many corresponding duties and obligations they have to have impacts on *several* forms of capital, not just one. Thus, business strategies should be thought of as inclusive of sustainability strategy, and not somehow superordinate to it.

It should also be clear that the odds of achieving an organization's monetary or financial goals will be higher in cases where it is meeting its non-financial duties and obligations, since the failure to do so can put the survival and/or profitability of an organization at risk. Strictly speaking, then, sustainability strategies need not be *aligned* with business strategy, and instead should be viewed as merely part and parcel of it. And just as strong financial performance can enhance non-financial performance – since strong non-financial performance often requires financial support – so can strong non-financial performance enhance financial performance in at least the medium to long term by helping to mitigate risk.

The result of this thinking is that organizations and their managers should feel completely free to define their stakeholders as they see fit, and to regard the duties and obligations owed to each of them as the proper basis of strategy. Strategy, that is, should certainly be geared towards maximizing profits, but it should also be aimed at meeting the needs of all stakeholders, not just shareholders, in terms of (a) who the organization's stakeholders, in fact, are, and (b) what its duties and obligations are to each of them to have impacts on vital capitals of importance to their well-being.

How far to take this, of course, is the real question – a question that essentially boils down to the challenge of determining what the scope or content of a corporate CSM program should be, and how to define it. As Porter and Kramer put it (2006, p. 91):

Strategy is always about making choices, and success in corporate social responsibility is no different. It is about choosing which social [and environmental] issues to focus on.

To say that a company should be free to focus on more than just money making, though, is not to say that it should be free to ignore the investment and earning interests of its shareholders. Rather, in our view, it is to say that a company should be free – if not *required* – to attend to the duties and obligations it has to *all* of its stakeholders to the best of its ability, including the profit-making duties it owes to shareholders.

On the basis of the discussion thus far, we take the position that CSM programs need not be subordinate to strategy at all, and that they receive their legitimacy instead from the stakeholder relationships and responsibilities they separately, if not already, have. To be sure, all organizations have stakeholder relationships with more than just shareholders or owners, and arguably always have had such relationships. Employees, for example, constitute one such non-shareholder group, as do surrounding communities in places where companies do business, and also customers, trading partners, and others. To the extent that business activities and operations have impact (or should have impact) on vital capital resources in the world, companies are duty-bound to manage such impacts in ways that ensure stakeholder well-being, if only by not diminishing it.

A stakeholder group for a company is any population or constituency whose interests and/or well-being are impacted – or *should* be impacted, as the case may be – by the company's actions or given the relationships that exist between them. Whenever such impacts occur, or should occur, duties or obligations for a company to act accordingly come into play and must be attended to. It is precisely the question of whether or not a company has lived up to such responsibilities that constitutes the substance of sustainability measurement and reporting, and it is precisely the process of fulfilling such duties and obligations that constitutes the business of sustainability management, or CSM, at least on the non-financial side of things.

Here it should be clear, then, that a duty owed to, say, employees to ensure safe working conditions is not trumped or washed away in some way by the fact that fulfilling such a duty might cause profits to decline. The fact is that duties to ensure safe working conditions for employees and maximize profits for shareholders both exist, and are equally legitimate and must be attended to. Whether or not doing so also happens to directly support strategy in the service of shareholder value in some way is largely irrelevant, although we certainly agree that CSM actions that result in both fulfilling duties and obligations to non-shareholder stakeholders *and* increasing profits are especially desirable.

In taking the position we have (i.e., that managing non-financial performance in business boils down to managing impacts on vital capitals of importance to stakeholder well-being), it should not be lost on the reader, we hope, that what we are arguing for on the non-financial side of business is precisely what managers have been doing for time immemorial on the financial side. Instead of focusing only on shareholders and monetary capital, though, what we are suggesting is that the scope of management should be expanded to acknowledge other stakeholders and other capitals of interest. What we are advocating for, then, as already mentioned above, is a kind of pluralistic form of capital-based management instead of the traditional monistic one. Indeed, the approach to CSM we are proposing is in a very real sense based on a classical pattern of historical and contemporary management, according to which performance in business is a function of how well managers manage their organizations' impacts on capitals of vital importance to stakeholder well-being. This should be very familiar territory for modern-day managers.

Notwithstanding the similarities between CBS and contemporary management models, managing non-financial performance differs from managing financial performance in terms of more than just the differences in the makeup of stakeholders and capitals. Planning horizons (or cycles) can also vary significantly. The most practical plans for dealing with greenhouse gas impacts on the global climate system, for example, can involve decades if not centuries, thanks to the pace at which the carbon cycle on Earth functions. Managing impacts on other capitals, too, will very often involve the need to think and act in terms of multi-year scenarios as opposed to the annual planning cycle so familiar to us on the financial side of performance. In any case, planning for impacts on all forms of capital starts with the identification of stakeholders and the duties an organization has to help ensure their well-being.

As we will further explain in Chapter 3, then, the proper criteria for determining the content of a CSM program under the context-based approach we favor starts with identification of a company's actual stakeholders, and the specific duties and obligations it owes to each of them to have impact on capitals of vital importance to their well-being. Thus, CSM does not start with the identification of corporate strategy followed by a systematic search for social and environmental initiatives that can support it. Rather, it starts with the identification of the organization's responsibilities to stakeholders and proceeds from there. In this way, CSM contributes to the achievement of an organization's primary mission – its business mission, that is – by helping to insulate the organization from the risks of not attending to the equally legitimate concerns of its stakeholders. It does this by (a) clarifying who such stakeholders are, and (b) specifying the organization's related responsibilities to have impact (or not have impact) on capital resources of vital importance to their well-being.

If, therefore, in the conventional practice of CSM (assuming there is such a thing) we can say that CSM is business-strategy-driven, under the context-based alternative put forward in this book, that is not entirely true: CSM strategy, instead, is better thought of as stakeholder-driven – where stakeholders may include, but are not limited to, shareholders. The sustainability performance of a company can, in turn, be seen as a function of its impacts on vital capitals, as such capitals are required by its stakeholders – not just shareholders – for their well-being. That said, it is also the case that strong sustainability performance addresses not only the interests of non-shareholder stakeholders, but also those of shareholders to the extent that it helps protect, if not enhance, the value of their investments.

When we take this position, we can see that what makes the poisoning of a public well by a company unsustainable is not that refraining from doing so instrumentally supports its strategy or serves its shareholders' interests – although it certainly does all of that, too, by mitigating risk – rather, it is that its neighbors comprise a legitimate stakeholder group with standing, whose interests are affected by the company's impacts on a vital capital resource important to their well-being – natural capital, in this case. This, in turn, gives rise to a duty or obligation on the part of the company to not contaminate its neighbors' well; the company's strategy has nothing to do with it, but benefits nonetheless in the exchange. Here we can simply say that responsible behavior enhances the achievement of strategy, if only by making it possible for a company to minimize and/or avoid the risks associated with *irresponsible* behavior. Beyond that, we can also say that duties owed to legitimate stakeholders must be attended to, whether they have anything to do with the achievement of strategy or not. The money-making purpose and intent of a company does not somehow absolve it of the responsibility to fulfill its obligations to stakeholders.

Notwithstanding the above, shareholder-oriented academics and management pundits are still prone to publishing opinion pieces in which they remind managers in business (and the CSR/sustainability consultants they sometimes hire) that the purpose of business is to make money for shareholders, and nothing else. Porter and Kramer, for example, put it this way (2006, p. 84):

> No company can solve all of society's problems. Instead, each company must select issues that intersect with its particular business ... The essential test that should guide CSR is not whether a cause is worthy but whether it presents an opportunity to create shared value – that is, a meaningful benefit for society that is also valuable to the business.

This, of course, is the shareholder primacy doctrine cloaked in softer, more conciliatory terms. The only legitimate social benefits a company might have in society, the authors seem to be saying, are those that can be justified *first* in terms of financial benefits to the business and its shareholders. Unless such an overlap exists, companies have no obligation to act in their non-shareholders' best interests or with their well-being in mind. Karnani (2010) makes a similar argument when he says (pp. R1 and R4):

> Companies that simply do everything they can to boost profits will end up increasing social welfare ... Still, the fact is that while companies can sometimes do well by doing good, more often they can't. Because in most cases, doing what's best for society means sacrificing profits ... Even if executives wanted to forgo some profits to benefit society, they could expect to lose their jobs if they tried – and be replaced by managers who would restore profit as the top priority.

These arguments are clearly rooted in the shareholder primacy school of thought, which holds that only social benefits that occur as a byproduct of maximizing profits for shareholders are legitimate. In other words, only coincidental social benefits should be recognized as legitimate non-financial impacts in business. Everything else arguably diminishes profits and should be scrupulously avoided.

Here we can see that a spectrum of views on CSR theory and practice exists and that there is anything but unanimity in the field. At one end of the spectrum can be found the shareholder primacy doctrine, according to which there is only one legitimate stakeholder group (shareholders); at the other end is the stakeholder primacy doctrine, according to which there may be many legitimate stakeholder groups, thanks to the fact that companies do indeed have impacts on vital capital resources of importance not just to shareholders but also to non-shareholders as well. And in between these two poles there are arguably many hybrid views, such as that duties are owed only to shareholders, but that companies should be encouraged to make discretionary contributions towards the well-being of others in view of the license to operate they receive from society, or out of a desire to simply do good in the world. What varies along this spectrum is (a) an understanding of to whom duties are owed, and (b) the degree of discretion an organization has to act accordingly.

Is there a business case for sustainability?

This is a question that often gets asked and is, in a sense, the same question already addressed above. Still, it is a bit less direct and comes with certain preconceptions neatly bundled in – such as the presupposition that a business case, whatever that might mean, is required in order for sustainability or CSM to be legitimate. This, of course, as we have explained above, is nonsense. CSM receives its legitimacy not from the positive effects it might have on a company's financial performance, but from the otherwise equally legitimate effects it can have on helping a company to fulfill its non-financial duties and obligations to stakeholders of all kinds. Such duties and obligations exist independently of financial duties and obligations to shareholders and must be attended to by a company, no matter what its primary business or financial goals happen to be.

That said, it should also be clear that a company's business interests can be well served by strong non-financial, or sustainability, performance, since such performance can generally help mitigate and/or avoid risks and thereby increase a company's profitability and longevity.

So rather than ask if there is a business case for sustainability, the more interesting question to us is: *is there a sustainability case for business?* In other words, instead of presupposing the need for a financial justification in order for CSM to be legitimate, let us consider the opposite. Can the pursuit of financial goals by a business be legitimate if its social and environmental impacts are chronically unsustainable? Further, can businesses collectively, or the economy as a whole, be legitimate if their social and environmental impacts are, in the aggregate, unsustainable? We don't think so.

But that, of course, is where CBS comes rushing into play, since it is only by including context in the measurement and reporting of a company's social and environmental impacts that its true, or literal, sustainability performance can be known. If what we need and want is a world in which businesses are socially and environmentally sustainable, then a very good place to start would be with the implementation of performance measurement tools that provide meaningful information as to what a business's social and environmental performance actually happens to be. Indeed, we will never achieve sustainability in the conduct of human affairs until or unless context-based CSM has become firmly ensconced in the daily routines of businesses and their CSM functions. Until then, as we have already said, businesses and the economies in which they operate are flying blind.

How CBS relates to measurement and reporting

Having considered the ways in which CSM relates to predominant forms of strategy formulation and management, we now want to turn our attention to the narrower issue of how context-based sustainability stacks up in terms of measurement and reporting. To do this, we have identified several key issues of importance in CSM today, each of which we will use as a foil, as it were, to help readers better understand how the CBS approach compares in practice with other, more conventional methods of CSM. The key issues we have in mind here are as follows:

1. Are economic and financial bottom lines the same thing?
2. How many bottom lines are there?
3. Are context-based metrics 'relative' or 'absolute' metrics?
4. Can a company be 'more' or 'less' sustainable?
5. Can products be sustainable?
6. Does context-based sustainability preclude cross-company comparisons?
7. According to what rules and principles should social sustainability performance be measured?

Are economic and financial bottom lines the same thing?

One of the more persistent and bedeviling issues in CSM is the common confusion between the financial bottom line and the economic bottom line, and the question of whether or not they are the same thing. The view that they are synonymous is often reinforced by the short-hand reference to the triple bottom line (TBL) as *people, planet and profit*. The *profit* part clearly suggests that the economic bottom line component of the TBL is the same thing as the financial bottom line; we, however, disagree (see our earlier reference to Jennings' distinction between the two in Chapter 1).

Further support for the non-financial interpretation of the economic bottom line can be found in the writings of Von Carlowitz (1713), who according to Edinger and Kaul (2003), as we noted in Chapter 1, 'saw economic activity as responsible for future generations' (i.e., not just current shareholders). Still, the financial interpretation of the economic bottom line persists, leading to no end of confusion about this in CSM.

Some of this can be attributed, we think, to the reinforcing (if not unintended) effects of prominent thinkers in the field. In laying out his vision of the economic bottom line, for example, John Elkington (1997) provided a definition that was inclusive of impacts on human capital, intellectual capital, natural capital and social capital, not to mention various aspects of financial performance, such as profit margins (pp. 74–75). In his treatment of issues and indicators for managing and measuring the economic bottom line, he wrote (pp. 76–77):

> Among the items you would expect to see in a company's report and accounts would be a profit and loss account, balance sheet and statement of total recognized losses and gains. When it comes to wider economic sustainability, however, there is a surprising lack of generally acceptable indicators. Key considerations here might include the long-term sustainability of a company's costs, of the demand for its products or services, of its pricing and profit margins, of its innovation programs, and of its 'business ecosystem'.

Notwithstanding his earlier interpretation of the economic bottom line as being inclusive of impacts on all sorts of capitals, this particular statement on Elkington's part seems mostly tied to the financial bottom line in its conventional monetary form. Thus, we think it fair to conclude that what Elkington had in mind for the economic bottom line was at least partly, if not mainly, composed of financial performance indicators. Again, we disagree with this particular interpretation, although we agree that people are free to define terms in any way they like. For our purposes, though, we do not think a new name or interpretation of the financial bottom line is or ever was needed, since the older pre-existing one was working just fine, except for the non-financial impacts that it fails to reflect, and which the newer non-financial bottom lines are designed to address. Indeed, if the economic bottom line component of the TBL is the same as the financial bottom line, why not just call it the financial bottom line and drop the 'economic' term altogether?

GRI, for its part, is more in line with our own thinking here. In the preamble to the indicators listed for economic disclosures in G3.1, GRI says (2011, p. 25):

> The economic dimension of sustainability concerns the organization's impacts on the economic conditions of its stakeholders and on economic systems at local, national, and global levels. The Economic Indicators illustrate:
>
> • Flow of capital among different stakeholders; and
> • Main economic impacts of the organization throughout society.
>
> Financial performance is fundamental to understanding an organization and its own sustainability. However, this information is normally already reported in financial accounts. What is often reported less, and is frequently desired by users of sustainability reports, is the organization's contribution to the sustainability of a larger economic system.

On the basis of this statement alone, it should be clear to any company using the GRI guidelines, or reading reports prepared in accordance with them, that the economic section of GRI is not about financial reporting at all.

What, then, can we say about the context-based view on this subject as put forward in this book? First is that it lines up behind Jennings and GRI on the question of whether or not the financial and economic bottom lines are the same thing – the answer is a resounding *no*, and the *people–planet–profit* slogan should be rejected accordingly, at least insofar as the *profit* piece is concerned. A better alternative might be *people, planet and (economic) prosperity*. Why? Because the capitals involved are completely different. The financial bottom line pertains to impacts on monetary or financial capital, per se; the economic bottom line pertains to impacts on human, social and constructed capitals in the economy (see below). The economy in society is not the same as an individual company's profitability or financial performance – they are apples and oranges.

The next thing we can say is that the context-based school of sustainability actually views the economic bottom line as merely a special case (or subset) of the social bottom line, which for reasons of high relevance to business has been called out separately from all the other kinds of social impacts an organization can have. In principle, other such sub-bottom lines could also be called out for separate treatment if we wanted to, such as an *educational* bottom line, a *healthcare* bottom line, a *housing* bottom line, a *government* bottom line, and so forth. Here it is important to remember that the social bottom line, like the environmental bottom line, is a broad category of impacts, and that it actually contains many social-type, sub-bottom lines, one of which happens to be economic in scope.

As we also briefly explained in Chapter 1, the social bottom line is a measure of impacts on three types of non-financial, non-natural capital (human capital, social capital and constructed capital), which together we refer to as anthropogenic capital, or *anthro* capital (McElroy, 2008), since all three types are human-made. Such impacts are, again, measured against standards or norms for what they need or ought to be in order to ensure stakeholder well-being. In some cases, those impacts pertain to stakeholder *economic* well-being. To that degree, we can separately measure and report economic-related social impacts on anthro capitals relative to levels required to ensure the economic well-being of certain stakeholder groups, such as a company's employees. By the same token, we can separately measure and report a company's human-health-related impacts, or its impacts on, say, a community's transportation systems. All of these are examples of social sub-bottom lines (see Table 2.1).

The resulting scores produced from taking such measures comprise social sub-bottom lines, including the economic bottom line – not to be confused with impacts on monetary capital separately reported in the form of the *financial* bottom line (see Table 2.2). What ultimately differentiates one bottom line category from another, then, is the kinds of capital(s) it pertains to. Any two or more bottom lines that pertain to the same capitals must, from this perspective, be of the same general kind or type, with some representing supersets or groupings of the type (e.g., the social bottom line is a superset of all social-type, sub-bottom lines) and others representing subsets of the type (e.g., the economic bottom line is a sub-type of the social bottom line). The fact that the social and economic bottom lines pertain to the same types of capitals means that they must be definitionally or conceptually related in some way. And in fact they are, just as we have described them.

TABLE 2.1 Examples of social sub-bottom lines

Stakeholder Group, e.g.	Social Bottom Line		Vital Capitals Involved		
	Specific Area of Impact, e.g.	Related Sub-Bottom Line	Human	Social	Constructed
Employees	Employee Wages	Economic	✔[1]		
Customers	Product Safety	Human Health		✔[2]	
Communities	Public Highways	Infrastructure			✔[3]

Notes:

1. Pertains to duties and obligations organizations have to engage in fair trade with employees, so as to ensure the quality of their employment situations, which is a form of human capital people rely on for their economic well-being. Related impacts therefore accrue to an organization's economic bottom line.
2. Pertains to duties and obligations manufacturers have to produce safe products, so as to ensure the physical well-being of customers. Often involves the creation of product safety programs and protocols (i.e., forms of social capital) in order to control the quality of manufacturing processes and products.
3. Pertains to duties and obligations organizations have to contribute to the creation and/or maintenance of public highway systems (i.e., a form of constructed capital) in ways that are proportionate to their use of them, so as to ensure the well-being of community members who also rely on such systems to satisfy their own day-to-day transportation needs.

TABLE 2.2 The four bottom lines and their capitals

	Social Bottom Line	Economic Bottom Line	Environmental Bottom Line	Financial Bottom Line
Natural Capital			✔	
Human Capital	✔	✔		
Social Capital	✔	✔		
Constructed Capital	✔	✔		
Monetary Capital				✔

How many bottom lines are there?

In the discussion just above, we spoke of categories of bottom lines on the one hand, and four bottom lines on the other. This raises the question of exactly how many bottom lines there really are. Are there four or are there more than four?

The answer to this question is ultimately informed, at least in part, by the content of the capital-based theory of sustainability upon which we are relying as a key foundation to CBS. According to that theory, the sustainability of human activity – *any* human activity, business or otherwise – is a function of its impacts on vital capitals in the world, relative to levels of such capitals required for human well-being. Those capitals are finite in type, and so the kinds of bottom lines will, in turn, be finite.

Now before we continue with this discussion, we want to be absolutely clear about the applicability of what we are saying to both financial and non-financial capitals and their bottom lines. Although it is indeed non-financial performance that is the primary focus of this book, the theoretical foundations we rely on as a basis for doing CSM are applicable to both forms of performance – financial and non-financial. What's more, we see this as a strength of the context-based school of thought, since in a very real sense its underpinnings have already been proven in practice on the financial side of management for decades, if not longer. Before returning to our non-financial discussion, then, it may be helpful if we take a moment to expand on this.

Instead of referring to the overarching idea described and advocated on these pages as *context-based sustainability*, let us consider the implications of what would happen if we were to expand the concept so as to include performance measurement, management and reporting *in general* – financial, non-financial and otherwise. Here, then, would be the basic tenets of that particular school of thought:

1. Performance is a function of an organization's impacts on capital resources of vital importance to stakeholder well-being.
2. Organizations therefore have specific duties and obligations to have impacts on such capitals in ways that are consistent with stakeholder well-being.
3. Such duties and obligations must also be specified separately for each stakeholder group according to the nature of the relationship the organization has with it.
4. Organizational activity can result in impacts on capitals that fall short of, exceed or exactly match related duties and obligations owed to stakeholders.

Now let us see what happens when we try to apply these principles more broadly to either financial or non-financial performance (see Table 2.3). In the case of financial performance, the relevant type of capital is monetary capital (money or other financial assets) that can be used to generate income (Black et al., 2009, p. 50). The related duty or obligation to have impact on monetary capital is to at least stay solvent and preserve shareholder capital or principal. Beyond that, shareholder well-being is generally enhanced if the value of monetary capital grows, or if profits are generated – or, better yet, maximized. This duty or obligation is owed to only one stakeholder group: shareholders. In cases where the duty or obligation is met in the context of financial management, we can say that the performance was 'profitable'.

Turning to the non-financial side of performance, the relevant types of capital involved are natural, human, social and constructed capitals, as earlier discussed. The related duties and obligations are to have impacts on such capitals such that they (the capitals) are sufficient for stakeholder well-being. In some cases, these duties and obligations are exclusive to the organization; in others, they are shared with other

TABLE 2.3 The capital/stakeholder basis of performance

	Relevant Vital Capital(s)	Relevant Duties and Obligations	Relevant Stakeholder Groups	Terms of Performance
Financial Performance	• Monetary	• Maintain levels of capital for stakeholder well-being	• Shareholders	• Profitability
Non-Financial Performance	• Natural • Human • Social • Constructed	• Maintain levels of capital for stakeholder well-being	• Employees • Customers • Communities • Trading Partners • Other	• Sustainability

parties (further discussed in Chapter 3). Moreover, these duties and obligations are owed to potentially many stakeholder groups, including employees, customers, suppliers, local communities, etc. In cases where the duties and obligations are met in the context of non-financial management, we can say that the performance was 'sustainable'.

From this discussion, we can see that both financial and non-financial management rely on a common capital-based theory of performance. The goal of management in each case is to use, produce and/or maintain stocks of capital at whatever levels are required to ensure stakeholder well-being. The capitals involved, however, vary materially, depending on the branch of management we are talking about. Non-financial management, or CSM, then, is nothing but capital-based management applied to the four types of non-financial capitals we have been discussing: natural, human, social and constructed. Beyond that, its theoretical roots and particulars are no different than those long used on the financial side of management.

Turning back to the question of how many bottom lines there are, we can see from the discussion above that the answer is at least four (one financial and three non-financial), and that each of the four, in turn, is liable to have multiple sub-bottom lines, depending on how many stakeholder groups an organization has, and the diversity of duties and obligations it owes to each of them. Each such duty or obligation will involve at least one measure of performance, the result of which will constitute a single sub-bottom line within one of the four categories. Specific examples of this will be provided in Chapter 3; for now, suffice it to say that the context-based approach to sustainability measurement, management and reporting is a multi-bottom-line scheme, according to which there are three broad categories of non-financial performance, each of which is liable to have some additional number of sub-bottom lines associated with it.

One final thought on this issue before we move on. *Does this multi-bottom-line orientation preclude the possibility of computing unitary or blended non-financial bottom lines, just as we do for financial performance?* Organizations, for example, routinely measure and report financial performance by product line, operating unit, facility, etc. on a distributed basis, but then roll them up into unitary or consolidated bottom lines – a single profit or loss figure for the organization as a whole. In that regard, we can say that an organization can have as many financial bottom lines as it likes without forgoing the opportunity to combine them into a single figure. Under the context-based school of CSM, the same is true for non-financial reporting. As long as we can assign or ascribe duties and obligations to have impacts on vital capitals to specific organizational departments, divisions, facilities, etc., we can measure and report non-financial performance at those levels, too, just as we do for financial performance.

And what about overall, rolled-up bottom lines? Can we compute them for non-financial reporting purposes at the enterprise level, just as we do for financial bottom lines? Indeed we can. And to that end, we will be presenting a methodology for doing so in Chapter 3. For present purposes, though, let us simply say that the manner in which such non-financial computations are made differs slightly from the financial case. How so? It differs in that in financial performance there is only one capital involved (monetary) and all forms of it are fungible and exchangeable. A financial bottom line for one operating unit can always be added to or subtracted from the financial bottom line of another in order to arrive at a blended or net measure of performance. This is not the case for non-financial performance, where there are four non-exchangeable and non-fungible capitals involved. To use an earlier example, a company cannot offset the effects of polluting its neighbors' well (natural capital) by simply increasing donations to the local soup kitchen (social capital). Impacts on one do not neatly translate into offsetting impacts on another. Thus, they must be managed and accounted for separately.

And even within the same categories of capital where the same kinds of resources are involved – such as water resources within the natural capital category – it is very often inappropriate to try to combine impacts into blended or net results because of the disconnectedness of the resources involved. If a company pollutes a body of water at its manufacturing facilities in France, but separately takes steps to rehabilitate or preserve the ecological integrity of another in America, are its deleterious effects in France any less deleterious by virtue of what it has done in America? Of course not. The contextual orientation makes this clear to us because, despite the fact that the impacts in both cases are on water resources, the two sites are physically disconnected from one another and therefore must be accounted for separately in our sustainability measurement and reporting system. Thus, even for a single area of impact, such as water, a company could have as many separate, water-related bottom lines as it has facilities in the world. All would belong to the same broad environmental category of impact, but would be separately measured and reported nevertheless. Still, there *is* a way to aggregate disconnected non-financial bottom lines, the particulars of which will have to wait until Chapter 3.

Are context-based metrics 'relative' or 'absolute' metrics?

As a distinct school of thought in the field of CSM, the context-based approach gives rise to its own style of metrics that should be used in measuring and reporting sustainability performance. We call these *context-based metrics*, or CBMs. More familiar to practitioners in sustainability management, however, are so-called *relative* and *absolute* metrics. In this section, we will examine the question of which of these two categories of metrics CBMs fall into, if any.

Starting with absolute metrics, these are perhaps the simplest form of measurement used in sustainability reporting, although they do have their problems. First, here's a definition of absolute metrics we can use:

> Absolute metrics express operational performance in terms of what overall levels of performance are in specific areas of interest (e.g., water use) for an organization as a whole – as in the *total volume of water consumed by an organization* during a specific period of time.

Although simple in form, issues abound in the use of absolute metrics when measurements are taken for different periods of time with the intent of comparing performance on, say, an inter-annual basis. This is because organizations rarely remain unchanged over time. The makeup and size of an organization, for example, will routinely vary from one year to the next, thereby undermining attempts to compare performance on an apples-to-apples basis. Indeed, an organization that doubles its carbon emissions in a year in which it has also doubled in size should hardly be seen as somehow having worsened its performance compared with the year before, since, to all intents and purposes, it is not the same organization anymore.

It is for these reasons that absolute measures, in order to be meaningful, must be normalized in a way that adjusts for changes in organizational makeup and size. One good way of doing so is to tie performance to a common denominator of some kind, such as the number of employees in a firm, thereby giving rise to a *per capita* unit of measurement. A per capita metric is particularly appropriate in this case because organizations, per se, are composed of individuals working together to achieve a common goal. If it is organizational performance we are concerned with, the normalized unit of measurement we choose should be one that is as descriptive of the organization as possible. By contrast, organizational performance expressed in terms of, say, office square footage (e.g., water consumed per square foot of occupied office space) makes about as much sense as *water consumed per pencil sharpener*. Neither constitutes a measure of the organization, per se, and instead focuses on some other thing that, at best, may be loosely correlated with the size of the organization, but which is not in any way a direct measure or descriptor of it.

Thus, absolute metrics, intended to support inter-annual comparisons of performance but which do not adjust for changes in the ways discussed above, are dubious and should be avoided. More important, even those that *are* properly constructed should not be regarded as sustainability metrics, per se. Why not? Because they typically fail to take context-based standards of performance (for impacts on vital capital resources and stakeholder well-being) explicitly into account.

Relative metrics are similar to normalized absolute metrics except that they, too, do not result in measures that describe the sustainability of organizations. Instead, they most often provide measurements of efficiency. Here, as we have already pointed out, it should be clear that there is a difference between sustainability and efficiency – the two are fundamentally different. For that very reason, a relative metric for water use in an organization, for example, need not be tied to the constraint earlier noted for absolute metrics (i.e., that the variable chosen for normalization purposes should be descriptive of the organization or of the activities being assessed). In the case of relative (or efficiency) metrics, no such constraint exists. Instead, the variable chosen for a relative metric must be descriptive of the non-organizational thing of interest, such as water consumption *per unit of production* or *output*, or water consumption *per hour of employee time*, or water consumption *per unit of revenue*.

Here, then, is a definition we can use for relative metrics:

> Relative metrics express operational performance in terms of how performance in one area (e.g., water use) correlates to performance in another area (e.g., revenue or total production) – as in *water consumed per unit of revenue* or *water consumed per unit of production* during a specific period of time.

Relative metrics are also sometimes referred to as intensity metrics, precisely because of their efficiency orientation. Once again, water provides us with an easy to understand example. Imagine a metric that reports water consumed per unit of production. This is an efficiency metric, pure and simple, or what some might refer to as a water intensity metric; it expresses the *intensity* of water use per product produced. The same thing can be done for greenhouse gas emissions, solid waste emissions, energy consumption, and material throughput, as well.

It should also be clear that an organization could have both an absolute and a relative metric in play at the same time for the same issue, such as water use. In that case, the absolute metric would be *water used by a company or manufacturing plant* in a year, and the relative metric could be *water used per unit of production* in the same year. And just as we can say that absolute metrics are not sustainability metrics, per se, so we can say that relative metrics are not sustainability metrics, either. To understand the efficiency of an organization's water use is not to know what the *sustainability* of its use is. Even reduced or optimal levels of water use can be unsustainable – without more information (i.e., context) to go by, one simply cannot tell.

This raises the question of what absolute measures really are, and whether or not they might be a kind of efficiency metric – or, if not, perhaps some other thing. In point of fact, we think it safe and valid to say that absolute metrics are merely a special type of relative metric since they express impacts in a normalized way, albeit at the level of whole systems. Instead of expressing impacts per underlying unit of production or what have you, they express impacts per unit of overlying organization, as in *water consumed by a company (a legal entity) from one year to the next*. Thus, for some purposes, the fact that organizations change in makeup and size from one year to the next is of no consequence. Imagine growth rates themselves, for example. A metric of that kind is already predicated on the assumption that organizations change in size every year; its very purpose is to measure by how much. So the fact that organizations change in size from one year to the next would in no way prevent a metric of that kind from being used.

The motivation behind most sustainability measures, however, is very different. Once again, take the case of water. Imagine a world in which one year there were only ten companies in business and one source of water. Imagine, as well, that each company used exactly one-tenth of the available renewable supply that year, and that the sustainability of their use was measured in absolute terms. Now imagine that the following year each company spins off a new division and transfers half of its employees to run it. In year number two, then, there would be twenty companies, not ten. Should each of the original ten companies in the second year be graded *sustainable* if their overall use of water resources remains unchanged? How could this be justified, since the original ten companies would be half the size of what they were, and the newer ten companies would have no water to use at all – not without dipping into non-renewable stocks, that is? All of these changes and contextual considerations, however, are hidden from view when using absolute metrics. And that is exactly what makes them so ill-suited for purposes of measuring sustainability.

A better solution in the imaginary case above would be to use a relative metric that measures organizational performance not on an enterprise-wide or legal entity level, but on a normalized per capita or per employee level. That way, the sustainability of a company's use of water resources could be expressed in terms of *water use per employee* (or *per employee hour worked*), and then be measured, reported and compared in those terms from one year to the next. Thus, despite the fact that a company might be half the size in year two of what it was in year one, its *water use per employee hour worked* might very well be the same.

To sum up what we have said thus far, we can say that the distinction between absolute and relative metrics is a fuzzy one, and that absolute metrics are merely a special case of relative metrics that operate at the level of the enterprise as a whole, or sub-groups within it. Thus, the thing being measured never really changes at a logical level from one period to the next – but does in a physical sense – which for some purposes poses no problems at all. Acme Widgets is Acme Widgets, no matter how many employees it has this year versus last.

For sustainability measures, however, variability in makeup, size and other factors matters greatly, as the example above makes clear. To help cope with such variability, other forms of relative metrics can be used, such as the ones already discussed – water consumption per employee, water consumption per unit of production, water consumption per unit of revenue, or what have you. But this, too, has its problems. If all we measured in the fictitious case above, for example, was water consumption per employee, the size and sufficiency of the shared water resource from which each company was taking its supplies would never be known, much less factored into the assessment. Thus, relative metrics, no matter what their statistical advantages over absolute measures might be, suffer – in all of their forms – from a fatal lack of context. It is precisely such context, however, that is so critical to the measurement of sustainability performance, notwithstanding its irrelevance to efficiency. This, of course, leads us to context-based metrics.

Contextual or context-based metrics (CBMs) measure and report sustainability performance in a literal or genuine sense. They do so by explicitly taking the *demand for* and/or *supply of* valuable goods and services from vital capitals explicitly into account. Using water once again as an example, a CBM would include a measure of an organization's proportionate share of available renewable supplies, given its location, its size in terms of headcount, contribution to GDP, or other factors that can be used in making such allocations (further discussed in Chapter 3). Actual water consumption can then be measured against the allocated level, resulting in a numerical score that is either less than or equal to the allocation (sustainable) or greater than the allocation (unsustainable).

Here, then, is a definition we can use for CBMs:

> Context-based metrics express organizational performance in terms of impacts on vital capitals, relative to norms, standards or thresholds for what such impacts ought to be (for specific periods of time) in order to be sustainable (e.g., total water consumed per employee per year compared with a fair or equitable allocation of available renewable supplies).

In a very important sense, then, context-based metrics are nothing but relative metrics with factual and normative context added (e.g., how much renewable water is there, and how much of it should an individual organization or facility be entitled to use?). The relative aspect of such metrics makes it possible to perform inter-annual analyses in order to resolve the problem of changes in organizational size, makeup, etc. that always come up, while the context element makes it possible to take the availability, quality and sufficiency of relevant vital capitals explicitly into account. The result is a powerful tool for measuring the sustainability performance of organizations in the real world, including all of the variations in capital resource conditions, human populations and company-specific stakeholder groups that must be fully accounted for if measurements are to be meaningful.

In our own work with clients, we have constructed CBMs in the form of numerical quotients, with denominators representing standards or norms of performance for impacts on capitals, and numerators representing actual impacts on the same capitals (see Figure 2.1). For environmental areas of impact, scores of less than or equal to 1.0 signify sustainable performance, while scores of greater than 1.0 signify unsustainable performance. This is because the *means* of natural capital is limited and we must therefore live within it.

In the case of non-environmental impacts, by contrast, the logic of scoring reverses, since, unlike natural capital, the other capitals associated with social sustainability (human, social and constructed) are human-made (i.e., are anthropogenic, or *anthro* capitals) and must therefore be created and maintained at certain minimum levels. Social sustainability performance, then, is largely a measure of capital *production*, whereas environmental sustainability, by contrast, is a measure of capital *consumption*. All of this will be discussed in more detail in Chapter 3.

Notwithstanding the important distinction we have made between sustainability and efficiency metrics, most sustainability measurement and reporting practices today

$$\text{Sustainability Performance*} = \frac{\text{A measure of impact on a vital capital}}{\begin{array}{c}\text{A standard or norm for what the impact}\\\text{on the same vital capital should be}\\\text{in order to ensure stakeholder well-being}\\\text{(i.e., for the impact to be sustainable)}\end{array}}$$

*Where:

- For impacts on *natural* capital, quotient scores of ≤ 1.0 = sustainable, > 1.0 = unsustainable
- For impacts on *human, social* or *constructed* capital, quotient scores of ≥ 1.0 are sustainable, < 1.0 are unsustainable

Source: McElroy, 2008

FIGURE 2.1 Context-based sustainability metrics.

fall into the efficiency category (i.e., they are context-free, relative metrics), while still clinging to sustainability terminology. That said, some important exceptions exist. Two formal (i.e., codified) exceptions, in particular, are worth noting. One is the *Ecological Footprint Method* (Rees, 1992; Wackernagel and Rees, 1996) already discussed in Chapter 1, and a second is the *Social Footprint Method* (McElroy et al., 2007; McElroy, 2008). Each of these context-based methods is currently being used to varying degrees, and will presumably – or hopefully – become more widely used as the shortcomings of context-free thinking become better understood.

Can performance be 'more' or 'less' sustainable?

We are all accustomed to hearing people refer to human behaviors as being more or less sustainable, such as the phrase: *Using compact fluorescent light bulbs is more sustainable than using incandescent ones.* Given the binary property of sustainability discussed above, however, this is not always appropriate, much less true. Using less fossil-fuel-based energy, for example, may not in the strictest sense of the term be *more sustainable.* Instead it may only be *less unsustainable.* What do we mean by this?

As discussed in the preceding section and also in Figure 2.1, measurements taken using context-based metrics result in scores that can either be less than 1.0, equal to 1.0 or greater than 1.0. These scores, in turn, can be plotted on a sustainability performance scale (see Figure 2.2). As will be discussed further in Chapter 3, scores associated with impacts on *natural* capital are interpreted such that any score of less than or equal to 1.0 signifies sustainable performance, since it means that the use of natural capital resources is less than or equal to an organization's fair share of them; scores of greater than 1.0, in turn, signify unsustainable performance, since it means an

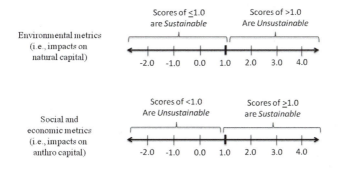

Source: McElroy, 2008

FIGURE 2.2 Sustainability performance scales.

organization's use is greater than its share. For impacts on anthro capitals, the logic reverses: scores of less than 1.0 signify unsustainable performance, since it means an organization's impacts on producing and/or maintaining them are less than they should be; any score of greater than or equal to 1.0, in turn, signifies sustainable performance, since it means an organization's impacts on anthro capitals are at least what they ought to be in order to ensure stakeholder well-being.

Now imagine a case where an organization's sustainability score for, say, an impact on natural capital of some kind was 1.7. According to the logic above, such a score would signify unsustainable performance because it would mean that a natural resource was being used at a rate that exceeds the organization's fair or proportionate share of it. Now let us imagine that a year later the organization's score improved to 1.3, still unsustainable but an improvement, nevertheless. Could we say that the score of 1.3 was more sustainable than 1.7? That is the question.

Strictly speaking, the answer is *no*, since in neither year was the organization's score sustainable – more, less or otherwise. The more correct characterization of the 1.3 score would be to say that it was *less unsustainable* than the year before, but still unsustainable. The phrase *more sustainable* can only be used to describe performance that, in fact, falls on the sustainable side of the performance scale, which is less than or equal to 1.0 for impacts on natural capital, and greater than or equal to 1.0 for impacts on anthro capital. If sustainability were an analog or variably progressive state of affairs, this would not be the case. But it isn't; it is a binary construct. A behavior and its impacts are either sustainable or unsustainable, with all actual states falling into one or the other category. There is no third or middling state of affairs.

Can products be sustainable?

Another very interesting implication of context-based sustainability pertains to products, and the question of whether or not they can be sustainable. The key issue here is to be clear about the type of thing to which the adjectives *sustainable* and *unsustainable* can be applied, and whether or not inanimate objects, like products, can be described in those terms. It is our contention that the answer is *no*, and that statements to the effect that a product is sustainable, or that one product is *more sustainable* than another, are meaningless and nonsensical.

The basis of our position is simply this: if sustainability performance is a function of impacts on vital capitals relative to corresponding duties or obligations to have such impacts, how can inanimate objects be held to such a test? How, that is, can an inanimate object have a duty or obligation? Of course they can't. Only living agents or actors capable of acting in accordance with norms or standards of morality (i.e., moral agents) can be regarded as such. Indeed, the object of sustainability assessments is not products or any other inanimate object; rather, it is human behavior or activity. When we speak of sustainability in business, then, what we are talking about – or *should* be talking about – is human activity, the actions that people take in the world and their corresponding impacts. In this regard, we can say that organizations are merely groups of people working together to achieve a set of common goals. To say that an organization is sustainable or unsustainable is to make reference to the joint actions of the people who work for it in their collective form.

To the extent that products come into play at all, it is really the sourcing, production and distribution of them by people in their organizational form, and not the products themselves, which matter most. Here it is important not to confuse the physical properties of products with the sustainability of the manufacturing processes used to produce them. The toxicity of a product, for example, has nothing to do with the sustainability of the processes used to produce it, in terms of either their environmental or social impacts. On the other hand, the act of using and/or disposing of a toxic product may also be sustainable or not, but again it is the human activity (using and disposing) that is being measured here, not the product itself.

The attribution of sustainability properties to inanimate objects is probably due in no small part to the growing use and popularity of life cycle assessments (LCAs) in business.[1] An LCA, as the name suggests, is a procedure by which the environmental impacts of a product can be determined from its inception to its disposal – starting with the sourcing of the raw materials used to produce it and continuing to its end of life or disposal stage. Thus, LCAs are an attempt to quantify all of the environmental impacts the manufacturing, use and disposal of a product have throughout the time and space of a product's life cycle, and to attribute such impacts to the product itself. Indeed, instead of attributing the effects of such actions to the people who produce, use and dispose of the products in question, LCAs shift the blame, so to speak, to the products themselves, as if the products are somehow responsible for the impacts humans have when they produce, use and dispose of them.

In light of the extent to which LCAs are being used in CSM, some further comment on them from the perspective of CBS is warranted. Here is what we have to say on the subject:

1. LCAs are fundamentally about eco-efficiency, not sustainability. They are designed to identify the environmental impacts of products and services, very often with the intent of comparing them in like terms, or to establish baselines for reference purposes as companies attempt to minimize or reduce the adverse environmental footprints of their products and services over time. But again, even a lowered impact of, say, producing a product can be unsustainable. Eco-efficiency and sustainability are simply not the same things. And while it may serve some purposes to perform LCAs, the results of LCAs cannot be used to express the sustainability performance of organizations. This is because they are (a) product/service-centric by design, (b) context-free, and (c) environment-only in scope. We comment further on each of these points below.

2. LCAs are product/service-centric; CSM is not. The object of interest, or reference, in CSM is primarily organizations, if not networks or chains of organizations. GRI, for example, is a framework for measuring and reporting the sustainability performance of organizations, not products or services. Assuming the issue of interest to us is how best to measure, manage and report the performance of organizations, LCAs have little to offer.

3. LCAs are also customer-driven, in the sense that they are often performed with the intent of informing buyers (or potential buyers) of what the environmental impacts are of products or services being offered. In that regard, LCAs are frequently designed to address the sustainability performance of customers not manufacturers, in that they make it possible for customers to better manage their own sustainability performance by disclosing to them what the environmental footprints of specific products and services happen to be.

   The flip side of all this is that the results of an LCA tell us very little about the sustainability performance of a company. At best, they tell us something – not much – about the product-specific environmental impacts a company (e.g., a manufacturer) has during the production stage of a product's life cycle. Any company's total environmental impacts, however, will always be greater than those associated with the production or handling of a single product. Thus, an LCA is no substitute for a corporate sustainability report, and should never be seen as such.

4. Like all methodologies in which efficiency is involved, LCAs are fundamentally context-free. They do not measure or express environmental impacts relative to norms or standards for what such impacts ought to be, because LCA was never designed to address sustainability performance, per se. Nor can products, as we have already said, be held accountable for anything. Since they are not morally accountable agents, any attempt to hold them accountable would be meaningless and nonsensical. This is because products are inanimate objects. And if, by contrast, it is the actions of people who make, use and dispose of products that we are really interested in assessing, LCA has nothing to offer; instead, we must turn to other methodologies that have human actions as their primary referents of interest, and which can help us measure the social and environmental impacts of people and their organizations relative to norms or standards for what such impacts ought to be. People make choices, products don't.

5. LCAs are, by definition, concerned only with the environmental impacts of products and services, although efforts are underway to develop a social LCA methodology.[2] Thus, to the extent that we are interested in applying a triple bottom line interpretation of sustainability, LCAs only get us so far. And even insofar as they do address one of the three bottom lines of interest to us – the environmental one – they only do so in terms of efficiency and with no context to go by, as separately noted above; and also for products and services only, not organizations, as also noted above.

That all said, LCAs do have a legitimate role to play in helping organizations to mitigate the environmental impacts of their products and services up and down the supply and demand chain, as well as helping users of products and services to improve their own sustainability performance. Our objective is simply to point out that the use of LCAs should not be confused with the separate need to measure, manage and report the sustainability performance of organizations in other ways; nor should it be viewed as a substitute or justification for not doing so.

Does context-based sustainability preclude cross-company comparisons?

Most people generally agree that a performance measurement and reporting system should make it possible both to understand the performance of an organization and to compare its performance with others in like terms. Generally Accepted Accounting Principles (GAAP), for example, make this possible with respect to financial performance, but what, if any, is the equivalent of GAAP on the non-financial side of performance? And what exactly is it that makes GAAP work in the first place? Let's deal with the second question first.

As argued above, financial measurement and reporting systems such as GAAP are fundamentally capital- and context-based. They are capital-based to the extent that they deal with organizations' effects or impacts on monetary capital, and they are context-based in the sense that they measure and report performance relative to the quality and sufficiency of such capital, while also measuring incoming monetary flows (revenue) against outgoing flows (costs). Like all context-based measurement, management and reporting systems, GAAP measures revenue against a threshold, which constitutes a financial standard of performance. That threshold, in the case of financial performance, is made up of costs or expenses, such that revenues should be no less than costs. Thus, revenues that fall below such a threshold diminish the stock of monetary capital, which if continued unabated will put capital, and therefore shareholder well-being, at risk. Income statements and balance sheets are, at least in part, predicated on these principles.

Once the theoretical underpinnings of a measurement model such as GAAP have been defined, templates or conceptual frameworks can be devised in order to operationalize them. Again, income statements and balance sheets, and the categories of measures they entail, fit this description in the case of financial management and

GAAP, in particular. Furthermore, rules can be devised that explain how to use such frameworks and how to record different kinds of transactions within them. GAAP, for example, helps us understand the difference between an asset and a liability, and how to reflect these and other transactions in our financial measurement and reporting systems.

Now assuming everyone is using the same conceptual frameworks and following the same rules for how to use them, the financial performance of one firm can be compared with the financial performance of another in like terms. Despite their imperfections, this is arguably one of the beauties of conventional accounting systems in use by businesses today – they make cross-organizational comparisons of performance possible, not to mention reporting of performance for purely internal, day-to-day management purposes. In other words, financial measurement and reporting systems not only make it possible for third parties to understand the financial performance of organizations; they also make it possible for organizations and their managers to understand their own performance so that they can manage it in an informed way.

Turning now to non-financial performance, what can we say about the state of the art in measurement and reporting systems? Well, the first thing we can say, as we already have, is that mainstream sustainability measurement and reporting systems arguably fail to do the one thing they set out to do, which is make it possible for third parties (e.g., stakeholders) and managers, alike, to understand the non-financial performance of their own organizations, or the ones they've invested in. They fail in this regard precisely because of the absence of context in their frameworks, despite the fact that, like all other performance management systems, they are capital-based in theory and therefore must be context-based in practice.

Even the closest thing we have to a GAAP-like standard in sustainability measurement and reporting, GRI, fails to make cross-organizational comparisons possible because of the absence of context. How can cross-organizational comparisons of sustainability performance take place when the measurement model being used at the level of individual organizations lacks context and therefore fails to measure and report sustainability performance at all? Still, much of the information routinely included in GRI reports is useful insofar as sustainability reporting is concerned. It only needs be put into context in order for genuine sustainability reporting to occur. Until or unless that happens, cross-organizational sustainability comparisons will not be possible using GRI or any other context-free methodology. For that, we need context, a fact that GRI ostensibly agrees with but has not yet acted on.[3]

Context-based sustainability, of course, does not suffer from this problem, and instead was born out of a desire to overcome it. All sustainability measurement and reporting, in order to be meaningful and authentic, must include context, in the sense that the social and environmental impacts of an organization should be measured against some quantification or standard for what they ought to be in order to ensure stakeholder well-being. And as we have said, this necessarily entails the measurement and reporting of impacts on vital capitals of four particular kinds: natural, human, social and constructed.

As we have also said, and will explain in more detail in Chapter 3, the choice or specification of standards for impacts on vital capitals should be driven by duties and obligations owed to stakeholders, the mix of which is potentially different for every company. In its most fully elaborated form, then, CBS begins with the identification and acknowledgement of stakeholder groups with whom an organization has relationships, and then continues with a systematic attempt to choose and/or create metrics that can be used to track performance against duties and obligations entailed by such relationships. Depending on how well an organization performs in terms of meeting its duties and obligations, its performance will vary accordingly – both its financial performance and its non-financial performance.

Turning more exclusively to non-financial performance, then, we can see that decisions about which metrics to use in the measurement and reporting of social, environmental and economic impacts have everything to do with who an organization's stakeholders are, and what it feels its duties and obligations are to each of them (by group) to have impact on vital capital resources of four different kinds. And since the answers to these questions are potentially different for every organization, one has to wonder if cross-organizational comparisons of non-financial performance can ever be possible. How, for example, can the non-financial performance of two organizations with two completely different sets of stakeholders and two different sets of obligations ever be compared, when the two will necessarily be managing and tracking performance against completely different duties?

The answer to this riddle is the same as it would be – and *is* – in the case of financial measurement and reporting. Indeed, are the charts of accounts for any two organizations in the world ever exactly alike; are their assets and liabilities the same; are their revenues and expenses the same? Of course not. And yet somehow we manage to measure and report financial performance in a way that takes cross-organizational differences in revenues received, expenses incurred and duties owed fully into account, while still making it possible to tally up the results in a consistent manner and compare financial performance between two or more very different organizations with ease. How is this possible?

It is possible precisely because of the shared use of common measurement models and rules for how to use them, as previously discussed. As long as two or more firms are using the same conceptual frameworks and models to measure and report their financial performance (i.e., capital- and context-based measurement models), and are also following the same rules for how to apply them, all of their otherwise very different financial transactions – and policies for how much to spend on one thing versus another – can be recorded in a way that makes cross-organizational comparisons possible. It is like saying in financial reporting that organizations are free to spend as much or as little as they like on the resources required to run their business (e.g., employees, office equipment, rent, etc.), as long as they categorize such transactions as expenses and report them accordingly in their income statements.

Thus, no standardization is required on the issue of whether or not, and if so how much, an organization should spend on such things, since all individual spending decisions can be converted to a common currency (i.e., money, an artificial proxy for value that we use in commerce). Thus, as long as we can compare the monetary value of revenue with the monetary value of costs, cross-organizational comparisons of profitability can be performed, despite the fact that no two organizations are incurring costs alike, receiving revenue alike, etc.

What, then, are the conceptual frameworks and associated rules for making *non-financial* measurement and reporting possible, in ways that might facilitate cross-organizational comparisons? In Chapter 3, we will discuss the details of these frameworks and rules further, but for now we can summarize our answer to this question as follows:

1. Non-financial performance is a function of how well an organization meets its obligations to its stakeholders to have impact on vital capitals of importance to their (its stakeholders') well-being. The first step in creating comparability in reporting, therefore, is for each organization to identify its own stakeholder groups. The fact that they may differ between organizations imposes no impediment to cross-organizational analysis; rather, it is their shared grounding in stakeholder well-being that has exactly the opposite effect, just as the shared grounding in shareholder well-being makes cross-organizational financial reporting possible.

2. Next comes the identification of duties and obligations to have impact on vital capital resources of importance to stakeholder well-being. This is expressed in terms of impacts on four specific capitals, or some subset of them, as the case may be. It is up to each organization to determine what its obligations are to each group, and to manage its performance accordingly. The fact that different organizations will have different duties and obligations to have impact on a different mix of vital capitals in order to ensure the well-being of their own sets of stakeholders in no way precludes cross-organizational comparisons. Rather, it enables them precisely because of the common underlying framework all organizations could use, consisting of the process of setting non-financial standards of performance that are stakeholder-driven and capital-based, against which actual performance can be measured and reported as such.

3. In terms of rules, what is required is that each organization define its own unique set of non-financial standards of performance; the fact that they are liable to be different from any other organization's is no more preclusive of cross-organizational comparisons than different revenues and expenses are in the case of financial reporting. There is no need for standardization at the level of specific duties and obligations in non-financial reporting either, only that stakeholder-driven standards for impacts on vital capitals be determined in a consistent fashion by all organizations, recognizing that the specifics of what follows for two or more organizations might be just as varied as they are on the financial side of things. It is consistency in the measurement and reporting *frameworks* and the *rules* for applying them that makes cross-organizational comparisons possible in the case of *both* financial and non-financial measurement and reporting.

To the extent that cross-organizational comparisons of performance are just as desirable for non-financial assessments as they are for financial assessments, it should be clear from the above that they are indeed possible to perform under the context-based approach to sustainability. Further, we can see that objections to such comparisons as not being possible because of the absence of commonly held standards of performance for impacts on vital capitals are unfounded. Not only does CBS make meaningful measurement and reporting possible at the level of individual organizations; it makes comparisons between them possible as well, thanks entirely to the use of common conceptual frameworks, and rules for applying them, that allow different organizations to communicate their variable performance in consistent terms.

According to what rules or principles should social sustainability performance be measured?

In Chapter 1 we called attention to three rules for sustainability performance put forward by Herman Daly, all of which deal only with impacts on natural capital. Here we want to address the question of whether or not there can be rules of a similar kind for impacts on anthro capital. Indeed we think there can be. Before explaining what we think they are, however, here again are Daly's rules for impacts on natural capital as neatly summarized by Meadows et al. in 1992 (p. 209):

> In order to be physically sustainable [a] society's material and energy throughputs would have to meet economist Herman Daly's three conditions:
>
> 1. Its rates of use of renewable resources do not exceed their rates of regeneration;
> 2. Its rates of use of nonrenewable resources do not exceed the rate at which sustainable renewable resources are developed;
> 3. Its rates of pollution emission do not exceed the assimilative capacity of the environment.

Daly's rules hinge on the distinction that can be made between renewable versus non-renewable natural capital resources. The first and third rules deal with renewable resources; the second deals with *non*-renewable ones.

In the case of anthro capitals, they are all, in a sense, renewable, since they are all human-made and can be re-made or expanded in supply at will. Because of this, there is only one rule required to characterize sustainable performance in the case of anthro capitals. That rule, we propose, is as follows:

> In order to be socially sustainable, a society's or organization's impacts on anthro capitals must meet the following condition:
>
> > Its rates of anthro capital production and/or maintenance must not fall below levels required to ensure human/stakeholder well-being.

The rates referred to in this formulation are allocated rates, in the sense in which we used the term in our definition of context at the end of Chapter 1 (i.e., per the third element of context we introduced there). In other words, the standard of performance for social sustainability – which, again, includes economic sustainability, since we regard economic sustainability as merely a form or type of social sustainability – is to produce and/or maintain anthro capital resources at levels that are fair and proportionate to an organization's place in the broader population responsible for preserving, producing and/or maintaining them (i.e., per the *Responsible Populations* element of sustainability context explained at the end of Chapter 1). In some cases, the broader population will include other parties, in which case an organization's share of the overall responsibility for producing and/or maintaining anthro capitals will be a partial one; in other cases, an organization will be the sole party responsible for such capitals, in which case its share of responsibility for them will be exclusive and absolute (see Chapter 3 for several illustrations of this rule in practice).

GRI and the prevalence of context-free sustainability

By some accounts, approximately half of the now thousands of corporate sustainability or CSR (corporate social responsibility) reports produced each year by organizations around the world are prepared in accordance with the GRI guidelines. As earlier noted, the GRI framework is reflective of the triple bottom line and includes sections, therefore, that call for the measurement and reporting of an organization's social, environmental and economic impacts. In that regard, GRI is highly compatible with the approach put forward in this book.

Of greater importance, however, is the extent to which GRI explicitly advocates for the inclusion of context in sustainability reporting, a position it has taken since it was first deployed in 2000. To be clear, then, the necessity to include context in sustainability measurement and reporting *is advocated by the leading international sustainability reporting standard in the world*, and has been so advocated for more than a decade. Why, then, is the inclusion of context in mainstream sustainability reports, including in the thousands of so-called GRI-compliant reports prepared each year, so rare if not virtually non-existent?

Below we offer our own perspective on this question as we consider the manner in which GRI actually advocates for the inclusion of context in reporting, what specifically it has to say about that, and how we could or should interpret it. Here, then, is what GRI has to say about context as found in a section of the latest version of the standard, entitled '1.1 Defining Report Content' (GRI, 2011, p. 11):

SUSTAINABILITY CONTEXT

Definition: The report should present the organization's performance in the wider context of sustainability.

Explanation: Information on performance should be placed in context. The underlying question of sustainability reporting is how an organization contributes, or aims to contribute in the future, to the improvement or deterioration of economic, environmental, and social conditions, developments, and trends at the local, regional, or global level. Reporting only on trends in individual performance (or the efficiency of the organization) will fail to respond to this underlying question. Reports should therefore seek to present performance in relation to broader concepts of sustainability. This will involve discussing the performance of the organization in the context of the limits and demands placed on environmental or social resources at the sectoral, local, regional, or global level. For example, this could mean that in addition to reporting on trends in eco-efficiency, an organization might also present its absolute pollution loading in relation to the capacity of the regional ecosystem to absorb the pollutant.

Now we would like to comment on each statement made in the quotation above, starting with the opening definition (GRI, 2011, p. 11):

Definition: The report should present the organization's performance in the wider context of sustainability.

Of course we agree with this claim, the truth of which can be demonstrated with a simple example. Imagine two different companies, one located in water-rich New England and the other in the comparatively dry southwestern United States. Let us assume, further, that the two companies involved are alike in every respect – size, revenue, facilities, number of employees, products produced, volume of production, etc. – and that they also consume the same amount of water from local sources each year. According to the way in which most companies report their sustainability performance today (i.e., in a context-free fashion), the water-related sustainability performance of these two companies would be reported as identical. But this couldn't possibly be the case, since the background water conditions at the two locations are dramatically different.

Indeed, the company in New England might be using water at rates that, if generalized to the population as a whole, fall well within the rate of water replenishment or regeneration each year (i.e., per Herman Daly's first rule of sustainability as discussed in Chapter 1), whereas the company in the southwest with the same rate of consumption might be contributing to the rapid decline, or even disappearance, of water resources there, even if its rate of consumption is falling. For all we know, the volume of water resources in the southwest might be declining at three times the rate of the company's own decreasing consumption, thanks to a combination of dry weather and a rapidly growing population.

Background conditions of these types matter greatly when attempting to assess and/or report the sustainability of water use, as do background conditions of many other kinds in other areas of sustainability performance. As GRI separately explains in the Technical Protocol section of its guidelines (GRI, 2011, TP section, p. 6):

Organizational performance [should be assessed] in relation to information about economic, environmental, and social conditions in relevant locations, e.g., discussing water consumption in relation to available supply in a particular location.

Sustainability reporting that fails to take such factors explicitly into account is no sustainability reporting at all. Rather, it begs the question.

The statement continues (GRI, 2011, p. 11):

> **Explanation:** Information on performance should be placed in context.

Again, we agree with this statement for the same reasons discussed above. Furthermore, it should be clear that GRI's use of the word 'should' establishes a normative requirement for reporting, in cases where the GRI standard is being used. Every report prepared under the auspices of GRI that does not conform to this requirement is arguably *not* in compliance with GRI to the required extent. Still, it is worth noting that reports prepared in accordance with GRI's guidelines can receive a rating of A+ from GRI itself, even though such reports may be entirely context-free. Here we begin to see why context, or *sustainability context* as GRI calls it, is so conspicuously missing from mainstream reporting. Why go to the trouble of including it when top-level ratings for the content of a report can be obtained without it? The requirement to include context is simply not enforced in this regard.

The inclusion of context in reporting also has the added benefit of helping to mitigate the possibility of false positives or negatives in terms of how content is interpreted. Water consumption rates that are steadily declining over time, for example, could be misinterpreted as a positive result when in fact the availability of underlying supplies might be decreasing at twice the rate (e.g., due to drought conditions, increases in human population, climate change, etc.).

Next comes a more specific indication of what GRI means by context (GRI, 2011, p. 11):

> The underlying question of sustainability reporting is how an organization contributes, or aims to contribute in the future, to the improvement or deterioration of economic, environmental, and social conditions, developments, and trends at the local, regional, or global level.

Here again we agree with GRI, but let us try to put a finer point on things. The specific 'economic, environmental, and social conditions' GRI speaks of should be interpreted as vital capitals in the world (i.e., the required levels of their stocks and flows), upon which people at the 'local, regional, or global level' depend for their well-being. The 'developments' and 'trends' GRI further refers to should, in turn, be interpreted as developments and trends related to the quality or sufficiency of such capitals. If, as we allege, the sustainability performance of an organization is a function of its impacts on vital capitals, then it must be vital capitals – and the carrying capacities of their flows – that comprise the specific local, regional or global conditions of interest to us when we measure and report an organization's sustainability performance, as well as the demands placed on them, as GRI also points out (discussed further below).

It should be clear by now, then, that our interpretation of GRI's treatment of context as a requirement for reporting is that it is consistent with our own position on the subject, as far as it goes. That said, GRI simply does not go far enough in terms of explaining context further, much less in providing guidelines for how to operationalize it. The term *capital* itself, for example, when used in the GRI standard only occurs in the narrow economic sense. There is no discussion of natural capital, human capital, social capital or constructed capital, despite the foundational importance of these concepts to sustainability performance and to the inclusion of context in related reporting. Exactly *how* to include context is largely left to the user's imagination, with or without capital theory to go by.

This, in our view, constitutes another major reason why GRI reports so often, if not always, omit context: there are simply no guidelines for how to do it. Given the utterly foundational and fundamental importance of context to sustainability measurement and reporting, though, it is hard to understand why the absence of such guidelines has been allowed to persist for so long. The consequence? Every GRI report – or every sustainability or CSR report, for that matter – from which context is missing (i.e., the majority of reports ever prepared) necessarily fails to achieve the one thing it sets out to do: report the sustainability performance of the organization it describes. Again, this is a little bit like issuing income statements for financial reporting that systematically exclude costs, and which therefore never really report profits or losses. Instead of triple bottom line reporting, a better description for this kind of disclosure might be triple *top* line reporting – no real sustainability reporting going on at all.

GRI continues as follows (GRI, 2011, p. 11):

> Reporting only on trends in individual performance (or the efficiency of the organization) will fail to respond to this underlying question.

Again, we completely agree with this statement. Of particular importance to its phrasing is its use of the term *efficiency*, which in sustainability management circles is more often referred to as eco-efficiency, a term first coined by the World Business Council for Sustainable Development (WBCSD) as follows (Schmidheiny and WBCSD, 1992, p. 10):

> Industry is moving toward 'demanufacturing' and 'remanufacturing' – that is, recycling the materials in their products and thus limiting the use of raw materials and of energy to convert those raw materials ... It is the more competitive and successful companies that are in the forefront of what we call 'eco-efficiency'.

As already mentioned, there is a world of difference between measures of efficiency and measures of sustainability. The first is a measure of resource use relative to some normalizing variable, such as water used *per unit of production* or *per year*; the second is a measure of resource use relative to resource supply. That the two are not the same is easily understood by contemplating a case where water efficiency, for example, is improving through conservation measures even as background water supplies are dropping at three times the rate. To say that an organization's use of natural resources is efficient or even optimal is not to say that its use is sustainable.

McDonough and Braungart (1998) make the same point in more dramatic terms as follows (p. 85):

> Eco-efficiency is an outwardly admirable and certainly well-intended concept, but, unfortunately, it is not a strategy for success over the long term, because it does not reach deep enough. It works within the same system that caused the [environmental] problem in the first place, slowing it down with moral pro-scriptions and punitive demands. It presents little more than an illusion of change. Relying on eco-efficiency to save the environment will in fact achieve the opposite – it will let industry finish off everything quietly, persistently, and completely.

The point here is that limited natural resources are still limited no matter how efficient their use is; and further, that advances in efficiency can easily be offset by even greater advances in overall consumption. To improve efficiency where steadily decreasing natural resources are concerned is simply to delay the inevitable – like putting *un*sustainability in slow motion: the same outcome is assured, just postponed for a bit.

There is also the not so insignificant matter of *Jevons' Paradox*, a name given to the observation that consumption tends to increase, not decrease, as efficiencies improve. As Jevons himself put it in his own investigation of fuel consumption patterns in the mid-nineteenth century (Jevons, 1866, pp. 123–24):

> It is wholly a confusion of ideas to suppose that the economical use of fuel is equivalent to a diminished consumption. The very contrary is the truth.
>
> As a rule, new modes of economy will lead to an increase of consumption according to a principle recognised in many parallel instances. The economy of labour effected by the introduction of new machinery throws labourers out of employment for the moment. But such is the increased demand for the cheapened products, that eventually the sphere of employment is greatly widened ... Now the same principles apply, with even greater force and distinctness, to the use of such a general agent as coal. It is the very economy of its use which leads to its extensive consumption. It has been so in the past, and it will be so in the future. Nor is it difficult to see how this paradox arises.

As gains in efficiency are made, including in *eco*-efficiency in business, demand for related products and services rises, thereby also increasing, not decreasing, the flow of natural resources in the economy – not to mention the production of wastes. Left unchecked, then, eco-efficiency can lead to lower, not higher, levels of sustainability performance, contrary to popular belief.

That said, managing for efficiency – or eco-efficiency – *can* be an important tactic for helping organizations to achieve sustainability. Using water resources more conservatively, for example, can contribute to a decrease in overall water use, such that the resulting levels of consumption fall within a sustainable range. Determining the sustainable range, however, requires something more than what the principle of eco-efficiency brings to the table; namely, a reference to context, which in the case of water involves things like watershed location and size, annual precipitation levels, human population size, and so forth. Eco-efficiency, of course, brings none of that to bear – it is entirely context-free. And that is why it, alone, cannot lead to sustainability and more often leads to the opposite.

It should also be clear that although eco-efficiency (when combined with a context-based perspective) can be an important contributor to achieving sustainability, it can only be so with respect to the environmental bottom line. Why? Because the capitals involved in social and economic sustainability (human, social and constructed) are completely different from the capital involved in environmental sustainability (natural).

Similarly, marginal improvements in social or economic impacts – measured in terms of what we might call *socio-efficacy* – also require context in order to be sustainable. To say that there is less poverty in the world, for example, is not to say that the levels involved are less enough. The same goes for education levels, employment, housing, and so forth. Here again there are thresholds to consider – dividing lines, if you will, between sustainable conditions on the one hand and unsustainable conditions on the other. Marginal measures tell us nothing about any of that.

Next in the GRI text comes the following statement (GRI, 2011, p. 11):

> Reports should therefore seek to present performance in relation to broader concepts of sustainability. This will involve discussing the performance of the organization in the context of the limits and demands placed on environmental or social resources at the sectoral, local, regional, or global level.

This is about as close to the capital-based theory of sustainability as GRI gets. Of particular importance here is the manner in which context is explained in terms of 'the limits and demands placed on environmental or social resources'. In our own formulation of context provided in Chapter 1, we used different words to express a similar idea: that organizations are, to one degree or another, responsible for preserving and/or producing vital capitals of importance to stakeholder well-being. Specifically, we said that *context* in sustainability is determined by following a three-step procedure:

1. **Carrying Capacities of Capitals**: First we identify the vital capitals (stocks) and their carrying capacities (flows) an organization is having impact on in ways that can affect stakeholder well-being, as well as capitals it *should* be having impact on in order to *ensure* stakeholder well-being.

2. **Responsible Populations**: Next we determine who the responsible populations are for ensuring the quality and sufficiency of such stocks and flows.
3. **Organizational Allocations**: And last, based on the first and second steps above, we allocate proportionate shares of available stocks and flows (in the case of natural capital) and/or burden shares for producing and/or maintaining them (in the case of anthro capital) to individual organizations.

As indicated in this particular explication of context, we took the position that the vital capitals we refer to yield flows of valuable goods and services required for human well-being, and that the volume or size of such flows can be expressed as the *carrying capacities of capitals* and can be measured as such. This concept does not appear at all in the GRI standard, but it is at least suggested or alluded to in the language quoted above in which the 'limits' of 'environmental and social resources' are mentioned. *Limits quantified in what way?* one might ask. *By their carrying capacities*, we would reply.

It is our contention, therefore, that the principle of sustainability context in GRI can be operationalized by embracing a combination of the capital-based theory of sustainability and the related concept of carrying capacity it simultaneously entails. In that sense, we can say that the context-based approach to CSM put forward in this book builds on the principle of sustainability context otherwise advocated by GRI and is completely compatible with it.

The final statement in the GRI text quoted above is as follows (GRI, 2011, p. 11):

> For example, this could mean that in addition to reporting on trends in eco-efficiency, an organization might also present its absolute pollution loading in relation to the capacity of the regional ecosystem to absorb the pollutant.

This statement, of course, is intended to provide an illustration of what the inclusion of context might look like in a case involving the emission of a pollutant, such as wastewater. In our terms, the illustration can best be understood as (a) one that refers to impacts on natural capital, and (b) one that specifically involves the carrying capacity of natural capital as expressed in Daly's third rule, which he explained as follows (Daly, 1990, p. 2):

> [A]ssimilative capacities [to absorb human wastes] must be treated as natural capital, and failure to maintain these capacities must be treated as capital consumption, and therefore not sustainable.

Thus, we can say that a body of water into which a wastewater stream is emitted has a limited assimilative capacity to withstand such emissions, beyond which the capacity is exceeded and the ecological integrity of the resource will be compromised. This, in turn, may put human well-being at risk, and that – by our definition – is precisely what makes related behaviors (and their impacts) unsustainable.

On this particular point where the assimilative capacity of water resources is concerned, it may also be useful to point out that many of the wastewater permitting systems in force in the U.S. and elsewhere are context-based regulatory systems writ large. This is true in the sense that individual wastewater permits are typically reviewed by regulators in the context of the so-called receiving waters that an emitter plans to use as a drain or sink for his or her wastes. The volume and toxicity of a would-be emitter's wastes are systematically compared with the carrying capacity of receiving waters (i.e., their assimilative capacity to safely absorb the wastes), and permits are thereby approved or denied, accordingly, depending on the outcome of related calculations. In this regard, we have had context-based sustainability management going on all around us for decades now, albeit mainly on the regulatory front.

To conclude this section's examination of the extent to which GRI has embodied the principle of sustainability context in its guidelines, we offer the following summary:

1. The principle of sustainability context is nothing new to sustainability measurement and reporting and has been advocated by GRI, the leading international standard for sustainability reporting in the world, for more than a decade now.
2. Despite its advocacy for the inclusion of context in sustainability measurement and reporting, GRI has (a) failed to provide guidelines for how to do so,[4] and (b) failed to enforce the requirement to do so while simultaneously granting superior ratings to reporters (and their reports) who don't.
3. The principle of sustainability context can – *and should* – be articulated in terms of the capital-based theory of sustainability and the concept of carrying capacity that it entails.
4. Taking the capital-based view would make it possible to operationalize the concept of sustainability context, as countless environmental regulatory and permitting systems have been doing for years, and as we ourselves do in this book.

In light of the above, we believe the time has come for GRI to take the sustainability context principle to the next level, and to codify guidelines that preparers of corporate sustainability reports can follow in practice. Until or unless that happens, corporate sustainability reporting will continue to fall short of its most basic purpose, which is to disclose the true sustainability performance of organizations in the social, environmental and economic sense of the term. An activity is sustainable if, and only if, its impacts on vital capital resources in the world can continue indefinitely without putting human well-being at risk. A sustainability report should inform readers accordingly. Most, however, do not. And so, as an institution, sustainability reporting has thus far failed to deliver, thanks entirely, we believe, to the chronic absence of context in related 'best' practices and the willingness of leading international standards organizations, such as GRI, to put up with this.

Summary: key issues and practice implications of CBS

In this chapter we have attempted to provide the reader with a better understanding of context-based sustainability (CBS) by (a) discussing the manner in which several key issues in CSM can be addressed, if not resolved, when viewed from a CBS perspective, and (b) critiquing the way in which context is currently handled in the world's leading sustainability measurement and reporting standard, GRI.

In addressing the question of how CBS can be applied to the analysis and resolution of several key issues in CSM, we differentiated between two classes of issues: one that pertained to how CBS relates to, or interacts with, both the business strategy of an organization and its conventional management practices, and another that dealt with sustainability measurement and reporting, per se, and how CBS can add value in that space. Our key conclusions were as follows:

How CBS relates to conventional strategy and management

- Rather than positioning sustainability, or CSM, as something that must be aligned with – and somehow subordinate to – strategy, we took the position that sustainability goals and objectives should be seen as legitimate components of strategy in their own right, and that the profit-making interests of shareholders must be balanced with the separate, but no less legitimate, interests of non-shareholders, or stakeholders of other kinds.
- We also took the position that attending to the non-financial impacts of an organization necessarily serves and supports the business mission and purpose of an organization, since it helps to insulate the organization from risks associated with its social and environmental impacts by ensuring that such impacts are consistent with stakeholder well-being.
- Next we argued against the shareholder primacy doctrine of strategy and management, and in favor of the stakeholder-centric alternative. Here we simply pointed out that organizations do, in fact, have more than just shareholders to contend with, if only because of their impacts on vital capital resources of importance to non-shareholder well-being. Because of this, it makes sense to recognize parties other than shareholders as stakeholders, and to define related duties and obligations to have impact (or not) on such vital capital resources in accordance with the principle of stakeholder well-being. Indeed, by doing so, the proper scope of a CSM function can be defined in a logically bounded fashion, instead of an arbitrarily unbounded one, as if the whole of the world's social and environmental problems are somehow the responsibility of any and all organizations.
- By rejecting the shareholder primacy doctrine, we also opened the door to the idea that planning horizons and cycles – which are typically one year or less on the financial side of management – can be 25 years or longer on the non-financial side, since change in the social and environmental domains proceeds at a much slower pace. Indeed, if planning horizons for both financial and non-financial management were, in fact, calibrated to the same longer-term time scales, the risks associated with subpar social and environmental impacts – not to mention the benefits of superior performance – would necessarily come into play more often in strategy-making and management, thanks to the coincidence of timing. As things sit today, by contrast, the social and environmental impacts of an

organization's performance rarely come up at all in the context of strategic planning and management, in part because of a mismatch in the timing of financial
versus non-financial planning horizons. The effects of an organization's social and
environmental impacts, that is, are always just far enough out into the future (if
not way out) to be of little or no concern to conventional, short-term planning.
Thus, embracing a *stake*holder, as opposed to *share*holder, primacy doctrine can
bring the two sides of performance closer together in ways that are beneficial for
both shareholders and other stakeholders.

- We also called attention to the fact that the context-based approach to CSM we
  are calling for can be seen as merely the extension of classical financial management principles into the non-financial domain. Here we pointed out that financial
  management largely boils down to managing monetary or financial capital on
  behalf of shareholder well-being. Similarly, non-financial management, we
  claimed, can be approached from the perspective that there is more than just one
  type of capital and one type of stakeholder to contend with in an organization,
  and non-financial management is best construed accordingly. More specifically,
  on the non-financial side of management, there are four additional capitals to
  consider (i.e., natural, human, social and constructed) and several more stakeholder categories of interest (e.g., customers, employees, regulators, community
  members, etc.). What's good for financial management ought to be good for non-
  financial management, and so context-based sustainability can be thought of as
  nothing more than an extension of capital-based management principles that have
  served business well for decades, if not centuries. Instead of taking a monistic view
  of capital, then, we argued for a pluralistic one in which there are many capitals
  and many stakeholder categories to consider, not just one of each.

How CBS stacks up in terms of sustainability measurement and reporting

- First in our discussion of how CBS stacks up in terms of sustainability measurement and reporting was the need to confront the frequent confusion in CSM
  between financial and economic bottom lines – in their colloquial usage, that is.
  The question arises because (a) we already have a financial bottom line and certainly did long before CSM arrived, and (b) confusion nevertheless reigns in the
  marketplace on this very topic. Our position – as informed by the context-based
  approach to CSM – is that there is a material difference between the financial and
  economic bottom lines, and that the interpretation most appropriate to sustainability management, which by definition deals with non-financial performance, is
  that the economic dimension of the triple bottom line has nothing to do with
  financial performance. Instead, the economic bottom line deals with the impacts
  of organizations in the broader economy, or with the economic well-being of
  stakeholders with whom an organization has a relationship, and to whom an
  organization owes certain duties and obligations to have impacts on vital capitals,
  accordingly.

Our position on this matter is also not unique, and is supported by the writings of others who see a clear distinction between financial performance and economic performance. Our capital-based perspective adds depth to this view as well, since financial performance deals with impacts on monetary capital and economic performance deals with impacts on human, social and constructed capitals (i.e., what we call anthro capitals because of their anthropogenic origins). Here we can also see that the economic bottom line is really a subset or sub-bottom line of the social bottom line. After all, the human economy is nothing but a subset or slice of human society that happens to involve trade and commerce, just as there are other subsets or slices that involve education, healthcare, law enforcement, government, justice, national defense, etc.

Once we see that there are sub-bottom lines that can be organized into broad categories, it is a short hop from there to realizing that there can be many more than three non-financial bottom lines to contend with in an organization. Indeed, if the economic bottom line is merely a sub-type of the broader social bottom line, there are really only two major categories of non-financial performance to consider: social and environmental – each of which is liable to contain many sub-bottom lines. What ultimately determines the actual number of bottom lines an organization must deal with is (a) the diversity of its stakeholder groups to whom duties and obligations are owed, and (b) the specific duties and obligations owed to each of them and the vital capitals involved. Again, we will explain this more fully in Chapter 3, along with the means by which scores received for multiple social and environmental bottom lines in an organization can be consolidated into unitary, non-financial bottom lines, much like we do in financial reporting.

- Next in our discussion of key issues in CSM came the subject of metrics, and the nuances between so-called relative and absolute measures. The question we raised here is what, if any, implications are raised by the context-based approach insofar as the types of metrics that should be used are concerned? In order to address this issue, we identified three types of metrics in particular (absolute, relative and context-based metrics), and then consolidated them into two variants of one type (context-free relative metrics and context-based relative metrics).

Absolute metrics express the performance of organizations from one year to another without making any attempt to adjust or normalize reports in ways that take changes in organizational size, make-up, etc. into account. This can lead to consistency problems, since most organizations at least change in size from one year to the next, thereby making apples-to-apples comparisons problematic. One good solution to this, we argued, is to express performance using a common denominator of sorts, such as expressing performance on a per capita (or per employee hour worked) basis.

Relative measures of performance tend not to be about sustainability performance at all, and instead pertain to efficiency or the marginal impacts of organizations. Here we might see metrics expressing such things as water consumed per unit of production, or dollars donated to philanthropy per employee. While these are indeed measures of performance of some kind, they are not measures of sustainability performance. Why not? Because they fail to take the demand for, and supplies of, vital capital resources explicitly into account, not to mention related duties and obligations owed to stakeholders. This takes us to context-based metrics.

Context-based metrics (CBMs) are, in effect, relative metrics with context added. Organizational performance is expressed in terms that make inter-annual comparisons possible (i.e., by expressing performance on, say, a per capita or per employee hour worked basis), while also expressing such performance relative to capital-based *standards* of performance. In other words, CBMs measure and express an organization's impacts on vital capital resources relative to what such impacts need to be in order to ensure stakeholder well-being.

In considering the differences between absolute and relative metrics, we also drew the conclusion that absolute metrics are merely a special type of relative metric. They are relative in the sense that they express performance relative to at least a specific period of time for an organization (e.g., organizational performance per year). Since CBMs are also relative metrics, albeit with context added, we can see that there really is only one type of metric in use today (relative metrics) but with two important variations: context-*free* relative metrics and context-*based* relative metrics.

- From here we went on to comment briefly on some further implications of the binary property of sustainability – namely, that the language of sustainability as being a *more* or *less* proposition is very often incorrect. We explained our thinking by introducing a *sustainability performance scale* (see Figure 2.2), on which the results of context-based measurements can be plotted. As indicated in Figure 2.2, scores pertaining to impacts on vital capitals are all expressed relative to a demarcation point of 1.0 on the scale, although the meaning of such scores will differ depending on the type of capital involved.

  Scores for impacts on natural capital, for example, are interpreted such that any score of greater than 1.0 signifies unsustainable performance. Thus, scores of 1.3 and 1.5 would both be unsustainable. With this in mind, it would be misleading and incorrect to say that a score of 1.3 is *more sustainable* given its closer proximity to 1.0. Rather, a score of 1.3 is better described as *less unsustainable* than a score of 1.5; in other words, it is not sustainable in any sense of the term – more, less or otherwise – since it falls on the unsustainable side of the sustainability performance scale to begin with. And although this point may seem overly pedantic to some, one can easily see how incremental improvements in performance on the unsustainable side of the scale could be misinterpreted as *more sustainable* given the shift towards the sustainable side of the scale. Indeed, this is arguably a symptom of mainstream thinking in CSM (i.e., context-free sustainability), under which there are no thresholds or demarcation points to refer to, and hence no ability to score or interpret performance in anything but *more* or *less* terms. Not so for the context-based school.

- We then took up the question of whether or not products, per se, can be sustainable (or unsustainable). Here it is important to be clear about the referents we have in mind when speaking about sustainability. The fact is that, in CSM, referents can vary – and very often without warning, as it were. In some cases, the thing of interest to us is organizations; in others, it is supply chains; and for others again, it is products. This point is perhaps best illustrated by reference to two leading measurement and reporting systems in CSM: the Global Reporting Initiative (GRI) and life cycle assessments (LCAs). Whereas GRI is decidedly organizational in focus, LCAs are aimed squarely at products and services. The two are in no way interchangeable.

Given products as a referent, it should also be clear, we argued, that sustainability is not an attribute that can be applied to them. Why not? Because products are inanimate objects. As such, they can have physical properties – such as being toxic, biodegradable, recyclable, etc. – but they cannot be held accountable to standards of performance, as if they are moral agents capable of choosing their own behaviors in order to comply with ethical norms of sustainability. When we find ourselves tending to speak in these terms, what we are really talking about is the way people manufacture, use and dispose of products. The referents in such cases are human actions and the consequences of taking such actions, not the products that humans happen to be making, using or disposing of.

- We further pointed out that performance measurement and reporting of all types – financial and non-financial, alike – is predicated on a stakeholder-centric model, according to which organizations have duties and obligations to their stakeholders to have impact on one or more types of capital on their behalf. How well they live up to such responsibilities is, in fact, what sustainability measurement and reporting is all about. It just so happens that on the financial side of performance there is only one stakeholder group to contend with (shareholders) and only one type of capital (monetary). Not so on the non-financial side of performance, where there can be many stakeholders and four types of capital (natural, human, social and constructed). Despite the differences between financial and non-financial management, then, performance on both fronts boils down to the same basic principles: impacts that conform to standards or norms for what they ought to be in order to ensure stakeholder well-being signify positive performance; impacts that do not signify the reverse.

- Armed with the kind of context-based metrics discussed in this chapter and a sustainability performance scale on which to plot and interpret numerical results, we then argued that the actual sustainability performances of organizations can be quantitatively determined, and then compared with one another just as we routinely do for financial performance. Here again the methodology, in principle, is the same for both financial and non-financial assessments: impacts on one or more capitals of vital importance are measured and reported against standards or norms for what they ought to be in order to ensure stakeholder well-being.

Since every organization's stakeholders are liable to be different from every other's – not to mention the duties and obligations owed to each of them – applicable norms or standards for non-financial performance will vary from one organization to another. This, however, does not preclude cross-organizational comparisons, since the basis of comparison is to determine the degree to which individual organizations meet their own standards of performance, regardless of whether they happen to be the same as any other's. After all, variation abounds on the financial side of things, and always has; yet cross-organizational comparisons on that front are no less possible and are routinely performed. Why should things be any different on the non-financial front?

- The final key issue we addressed was the question of whether or not there can be the equivalent of Daly's rules for impacts on anthro capitals, since Daly's rules deal only with impacts on natural capital. The answer we gave was *yes*, although only one such rule is needed – that a society's or organization's rates of impacts on anthro capitals should be no less than those required to ensure human/stake-holder well-being. Determining what those rates should be and measuring performance against them, however, require a structured methodology of some kind for practicing context-based CSM, a vision for which we will present in Chapter 3.

We concluded this chapter with a detailed discussion of how GRI defines and presents the subject of context in its sustainability measurement and reporting guidelines. Briefly, our major conclusions were as follows:

- Although GRI argues strongly, as we do, for the need to include context in sustainability measurement and reporting, it fails to enforce its position on the matter. It fails to do so by (a) not providing guidelines for how to incorporate context in reporting,[5] and by (b) excluding consideration of context in its formal rating system for assessing the quality of sustainability reports. Thus, even reports that are completely devoid of context can receive A+ ratings under the GRI system.
- In order to resolve this problem, we believe GRI should (a) embrace the capital-based approach to CSM, (b) develop related guidelines for including context in sustainability reports, and (c) modify its rating system for reports so as to include consideration of whether or not context has been properly or sufficiently included.

Having discussed the meaning and origins of context-based sustainability in Chapter 1, and the application of it to key issues in CSM in Chapter 2, it is now time to explain how, in fact, CBS can be operationalized in an organization. That is the subject of Chapter 3.

Notes

1. Life cycle assessment, or LCA, is a technique for quantifying and assessing the environmental impacts of products or services from their inception to their end of life or disposal stage (e.g., from raw material extraction to disposal in solid waste facilities). Detailed procedures for performing LCAs are spelled out as part of the ISO 14000 environmental management standards.

2. Social LCAs, in principle, are intended to augment environmental LCAs by quantifying the social impacts of products and services throughout their life cycles. An effort is currently underway under the auspices of the United Nations Environment Program (UNEP) and the Society for Environmental Toxicology and Chemistry (SETAC) to develop a standard methodology for performing social LCAs. At the time of writing, the development of the methodology was still very much a work in progress.
3. See note 3 in Chapter 1.
4. See note 3 in Chapter 1.
5. See note 3 in Chapter 1.

3

HOW TO DO CSM

Introduction

We now turn our attention to the practice of context-based sustainability, which is fundamentally about managing the sustainability performance of organizations in a way that takes vital capitals and stakeholder well-being explicitly into account. Here we should first acknowledge that the approach we advocate in this chapter is by no means the only approach to managing the sustainability performance of organizations; rather, it is the one we think is the best and most legitimate at this time, and which logically follows from the capital- and context-based school of thought.

In using the term *sustainability performance*, we mean to refer to the degree to which an organization's non-financial performance, consisting of its impacts on vital (non-monetary) capitals in the world, is sustainable. By *sustainable*, we mean that such impacts can continue indefinitely without putting human well-being at risk, and instead have the effect of preserving, producing and/or maintaining vital capitals at levels required to *ensure* it. Corporate sustainability management (CSM), therefore, is a management discipline that seeks to manage or control the impacts of organizations on vital capitals in the world, such that they (i.e., the impacts and the activities that produce them) are sustainable.

Of central importance to the sustainability of business is the question of how organizations and their sustainability management functions should, in fact, go about the business of managing their sustainability performance. In order to do so, a methodology of some kind is required – one that is predicated on a particular *theory of change* or *practice* of some kind, and a corresponding *theory of system* that lies behind it.

A theory of change, or practice, is a kind of *if–then* set of beliefs, which says *if we do x, y will happen*. It's like saying the way to stimulate the economy is to lower interest rates. In the case of CSM, the more relevant assertion might be something like: *the way to achieve sustainability in business is to manage impacts on vital capitals in ways that ensure stakeholder well-being*. That, in a nutshell, is in fact the theory of practice put forward in this book under the banner of *context-based sustainability*, or CBS. Exactly how to practice CBS is the subject of this chapter.

Theories of practice, in turn, are grounded in theories of system. A theory of system is a set of propositions about how the world works, what's in it and how the parts of the world of interest to us in it interact with one another. Having a theory of system is therefore a necessary precondition for having a theory of practice. One can hardly have a compelling theory for how to manage events or conditions in the world if one doesn't first have a theory of what's in the world and how the world works. The specific parts of the world that interest us in our own particular theory of system are people, organizations, societies, economies and the natural environment.

According to our theory, there are various forms of capital in the world that people rely on for their well-being. Organizations, in turn, can and do have impacts on the quality and sufficiency of them (the capitals) – both positive and negative – the results of which affect human well-being. What's more, organizations, because of their disproportionate impacts on people and the environment, constitute a significant point of leverage in the general push for sustainability, and that is why we have chosen to focus on them so heavily in this book and in our general application of CBS. On top of that, the fact that organizations can and do have such disproportionate impacts on vital capitals in the world – thereby affecting human well-being – obligates them, we feel, to manage their impacts accordingly.

The question we will address in this chapter, then, is how best to do that. What we will provide is a structured methodology that CSM practitioners can use in their own organizations to manage their impacts on vital capitals, and thereby manage their sustainability performance. Of key importance to this methodology will be the manner in which CSM should be conceived, and also how the sustainability performance of an organization should be measured and assessed. This means we will be placing a heavy emphasis on metrics – *context-based metrics* in our case – and also on how to interpret the results of related measurements, so as to inform CSM practitioners and others.

The approach put forward in this chapter is one that envisions sustainability managers interacting with their own organizations in order to manage or control their impacts on vital capitals in the world. Vital capitals, in turn, are seen as critical resources that people rely on for their well-being, the quality or sufficiency of which organizations can have impact on. Thus, the purpose of CSM is to (a) understand what an organization's impacts on vital capitals are, (b) further understand what they *should* be, and (c) take steps to bring such impacts into conformance with standards or norms for what they ought to be in order to ensure stakeholder well-being. To explain how to do this, we will be introducing a six-step methodology for performing CSM, including detailed instructions for each of the steps and examples of how they have been performed before.

A case study in CBS: Cabot Creamery Cooperative

Throughout this chapter, we will be using examples taken from a case study involving Cabot Creamery Cooperative, a prominent dairy food producer in New England best known for its award-winning cheddar cheese (see box for background on Cabot).

Cabot Creamery Cooperative

It goes without saying that the cooperative known for making the 'World's Best Cheddar' would have undergone some natural aging of its own.

The Cabot story reaches back to the beginning of the twentieth century. In those days, the cost of farming was low and many farmers produced more milk than they could use themselves.

So in 1919 farmers from the hillsides around the village of Cabot, Vermont figured that if they joined forces, they could turn their excess milk into butter and market it throughout New England. They bet that through combined effort, they could create opportunity.

Ninety-four enterprising farmers created the cooperative – at a cost of $5 per cow, plus a cord of wood to fuel the boiler. These intrepid dairy farmers purchased a creamery, which had been in operation since 1893, and began producing butter under the Rosedale brand name.

Over the next two decades, as the nation's population increasingly migrated to urban areas, Cabot's farmer-owners thrived by shipping their milk and butter south. While the national economy shifted further away from agriculture, the Vermont economy was still largely dependent on dairy farming.

In fact, in 1930 cows outnumbered people nearly 4 to 3. It was at this time, just prior to the Great Depression, that the company hired its first cheesemaker and cheddar cheese joined the Cabot product line.

With the introduction of widespread, on-farm refrigeration in the 1950s and 1960s, cooperatives throughout the region began to consolidate. Cabot's membership reached about 600 farm families at its peak, although the total number of operating farms in Vermont, as in the nation, was in steady decline.

The trend continued into the 1980s when the total number of farms in Vermont sank below 2,000, less than one fifth of what it had been just a few decades earlier. By this time, Cabot was marketing all of its high-quality, Vermont cheeses and butter under the Cabot brand.

The company also began entering its cheddar in national cheese competitions. In 1989 Cabot took first place in the cheddar category at the U.S. Championship Cheese Contest held in, of all places, Green Bay, Wisconsin. That marked the first in what has now become an established tradition of Cabot cheese winning every major award for taste.

A pivotal year in the company's history was 1992, as Cabot's farmer-owners merged with the 1,800 farm families of Agri-Mark, a fellow New England cooperative that traces its roots to 1916. Together, at the time of their marriage, the combined co-ops represented more than 2,000 farms, four creameries and an expanding product line.

Today the future looks bright for Cabot, the leading brand for Agri-Mark, now a 1,200 farm family dairy cooperative with members throughout New England and upstate New York. The cooperative blends state-of-the-art facilities and a savvy entrepreneurial spirit with the timeless values of a personal commitment to quality – the very values that come from being 100 percent owned by dairy farm families.

It's a special combination that produces the highest quality dairy products, including the cheese that has been widely hailed as the 'World's Best'.

In 2007, Cabot formally launched a sustainability program that is perhaps more emblematic of context-based thinking than any other CSM program in the world. All of the company's sustainability performance goals and objectives are defined, managed and measured in terms of impacts on vital capitals, with stakeholder well-being squarely in mind. In this regard, Cabot has arguably pioneered the development of context-based CSM more extensively than any other company, the results of which are exemplary. For that reason, details concerning the development and implementation of Cabot's CSM program will be frequently cited throughout this chapter (see Appendix A for a summary of Cabot's commitment to CBS, and what it means to the company in terms of how CSM is handled there).

In terms of overall structure, Cabot is a vertically integrated organization in the sense that it is composed of both dairy food producers who produce milk at the farm level and dairy food processors who take delivery of fluid milk at the plant level and turn it into products. Once produced, products are then shipped to customers, which for Cabot includes retailers like Walmart, Costco and many others. Because of the dramatically different nature of its operations throughout its value chain, Cabot routinely differentiates between the farm side of the company and the manufacturing or brand side. For the same reason, its sustainability management efforts were similarly split, one part dealing with the cow-to-creamery side of its operations, the other part dealing with the creamery-to-customer side (see Figure 3.1).

In total, Cabot is made up of close to 1,200 dairy farms in New England and upstate New York and four manufacturing plants: two in Vermont, one in Chateaugay, NY, and a fourth in West Springfield, MA. Its main distribution facility is located in Montpelier, VT, as is one of its corporate offices. The other corporate office is located in Methuen, MA. At present, the company has close to a thousand employees on the brand side of the operation, which is where most of the context-based CSM program has been deployed. Assisting Cabot with all of this since late 2007 has been one of us (McElroy), as shown in Figure 3.1, working closely with a non-profit advisor on the farm side, Manomet Center for Conservation Sciences.

In early 2008, Cabot formally designated a new Director of Sustainability position and appointed to that post Jed Davis, a Cabot employee for eighteen years in the company's marketing department. It ultimately fell to Davis, then, working in

COW-TO-CREAMERY-TO-CUSTOMER

Source: Cabot Creamery Cooperative

FIGURE 3.1 Scope of CSM program at Cabot.

concert with McElroy and Manomet, to more fully define and operationalize the company's CSM function and all of its programs in the image of context-based sustainability. To a very large extent, this chapter comprises the story of the first three years of Davis' and Cabot's efforts, the particulars of which make for an excellent case study in the implementation of context-based sustainability.

A methodology for practitioners – the CSM cycle

The first step in developing a methodology for anything, especially a branch of management, is to be absolutely clear about the nature of the system we are trying to affect and our theory about how to do so. We earlier referred to this as the distinction between a *theory of change* or *practice* and a *theory of system*. Logically, it is the latter that must be determined first. In other words, we should first have worked out the nature and behavior of the system we have in mind to affect before we can say how we think we can manage it. What, then, is the theory of system in context-based CSM? In what sense, in other words, can organizations be seen to be sustainable or not in their operations under the context-based view?

The theory of system we rely on in CBS has already been referred to several times in Chapters 1 and 2 as the *capital-based theory of sustainability*. According to the capital-based theory of sustainability, human well-being is inextricably tied to the quality and sufficiency of vital capitals in the world, which such capitals are productive in the sense that they produce flows of valuable goods and services people need in order to meet their basic needs. Capital, as we have explained, is a stock of anything that produces a flow of valuable goods or services that people need and use in order to ensure their own well-being.

The quality or sufficiency of vital capitals in the world, however, can be affected by the actions people take in their lives, including in their working lives. Organizations, in particular, can have impact on vital capitals – sometimes positive, sometimes negative – such that human well-being can be affected. Negative effects on the functioning of natural capital, for example, such as the regulative function of the climate system on Earth, can put human well-being seriously at risk. Indeed, there are many goods and services produced by natural capital that we rely on for our very survival, including the following (Daily, 1997, p. 3):

- purification of air and water
- mitigation of floods and droughts
- detoxification and decomposition of wastes
- generation and renewal of soil and soil fertility
- pollination of crops and natural vegetation
- control of the vast majority of potential agricultural pests
- dispersal of seeds and translocation of nutrients
- maintenance of biodiversity, from which humanity has derived key elements of its agricultural, medicinal and industrial enterprise
- protection from the sun's harmful ultraviolet rays
- partial stabilization of climate
- moderation of temperature extremes and the force of winds and waves
- support of diverse human cultures
- providing of aesthetic beauty and intellectual stimulation that lift the human spirit.

The other forms of capital we have discussed (i.e., the *anthro* capitals of human, social and constructed capital) also provide critically important goods and services that people rely on for their well-being. Our individual and shared knowledge, for example – instances of human and social capital, respectively – makes it possible for us to take effective action day in and day out. The tools and technologies we use – instances of constructed capital – significantly improve the quality of our lives, and even the length of them. Organizations, too, of all kinds constitute instances of social capital, in which human capital is also embedded, not to mention constructed capital (buildings, equipment, technology, etc.). Any network of individuals working together to achieve some common purpose and the human-made material resources they use can be described in these terms.

The theory of system we subscribe to in context-based sustainability is therefore one in which the following claims are made:

- The world includes stocks of resources that produce flows of valuable goods and services that are vitally important for human well-being. We call these stocks *vital capitals*.

- Some vital capitals are anthropogenic (human, social and constructed capitals); others are not (natural capital).
- People, and the organizations they create and work for, can have impact on the quality and sufficiency of vital capitals, such that levels of human well-being can be affected, positively or negatively (see Figure 3.2, and compare it with Figure 1.1).

Next comes our theory of practice – in other words, a theory about how to manage the sustainability of organizations in the kind of world described in our theory of system. Here we take the position that the sustainability performance of an organization is a function of what its impacts on vital capitals are. Of course we couldn't take such a position if we didn't first have a theory of system in which vital capitals exist – hence our earlier point that a theory of system must logically precede our theory of practice.

According to the context-based theory of practice, the sustainability performance of organizations can be determined by (a) examining their impacts on vital capitals, and (b) determining what such impacts on vital capitals would be if they were generalized to the population as a whole (within the boundaries of our analysis, that is, as the case may be).

This latter step is critically important, for without it there can be no meaningful assessment of sustainability performance at the level of individual organizations. Why not? Because each organization is only one of many parties having impacts on vital capitals. Thus, in order to determine their individual sustainability performance, we must look at them from a kind of *what if everybody did it* point of view. In this way, we can assess the sustainability of an organization's actions and impacts in the world by actively considering the question of what the effects on vital capitals would be if

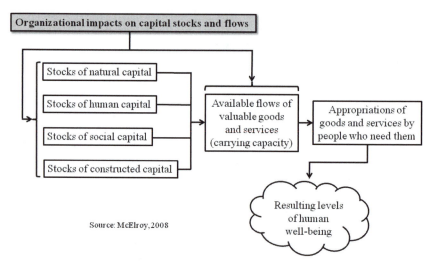

FIGURE 3.2 Organizational impacts on vital capitals.

every other actor in the social or environmental space of interest to us had the same effects. In other words, we ask: *are the impacts generalizable within the boundaries of interest to us, such that if they were, the quality and sufficiency of vital capitals in the world would still be adequate to ensure human well-being?* If the answer is *yes*, then the impacts are sustainable; if *no*, they are not.

In this regard, there is an element of social contract theory[1] going on in our own theory of CSM practice, in the sense that our approach to measurement holds organizations accountable to a kind of public fairness and equity doctrine. When it comes to impacts on vital capitals, fairness and proportionality are key. If there is only so much water to go around, organizations that use it should use no more than their proportionate share; otherwise they are depriving others of *their* proportionate share, and to do so would be unfair and unjust. If everyone used more than their proportionate share, water resources would rapidly disappear and human well-being would suffer because of it. Thus, to have disproportionately negative impacts on vital capitals – including a failure to create and/or maintain them in the case of human-made, or anthro, capitals – is unsustainable.

What all of this tells us, then, is that, in order to be sustainable, an organization must systematically manage its impacts on vital capitals such that its impacts are fair and proportionate, or at least not disproportionately unfair, and that its impacts, if generalized to the population as a whole, would not put human well-being at risk. This, in sum, is our theory of practice. It is the theory of practice that gives rise to context-based CSM, since it is precisely the state of vital capitals and the fair and proportionate impacts organizations should have on them in order to ensure human well-being that constitute the context of interest to us in the phrase itself: *context-based CSM.* What we must have, therefore, is a methodology that makes it possible for CSM practitioners to measure, manage and report their impacts on vital capitals in the ways we have been discussing. Let us now turn to just that.

In Figure 3.3 we present the CSM cycle we will be discussing in the remainder of this chapter. Not counting external reporting (as a separate step), the cycle consists of six steps, three of which are foundational or *policy*-oriented (steps 1 through 3), in the sense that they lay the groundwork for the day-to-day business of CSM, and the other three of which (steps 4 through 6) are more *operational*, in the sense that they describe the work that we believe CSM managers should be doing on a day-to-day basis.

The logic of the CSM cycle is fairly straightforward and proceeds along the lines of a gap analysis, given the theories of system and practice we have described here. Thus, it is process driven and can also be characterized as an *adaptive learning cycle*,[2] in which gaps are discovered and solutions are formulated for closing them – continuously. In other words, targets for performance are first defined on the policy side of the cycle, after which performance relative to targets is measured (continuously or cyclically) to determine whether or not performance conforms to the targets, and if not what the size of the gap is. In cases where gaps are found, management strategies and interventions are devised and implemented in order to close them and to meet the targets. Afterwards measurements are taken again, and the cycle repeats itself

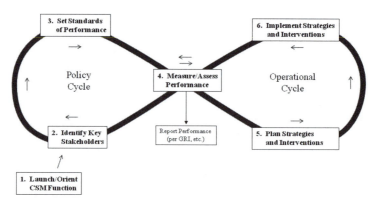

FIGURE 3.3 The (double-loop) CSM cycle.

endlessly, if only to ensure that performance relative to meeting the targets is being maintained. This more routine, day-to-day activity is portrayed in steps 4 through 6 on the operational side of the cycle.

At the very least, then, the performance of CSM reduces to steps 4, 5 and 6 on a continuing basis, whereby gaps in performance are first identified (step 4); plans are made to close them (step 5); and actions are taken to do so (step 6). Once performance has been reassessed (step 4 again), new or remaining gaps, if any, can be identified, followed by re-planning (step 5 again), more actions and implementations (step 6), and reassessment once again. As we say, the cycle potentially repeats itself endlessly as organizational circumstances routinely change and evolve, and the need for new CSM strategies and interventions continually presents itself.

The CSM cycle we describe is also a recursive one, not just an iterative one. In other words, CSM practitioners can at any time back up in the cycle to any prior step, as opposed to always having to back up to step 1 or 2 from, say, step 5 in order to revisit step 3 or 4 in the cycle, or to reformulate step 5 itself. Strategies and interventions devised in step 5, then, could be placed on hold while the underlying standards of performance that led up to them are revisited in step 3, or while the assessment performed beforehand in step 4 is repeated.

It should also be clear that step 1 will very likely only need to occur once, typically in the formative stages of a CSM function. That said, CSM functions also evolve, and so it may be necessary to return to the beginning of the cycle in some cases, not to mention the policy-making steps that follow (steps 2 and 3). We will have more to say about this shortly.

As earlier explained – and as explicitly indicated in step 2 of the CSM cycle – the methodology we propose is heavily oriented toward the relationships organizations have with their stakeholders. Stakeholder engagement (or at least consideration) therefore plays a critically important role in the performance of CSM. Although not explicitly shown in the CSM cycle in Figure 3.3 (except for step 2), there are five places where this occurs. The first is in step 2, where the identity of stakeholder groups is determined; the second is in step 3, where specific duties and obligations owed by an organization to its stakeholders are identified; the third is in step 4, where performance relative to such duties is assessed and possibly reported to stakeholders; the fourth is in step 5, where strategies and interventions involving impacts on vital capitals are planned; and the fifth is in step 6, where the strategies and interventions planned in step 5 are implemented. Thus, there is a very important thread of stakeholder engagement incorporated into the CSM cycle when viewed from a top-down perspective, the details of which we will discuss in more detail at the end of the chapter.

Practicing the cycle

In the remainder of this chapter, we will be discussing the steps involved in practicing the CSM cycle in great detail. This will include not only processes to be followed, but the specification, design and use of metrics for measuring the sustainability performance of organizations – *context-based metrics*, that is. By now it should be clear, we hope, that the purpose of the CSM cycle we will be describing is to make it possible for organizations to manage their impacts on vital capitals, in order to ensure stakeholder well-being. A CSM cycle of that kind must make it possible, therefore, to measure impacts on vital capitals, manage them and, to some degree or another, report them. But in order for a CSM cycle to be practiced in an organization, a CSM function must exist, the formation and launch of which comprise the first step in our six-step cycle.

Step 1: Launch and orient the CSM function

The first step in the practice of CBS in an organization is to formally establish a CSM function and orient it towards the context-based point of view. In some cases where pre-existing CSM functions are in place, this may translate into a need to *re*-orient CSM so as to embrace the context-based perspective.

Either way, embracing the context-based view of things has its own set of challenges. The fact is we live in a world of *context-free* sustainability. Organizations are simply not used to thinking in context-based terms, and more often prefer to think in terms of *discretionary* impacts and *marginal* improvements, instead of *obligatory* impacts and *sufficient* improvements. From a context-based perspective, for example, it is not enough simply to increase one's energy efficiency or decrease one's wastes. Rather, one must decrease energy use and waste emissions by sufficient amounts in order to ensure stakeholder well-being. Anything short of that is unsustainable, no matter how favorably it might compare with last year's numbers, as it were.

By this standard of thinking, very few, if any, organizations in today's modern world are sustainable. Most emit wastes in excess of Earth's assimilative capacity to absorb them; consume materials in similarly unsustainable amounts; and quite possibly fail to contribute to any or all of the anthro capitals of importance to stakeholders to a sufficient degree. And since impacts on vital capitals are generally not revealed in these ways in conventional sustainability reports, most of this goes unnoticed, both by stakeholders and the organizations themselves, whose true sustainability performance is very rarely known.

Unlike the practice of conventional CSM, then, context-based CSM involves the very strong possibility that many of an organization's impacts in the world will be unsustainable, if not intractably so. Publicly disclosing as much can test the courage of even the most progressive organizations. At the same time, however, it can reveal the truth and thereby provide managers with the information they need if they are to have any chance of achieving sustainability in the conduct of their business. Conventional sustainability measurement and reporting accomplishes no such thing, and because of that is quite possibly a monumental waste of time. The question organizations must ask themselves is: *are we truly interested in understanding and managing the sustainability of our operations in a literal or genuine sense?* Indeed, organizations can either ask this question proactively of themselves or, if not, wait for it to be forced upon them by others. If the answer to the question is *yes*, then the approach to CSM must be context-based, for there simply is no other way of assessing and managing the sustainability performance of organizations than by including context in the mix.

At Cabot Creamery Cooperative (Cabot) we had the good fortune to be present at the birth of the CSM function there, and indeed were instrumental in helping to make it happen. We therefore had the opportunity to present the company's management with the stark reality of the facts, as it were. In late 2007, as the urgency of the sustainability imperative, so to speak, was making itself known at Cabot (i.e., largely through customer pressure on the company to actively mange the sustainability of its operations and the 'greenness' of its products), a half-day sustainability briefing with the CEO and a team of the company's senior managers was arranged, in which the basics of context-based versus context-free thinking were laid out. Out of that meeting came a commitment on the part of Cabot's management to embrace the context-based approach.

Because of where we are in the evolution of CBS, most organizations have not yet fully embraced it – nor even heard of it, most likely – despite the prominent mention it receives in the GRI standard. What we see in most organizations, instead, is an orientation to CSM that, apart from being context-free, is grounded in either eco-efficiency, social benevolence or both. The eco-efficiency orientation, as the name suggests, is concerned only with the rate at which energy and materials are consumed on a relative basis (e.g., per unit of production or revenue) and simply strives to improve such efficiencies from one period to the next. The social benevolence orientation, for its part, is similarly incremental in its orientation and seeks to improve the human condition, if you like, through contributions to social services organizations and other acts of philanthropy.

As earlier noted in Chapter 2, the eco-efficiency orientation to CSM is an especially dubious one, since, apart from being context-free, it merely slows down the unsustainable use of energy and materials in business, but not necessarily to levels that are sustainable. Given the absence of context in related measurements, there simply is no way to tell. In any case, to say that an organization is eco-efficient, or even more eco-efficient, is not to say that it is sustainable or even more sustainable. At best it might simply be *less unsustainable*, but again, without context included in the assessment, there is no way to tell for sure.

The social benevolence orientation to CSM is similarly dubious in the sense that although philanthropy is clearly a good thing, the practice of it by itself does not necessarily mean that the organization is living up to its duties and obligations to have impact on vital human, social or constructed capitals of importance to stakeholder well-being. Those are the capitals we refer to as anthro capitals – because they are human-made – and they are also the ones that pertain to the social benevolence orientation. The other non-financial capital, natural capital, pertains to the eco-efficiency orientation.

As we said, management at Cabot ultimately opted to embrace the context-based school of practice. But it was not without difficulty. Along the way, management there struggled to understand the basis for measuring performance against standards of performance, since, strictly speaking, there are no industry or universal standards of performance for sustainability, only self-defined, voluntary ones. Indeed, the very need to manage, not to mention measure and report, sustainability performance at all is still not mandatory in any sort of regulatory sense throughout most of the world. How, then, could one establish a sustainability management function in which standards play such an important role?

The answer, we explained (to management at Cabot), is the same as it is on the financial side of performance. The only standard of performance there, such as there is one, is that companies are expected to be solvent, according to which their assets are greater than their liabilities. Beyond that, there are no regulated standards for how much a company should spend on rent, salaries, raw materials, etc. Companies set their own standards for such things, subject to the limitations of their assets. In other words, they first determine what the limit of their monetary capital is, and then they plan their actions accordingly.

What works for financial management can and will work for non-financial management, too. First we determine what the limitations in capital are (e.g., for natural capital) or what the demands of capital production and/or maintenance are (i.e., for human, social and constructed capitals), and then we plan accordingly. The basis for making such determinations is also consistent on both sides of the court, as it were. Namely, we base the determinations on considerations of stakeholder well-being. In other words, we determine what the capital needs of stakeholders are, and then we take steps to ensure the quality and sufficiency of related supplies. Since every organization has its own set of stakeholders which may or may not be the same as any other's, it is highly unlikely that there will be – or *can* be – common standards of performance insofar as ensuring stakeholder well-being is concerned.

Thus, the absence of industry or regulatory standards as a barrier to context-based sustainability is a red herring – a false problem that in no way inhibits the measurement of non-financial impacts against standards of performance for what such impacts ought to be. Instead, it simply tells us that each organization must set its own standards, which is what they do, and always have been doing, on the financial management side of the fence. Why should *non*-financial management be any different?

Indeed, it shouldn't. The implication, therefore, is not that CBS can't be done because of a lack of standards; rather, the implication is that a methodology is needed that makes it possible to (a) identify an organization's stakeholders, (b) formulate standards of performance for what impacts on vital capitals of importance to their well-being should be, and (c) provide a way of measuring actual impacts against such standards so that strategies and interventions can be devised to manage them accordingly. This, of course, is a good description of the CSM cycle as we have defined it in this chapter, and it also serves as a basis for how to orient the CSM function – a context-based one, that is – once it has been launched.

And that is precisely what we did at Cabot, having resolved the false problem of the absence of industry standards. In effect, what we did was to show that just as there is a regulative ideal of *solvency* in financial management, so can there be a similar principle of *sufficiency* in non-financial management. The parallels between the two are striking, and of course the common underlying element is the presence and function of capital – a stock of anything that produces valuable goods or services that people rely on for their well-being. The key principle in context-based sustainability, then, is the same as it is in (context-based) financial management (i.e., the quality and sufficiency of capital must be produced and/or maintained at levels required to ensure stakeholder well-being).

Next in the orientation of the CSM function and the sustainability strategy it entails is to define its relationship to the broader business strategy and to financial management, in particular. Insofar as the first issue is concerned, we have already presented our position in Chapter 2 that sustainability performance should in no way be subordinate to financial performance, or somehow discretionary in practice. Here we make the conscious decision to think in terms of stakeholder primacy instead of only shareholder primacy. To the extent that organizations have relationships with more than just shareholders – which they *do* – such relationships involve certain duties and obligations to act with the best interests of stakeholders in mind; in other words, to act in ways that help ensure their well-being.

This, by definition in sustainability, translates into a responsibility to have impact on vital capital resources in ways that do not diminish, and in fact help to ensure, the quality and sufficiency of them for stakeholder well-being. Moreover, such responsibilities are not secondary in importance or somehow less legitimate than the responsibility owed to shareholders to maximize profits or what have you. All responsibilities to all stakeholders must be attended to, even if it means one's own profits must be lowered.

Out of the stakeholder primacy perspective comes some additional insight into how and where CSM should be positioned in an organization. If non-financial performance is, as we say, equal in legitimacy to financial performance, then it should logically be positioned as such in the structure of an organization and in the hierarchy of management. The key underlying concept here is organizational performance and the definition of standards for performance that stem from duties and obligations owed to stakeholders. Given the manner in which financial performance management is positioned in an organization, the most logical choice for the CSM function would be to position it, too, in a similar fashion – in parallel with, or as a peer to, the financial management function.

Indeed, one can take the position that performance, in general, translates into a measure of impacts on vital capitals, in both a financial and non-financial sense. No performance management system can be complete, therefore, unless it includes measures of both financial and non-financial impacts for virtually every area of an organization's operations. Here we begin to see how CSM, like financial management, should be pervasive in an organization. Not only should the financial impacts of organizational actions and operations be measured, managed and reported every step of the way, so should the non-financial impacts – and always against standards of performance, just as in the case of financial impacts. Again, a good first step here would be to clearly identify the manner in which financial management is organized and deployed in the organization, and consider the possibility of establishing an equivalently empowered non-financial counterpart alongside of it.

Related to all of this is the issue of how to resolve the boundary question in CSM. In other words, *what should the boundaries of the organization or system be whose sustainability performance CSM is concerned with?* Here we find somewhat less consistency in terms of how this question is answered than one might think. In fact, we see three competing answers in play. The first is that CSM should concern itself with the boundaries of the organization, per se, just as financial management does for its part. The second is that CSM should be focusing, at least in part, on the sustainability performance of the organization's supply chain. And the third is that CSM should be focusing on the sustainability performance of products, which for reasons we explained in Chapter 2, is nonsensical – not because the impacts of products in the world is not a legitimate concern, but because the adjective *sustainable* simply does not apply to inanimate objects, and only applies to the actions of moral agents who make choices, like humans. In addition, even if we were to stretch the applicability of the term to cover products and their life cycles, the prevailing life cycle assessment methods (i.e., the LCA type of methodology we covered in Chapter 2) are not context-based and are predominantly environment-only in scope. Sustainability management, by contrast, is much broader than that.

This leaves us with the first two boundary scenarios (i.e., the organization and the supply chain) to contend with. For our part, we prefer the organizational boundary and sometimes wonder about the usefulness of CSM functions focusing on supply chains. After all, organizations do not in any direct sense control the sustainability performance of their suppliers, and they almost never expect them (their suppliers) to manage the sustainability of their operations in a context-based fashion. In a very real sense, then, there is no supply chain sustainability management going on, much less context-based measurement and reporting at that level. And since most organizations themselves are also not managing their sustainability performance in a context-based fashion, wouldn't they be more effective in their efforts to nudge their suppliers in the direction of sustainability if they first set the example by doing so themselves (i.e., if they embraced CBS)? We will frankly never get to a point where we have meaningful supply chain sustainability measurement, management and reporting going on until or unless we first get to a point where we have true organizational sustainability going on, as viewed from a context-based perspective.

Turning back to the *organizational* boundary, then, this, of course, is the boundary condition that pertains to the use of the Global Reporting Initiative (GRI), although, at the time of writing, we understand GRI is somewhere in the midst of developing a new set of guidelines for supply chain measurement and reporting, too. Nonetheless, our concerns about the legitimacy or usefulness of such reporting stand, since we presume the supply chain reporting guidelines will be just as context-free as the organizational guidelines have been (in practice). Time will tell.

It is our position, then, that the orientation of CSM must, first and foremost, be an organizational one. Moreover, if non-financial management is simply another form of performance management that should be co-organized, so to speak, with financial management, then it should also have the same boundary orientation that exists for financial management for that very reason. Indeed, if in fact it is the purpose of CSM to contribute to the broader understanding and management of the performance of an organization, how can we have one definition of boundaries in use for financial management and another one in use for non-financial management? Shouldn't they be the same? How else will we be able to see the performance of an organization measured, managed and reported in a comprehensive and consistent fashion unless they are?

One final word on the supply chain issue is warranted before we continue. We have argued above that the supply chain orientation is a questionable one for the CSM function to be focusing on for a variety of reasons, not least of which is that it includes organizations in a supply chain that a CSM function in only one organization does not control. Suppliers control their own sustainability performance, for which they (the suppliers) should be solely responsible, not their customers. That said, buyers of products and services from such suppliers are completely in control of their own purchases. They always have the option of buying from suppliers whose sustainability performance is superior.

One could think of this as *sustainable procurement*. Thus, procurement functions that procure from sustainable suppliers are sustainable; procurement functions that don't are not. This perspective on supply chain considerations in CSM fits neatly within the organizational orientation, since the sustainable procurement policies we're talking about fall squarely within the purview of an organization's own operations. And, of course, we now see this going on all around us as the use of *business to business scorecards* is becoming increasingly common in supply chain transactions.[3]

To sum up step 1, then, the purpose of CSM, as we see it, is to make it possible for an organization to measure, manage and report its own impacts on non-monetary capital resources of vital importance to its stakeholders' well-being. In this regard, not only should CSM take a capital-based approach to the subject, but because of that should also embrace a context-based view, according to which there are thresholds for impacts on vital capitals against which actual impacts can be measured, managed and reported.

We also hold to the view that because sustainability performance is a function of impacts on vital capitals of importance to stakeholder well-being, the idea that there must be universal standards of some kind for CBS to be workable is a red herring. Are all organizations' stakeholders the same? No, of course not. Just as we have had variable standards of financial performance in use by organizations for centuries now, so we can have – if not *must* have – variable standards of *non*-financial performance for today's organizations. Indeed, that is the point of CBS: the relevant context for every organization is liable to be different from every other's. Our management systems must therefore be flexible and adaptable in order to be effective.

We further reinforced the view first expressed in Chapter 2 that CSM must not be a handmaiden to strategy in the broad sense, or to profit-making more narrowly. Instead, the approach we advocated is one that is predicated on a doctrine of stakeholder primacy, not shareholder primacy, under which responsibilities owed to all stakeholders are equally legitimate and must be attended to. The CSM function should, in that regard, be on an equal footing with financial management.

And finally, with such equal footing in mind, we advocated for arriving at positioning and boundary determinations that are consistent with those used for financial management. This will only enhance the ability to do integrated performance measurement, management and reporting, and makes sense for all the same reasons of control and so forth that have long been in force for financial reporting. Once the CSM function has been launched and oriented in these ways, it is time for step 2 in the CSM cycle.

Step 2: Identify key stakeholders

Once a CSM function has been launched and oriented, there remains the essential task of determining what the scope of its programs should be. Scope, for our purposes, has three sides to it: type of sustainability, specific areas of impact, and social/geographic reach. Each of these dimensions of scope is defined as follows:

- *Type of sustainability* – Here we are referring to the basic distinction between social and environmental sustainability, the former of which also includes economic sustainability as discussed in Chapter 2. Thus, the first question of scope is: *will the CSM function be concerning itself with the full triple bottom line performance of the organization, or will it, instead, only be dealing with a narrower slice of the subject – perhaps environmental sustainability only?* For our purposes, we will be taking the broader view; the sustainability scope of the methodology we describe in this chapter, then, is grounded in the broadest view of the *triple bottom line*.
- *Specific areas of impact* – As we also discussed in Chapter 2, each of the three bottom lines represented in the triple bottom line model is actually a category of many different sub-bottom lines. The social bottom line, for example, includes an economic sub-bottom line, as well as many others that deal with organizational

impacts on human, social and constructed capitals of various kinds. The environ-mental bottom line, too, is multifaceted, and at the very least includes sub-bottom lines that deal with impacts on land, water, the atmosphere and living organisms, not to mention natural resources and ecosystem services (i.e., natural capital). So even a narrowly defined CSM scope that is limited to, say, impacts on natural capital still leaves many questions open as to what the specific areas of impact will be, or should be, for a CSM program. Will the organization's CSM program be concerning itself with natural capital in all of its forms or only a subset of them? More important, what criteria should we use to arrive at an answer?

- *Social/geographic reach* – Next in addressing the scope issue is to determine what the social and/or geographic reach of an organization's CSM efforts should be. If an organization chooses to focus on the quality of healthcare, for example, should it be for healthcare programs in one's own city, the region, the country or the world? Similarly, if a company chooses to address water issues as the centerpiece of its environmental sustainability efforts, what should the geographic reach of its efforts be? And again, what criteria should be used to answer these questions?

The breadth and depth of sustainability problems in the world are vast, certainly more than any single CSM function can take on. Organizations' resources, too, are fundamentally limited and are always subject to competing priorities, if only in the form of competition between financial and non-financial goals. All of this combines to force the issue of scope in the CSM function and what it should be. What's required, then, are guidelines or a set of criteria for making related (materiality) deci-sions. Here, for example, is how Porter and Kramer say we should approach this issue (2006, p. 92):

> Corporations are not responsible for all the world's problems, nor do they have the resources to solve them all. Each company can identify the particular set of societal problems that it is best equipped to help resolve and from which it can gain the greatest competitive benefit. Addressing social issues by creating shared value will lead to self-sustaining solutions that do not depend on private or government subsidies.

What Porter and Kramer are arguing for, then, is a kind of opportunistic and instru-mental approach to determining the scope of a CSM program. The scope of a program, they seem to be saying, should be determined on the basis of what will best serve the strategy and profit-making interests of the company, while coincidentally addressing a social need of some kind. In other words, they are arguing for shareholder primacy as a basis for making CSM scope decisions.

As we have already explained in Chapter 2, we believe a different approach than shareholder primacy is required as a basis for determining the scope of a CSM pro-gram. Under the context-based school of thought, the more appropriate and pre-ferred approach is one that puts stakeholders of all kinds on an equal footing with shareholders, and which regards all of an organization's responsibilities to all of them as of equal legitimacy. Once a duty or obligation to act, or not act, in a particular way on behalf of a stakeholder has been established, it is no longer discretionary; it is obligatory. Thus, either an organization has a duty or obligation to act (or not act) or it doesn't. Not only do Porter and Kramer – and the so-called 'shared value' school of thought they subscribe to – seem to gloss over the existence of affirmative (and non-financial) duties and obligations to stakeholders, they seem to treat all possible non-financial impacts an organization can have as discretionary – there to be picked and chosen from for purely instrumental and ulterior purposes in the narrow pursuit of profits. We couldn't disagree with that more.

Instead, we take the position that all three of the scope dimensions discussed above can be defined by (a) identifying who an organization's stakeholders are, and (b) determining what the organization's duties and obligations are to have impacts on vital capital resources of importance to their (the stakeholders') well-being. Thus, the specific scope of an organization's CSM program can and should be determined by explicit reference to an organization's stakeholders, and to the substance and implications of the relationships the organization has with each of them.

At the conclusion of the initial sustainability briefing we held with management at Cabot, for example, we concluded the session by identifying seven primary categories of stakeholders germane to their business. Their identities were determined by reference to (a) parties with whom Cabot has explicit legal or contractual relationships, and (b) parties who rely, to one degree or another for their well-being, on vital capitals affected by Cabot's operations. The stakeholder groups identified were as follows:

- farmers/owners (Cabot's shareholders)
- customers (e.g., major retailers)
- consumers (end users of Cabot's products)
- employees
- suppliers
- communities (local, regional and global)
- visitors (to company-owned stores and manufacturing plants).

Cabot clearly has relationships with each of these groups and a corresponding set of non-financial duties and obligations to act in their best interests. For its shareholders, for instance, the company is expected to participate in industry-related forums that generally promote the dairy industry and its products; for customers, it is expected to measure, manage and report its sustainability performance to some degree; for consumers, it is expected to produce safe products; for employees, it is expected to maintain safe working conditions; for suppliers, it is expected to behave in a commercially responsible fashion; for communities, it is expected to refrain from harming the environment; and for visitors, it is expected to ensure the safety of its facilities. These are only a few of the many non-financial duties and obligations Cabot has identified for itself, as we will further discuss later in this chapter.

Let us now try to be even clearer about what we mean by the term *stakeholder*. There is, in fact, a long tradition in what is known as stakeholder theory (see, in particular, Freeman et al., 2010 for a deeper discussion of the meaning and intellectual history of stakeholder theory). Competing definitions of the term abound. According to Freeman and Reed (1983, pp. 89 and 104), the term stakeholder was first coined in the business context in an internal memorandum at Stanford Research Institute in 1963, where it was defined as 'those groups without whose support the organization would cease to exist'. Freeman, a leading scholar on the subject, defines the term differently (1984, p. 46):

> A stakeholder in an organization is (by definition) any group or individual who can affect or is affected by the achievement of the organization's objectives.

Although we find Freeman's definition entirely consistent with our own, we prefer to put a finer – and, not surprisingly, capital-based – point on things. Our preferred definition is as follows:

> A stakeholder in an organization is anyone whose vital capitals – and whose interests and well-being, therefore – are affected by the organization's actions, or whose vital capitals ought to be so affected by virtue of the relationship that exists between them.

Returning to the list of stakeholders identified at Cabot (discussed above), all seven constituencies satisfied this definition in either a statutory sense (i.e., by contract or by law) or a non-statutory, purely moral sense. All that is required here is that an organization be able to satisfy itself that it has identified every constituency that fits the criteria set forth in our definition, and to whom it therefore owes a duty or obligation to manage its impacts on vital capitals. Stakeholders, then, receive their standing and legitimacy from the nature of the relationships they have with organizations, and the implications of those relationships insofar as how organizations should be expected to manage their impacts on related vital capitals.

Here it should be clear, again, that this is not a uniquely non-financial principle or standard of performance; rather, it is one that applies to both financial and non-financial performance alike, as earlier indicated in Table 2.3. While it is true that the specific capitals and the stakeholders involved in financial and non-financial performance will differ, the general principle of determining who should have stakeholder standing and what they are entitled to does not. Stakeholders are determined according to the criteria contained in our definition, and what they are entitled to is respect for their vital capitals.

Next in our discussion of the relevance of stakeholder theory to context-based CSM is the issue of materiality and how it relates to stakeholders. Materiality is a core concept in accounting and is defined as follows (*Oxford Dictionary of Accounting*, 2010):

materiality The extent to which an item of accounting information is material. Information is considered material if its omission from or misstatement in a financial statement could influence the decision making of its users.

Clearly, the context of the definition above is financial reporting, not sustainability reporting, but the same issue arises, just the same, in non-financial reporting. Indeed, it is treated as a core reporting principle in the GRI guidelines for determining the content of a report and is defined therein in a section entitled '1.1 Defining Report Content' (GRI, 2011, p. 8):

MATERIALITY

Definition: The information in a report should cover topics and indicators that:
- reflect the organization's significant economic, environmental, and social impacts or that
- would substantively influence the assessments and decisions of stakeholders.

Here we have nothing but praise for GRI, given the consistency and alignment between their definition of materiality and the stakeholder-driven approach we subscribe to for determining the scope of CSM. On the other hand, whereas GRI does not specifically define 'impacts' in terms of *impacts on vital capitals of importance to stakeholder well-being*, we do. Beyond that, we are in harmony with GRI on this issue. We, and they, see the sustainability performance of organizations in terms of a triple bottom line; we, and they, see CSM constituents as consisting of stakeholders, not just shareholders; and we, and they, see materiality as being a function of what matters to stakeholders, not just the company itself or, again, shareholders alone.

We further take the position that despite GRI's failure to specify impacts in terms of vital capitals, as we do, and its further failure to tie impacts to stakeholder well-being, per se, its reference to stakeholder 'assessments' is close enough for us. In other words, we think it perfectly reasonable to interpret GRI's reference to stakeholder assessments as being inclusive of *stakeholder assessments of an organization's impacts on capitals of vital importance to their well-being*. Our interpretation simply puts a finer point on things.

We should also like to observe that GRI's principle of *sustainability context* (discussed in detail in Chapter 2) appears in the same section on 'Defining Report Content' in which the *materiality* principle is also found, and yet the connection between the two (i.e., between stakeholders and context) is never explicitly made or acknowledged in the *Guidelines*. This is unfortunate, because it is precisely the impacts on vital capitals of importance to stakeholder well-being that drive the context of such importance to CSM, and which, in turn, determine what the scope of its focus should be. In other words, sustainability context determines materiality, and *that*, in turn, tells us what the content of a CSM program should be, including its measurement and reporting efforts.

In sum, if an organizational impact of some kind cannot be tied to a vital capital of importance to a stakeholder's well-being, it has no place in a CSM program. By taking this position, we offer CSM functions a compelling basis for determining what's material to their programs, and a logic for delineating an otherwise arbitrary if not wandering scope. Here we see in graphic terms the difference between sustainability and philanthropy. Since most acts of philanthropy are discretionary and have nothing to do with duties to have impacts on vital capitals of importance to stakeholder well-being, the fact of their existence and the impacts they have in the world are, strictly speaking, of no relevance to CSM. The same goes for employment and other discretionary or social impacts – as positive as they may be. What's most relevant to CSM is performance against standards or norms for what performance *ought* to be, the latter of which is grounded in stakeholder well-being.

Step 3: Set standards of performance

Perhaps the most distinguishing feature of CBS is not so much the context to which the name refers as the manner in which performance is measured against *standards* or *norms* for performance. It is one thing, for example, to say that if a certain rate of water use continues, water resources will disappear; it is quite another to then suggest that the same rate of water use ought not to continue. The former is a factual claim; the latter is a normative one – one that tells us not what is, but what *ought* to be.

It is our position that CSM requires the specification of such norms or standards of behavior as a basis for measuring, managing and reporting sustainability performance, *even if the standards used are entirely self-selected and are in use by no other organization.* Indeed, some might say that the very possibility of applying externally developed standards to an organization – or to all organizations – is highly questionable, given the extent to which standards must be tied to an organization's own stakeholders and to the particular duties and obligations it, alone, has to them. It is more likely the case, we think, that some standards will be broadly applicable to all or most organizations and others will not, the latter of which must be locally developed and self-selected. Time will tell.

In any case, the specific kind of standards or norms of performance we are talking about here are those that relate to an organization's impacts on vital capitals of importance to stakeholder well-being. Context comes into play in the sense that such norms or standards of behavior must be determined by reference to (a) related social, economic and environmental conditions in the world, and (b) the corresponding impacts or contributions an organization must have (or not have) in order to ensure stakeholder well-being. An organization whose impacts on water resources, for example, affect stakeholder well-being must limit its impacts on such resources according to how much water is available, what the relevant watersheds are, how many other people and organizations rely on the same resources, how much precipitation occurs each year, what the size of its operations are, etc. These contextual considerations are factual; the conclusions we reach about how an organization should behave in recognition of them are normative.

Formulating duties and obligations to stakeholders

The purpose of step 3 in the CSM cycle we are describing here is to determine what an organization's specific norms or standards of behavior should be as a basis for measuring and reporting its sustainability performance. This is the step that is so essential for sustainability measurement, management and reporting, and yet ironically it is precisely the one that so few organizations actually take. And even though it is true that the GRI guidelines for sustainability reporting call for the inclusion of context in related efforts – as we ourselves do – they do not explicitly state that such context should be used as a basis for determining what an organization's standards of performance should be relative to its impacts on social, economic and environmental conditions in the world. Moreover, as we have already said, GRI also does not call for a reference to stakeholder well-being as a basis for determining materiality in the CSM function. To be clear, then, step 3 of the CSM cycle is predicated on the following important principles:

1. The scope of a CSM function and the non-financial impacts it seeks to measure, manage and report should be determined by reference to an organization's stakeholders (identified in step 2), and the impacts on vital capitals of importance to their well-being that an organization is either already having or should be having.
2. Insofar as normative impacts are concerned, such impacts must be determined by reference to the state of the vital capitals of interest, the levels of such capitals required to ensure stakeholder well-being, and the degree of responsibility an organization has to preserve, produce and/or maintain them. The purpose of considering context in CSM, then, is so that fair, just and proportionate standards of performance for impacts on vital capitals can be determined at the organizational level, as a basis for measuring, managing and reporting sustainability performance.

On the basis of the above, it should be clear that the particular norms or standards of performance of interest to us, and to the CSM approach we are describing, are ones that consist of duties and obligations owed by an organization to its stakeholders to have impacts on vital capitals of importance to their (the stakeholders') well-being. The purpose of step 3, then, is to define what such duties and obligations are as a precursor to measuring actual impacts. Only by comparing actual impacts to normative ones can any real or meaningful sustainability conclusions be drawn, since, without standards of performance grounded in context and stakeholder well-being, measurements of impacts on vital capitals are incomplete – certainly inadequate for purposes of determining whether or not an organization's impacts are sustainable.

Before continuing with our discussion of step 3, it should be helpful to remind readers of the specific forms of non-financial capitals of interest to us as earlier discussed. In total there were four:

1. **Natural capital** consists of natural resources, living organisms and ecosystem services that humans and non-humans alike rely on in order to take effective action and for their physical well-being.
2. **Human capital** consists of *individual* knowledge, skills, experience, health and ethical entitlements that enhance the potential for effective individual action and human well-being.
3. **Social capital** consists of *shared* knowledge and organizational resources (e.g., formal or informal networks of people committed to achieving common goals) that enhance the potential for effective individual and collective action and human well-being.
4. **Constructed capital** (or built capital) consists of *material objects and/or physical systems or infrastructures* created by humans. It is the material world of human artifacts in which human knowledge is also embedded, and which humans use in order to take effective action.

Here again, it is not necessarily the case that any one organization ought to be having impacts of some kind or another on all four capitals; rather, an organization should only be having impacts on capitals of importance to its stakeholders – which might involve no impacts, in some cases – and only impacts that pertain to its relationships with them.

We have also made the very important point that natural capital differs from the other three capitals listed above in the sense that they (the other three) are human-made or anthropogenic capitals, whereas natural capital is not. Because of the anthropogenic nature of human, social and constructed capitals, we refer to them collectively as anthro capitals. The fact that anthro capitals are human-made and natural capital is not is significant in the context of our discussion of step 3 in the CSM cycle, because it means that whereas duties or obligations to have impacts on natural capital will typically be expressed in terms of not-to-exceed or maximum impacts, duties or obligations to have impacts on anthro capitals will be expressed in terms of minimums, or not-to-fall-below impacts (see, again, Figure 2.1).

The procedure for determining what an organization's impacts on vital capitals should be starts with the use of templates that correlate potential impacts on vital capitals with each stakeholder group. There are three such templates in recognition of the fact that the CSM cycle is oriented to the triple bottom line (see Tables 3.1, 3.2 and 3.3). In other words, we want to be able to correlate impacts on vital capitals in terms of (a) impacts that relate to social performance, (b) impacts that relate to economic performance, and (c) impacts that relate to environmental performance. And as earlier discussed (see Table 2.2), the vital capitals orientation to the context-based approach lends itself to this structure because the four capitals involved map explicitly into the three broad areas of impact (i.e., the three non-financial bottom lines) as further indicated in Tables 3.1, 3.2 and 3.3. They are, in fact, what gives rise to the three bottom lines and what differentiates them from one another and/or makes them similar (as is the case for the social and economic bottom lines).

In combination with the three templates referenced above, the checklist with more specific areas of impact provided in Appendix B (Areas of Impact Checklist) should

TABLE 3.1 Social bottom line template

	Stakeholder Group A	Stakeholder Group B	Stakeholder Group n
Internal Capitals: *			
Human			
Social			
Constructed			
External Capitals: *			
Human			
Social			
Constructed			

Here the question that should be asked is: *What are our duties and obligations to have impact on vital anthro capitals of broad importance to our stakeholders' well-being?*

*See Appendix B for specific examples of impacts on anthro capital.

Source: Center for Sustainable Organizations

TABLE 3.2 Economic bottom line template

	Stakeholder Group A	Stakeholder Group B	Stakeholder Group n
Internal Capitals: *			
Human			
Social			
Constructed			
External Capitals: *			
Human			
Social			
Constructed			

Here the question that should be asked is: *What are our duties and obligations to have impact on vital anthro capitals of economic importance to our stakeholders' well-being?*

*See Appendix B for specific examples of impacts on anthro capital.

Source: Center for Sustainable Organizations

be used. One would first start with one of the three templates – say, the Social Bottom Line template (Table 3.1) – and fill in the names of the stakeholder groups identified in step 2 of the CSM cycle across the top. One would then systematically ask the question highlighted in the template, which in the case of the social bottom line is:

What are our duties and obligations to have impact on vital anthro capitals of broad importance to our stakeholders' well-being?

TABLE 3.3 Environmental bottom line template

	Stakeholder Group A	Stakeholder Group B	Stakeholder Group n
Internal Natural Capital: *			
Natural Resources			
Living Organisms			
Ecosystem Services			
External Natural Capital: *			
Natural Resources			
Living Organisms			
Ecosystem Services			

> Here the question that should be asked is: *What are our duties and obligations to have impact on vital natural capital of broad importance to our stakeholders' well-being?*

*See Appendix B for specific examples of impacts on natural capital.

Source: Center for Sustainable Organizations

This should be done for each stakeholder group. Responses to the question should, in turn, be driven by the nature of the relationship the organization has with each stakeholder group, and should be correlated with the vital capitals shown in the row headings and the corresponding areas of need (illustrative only) listed in Appendix B. Each duty or obligation identified should be either explicit in the relationship the organization has with a stakeholder, such as a company's obligations to comply with environmental regulations (where the stakeholder group is a municipality or a regulator of some kind), or implicit instead, such as a duty to pay employees a fair and livable wage (where the stakeholder group is employees and such a duty is believed to at least morally exist).

To help improve the quality and legitimacy of the duties and obligations identified, organizations should also take steps to review them with the stakeholders involved (further discussed in the 'Stakeholder Engagement' section below). Until then, the responsibilities identified should be regarded as presumptive, possibly incorrect or incomplete, and not yet fully vetted – not that any of that, however, should disqualify a list as being possibly insufficient for starting purposes. Indeed, there is no certainty in any of this, nor is there any need for it as a basis for taking action. All that is required are claims about duties and obligations that have at least survived an organization's own internal tests and evaluations.

Developing context-based metrics (CBMs)

Table 3.4 contains summarized results of the procedure for determining duties and obligations owed to stakeholders after it was applied at Cabot. Included in the table

TABLE 3.4 Some sustainability standards at Cabot

Stakeholder Group	Related Duty or Obligation (i.e., Sust. Perf. Standard)*	Related Stakeholder Need*	Vital Capitals Involved*	Related Bottom Lines*
Consumers	Produce Safe Food	Nutrition	H-S-C	Social
Consumers	Provide Information	Nutrition	H-S-C	Social
Customers	Meet Commitments	Comm. Health	H-S-C	Econ.
Customers	Keep Employees Safe	Personal Health	N-H-S-C	Soc./Env.
Employees	Keep Employees Safe	Personal Health	N-H-S-C	Soc./Env.
Visitors	Keep Visitors Safe	Personal Health	N-H-S-C	Soc./Env.
Community (Local)	Use Water Fairly	Personal Health	N-H-S-C	Soc./Env.
Community (Regional)	Limit Solid Wastes	Waste Facilities	N-H-S-C	Soc./Env.
Community (Global)	Lower GHG Wastes	GHG Mitigation	N-H-S-C	Social
Farmer/Owners	Promote Industry	Comm. Health	H-S-C	Econ.

*Legend: Sust. = Sustainability, Perf. = Performance, GHG = Greenhouse Gas, Comm. = Commercial, N = Natural Capital, H = Human Capital, S = Social Capital, C = Constructed Capital, Soc. = Social, Econ. = Economic, and Env. = Environmental

Source: Cabot Creamery Cooperative

are ten specific duties and obligations we identified. As the table shows, we began by first acknowledging the stakeholder groups of interest to us (i.e., the ones identified in step 2), and then proceeded to ask ourselves about the duties and obligations owed to each using the templates shown in Tables 3.1, 3.2 and 3.3. Then, for each duty or obligation identified, we correlated it to a specific area of stakeholder need as a way of validating the legitimacy of the duty in terms of stakeholder well-being (again, see Appendix B for an illustrative listing of such needs). Next we specified the types of capital involved in fulfilling the duty or obligation, and on that basis classified the duty as pertaining to one or more of the three non-financial bottom lines.

Not shown in Table 3.4 is the final step in the procedure, in which specific metrics were identified for measurement and reporting purposes. For that we must turn to Table 3.5 in which metrics for a sampling (five) of the ten duties and obligations summarized in Table 3.4 are shown. Thus, relevant metrics in a CSM program are specified by a chain of reasoning that starts with the specific duties and obligations owed by an organization to its stakeholders to have impacts on vital capitals (or not), and concludes with the determination of those things that require measurement. At the end of the day, then, what metrics are measuring in CSM is impacts on vital capitals, and whether or not such impacts conform to standards for what they ought to be in order to ensure stakeholder well-being. (See Appendix C for a more exhaustive discussion of the duties and obligations identified at Cabot Creamery Cooperative, and the basis, rationale and vital capitals associated with each.)

As Table 3.5 also shows, we distinguish between metrics that measure causes and metrics that measure effects. Effect metrics, in our scheme of things, measure impacts on vital capitals that are directly appropriated by stakeholders. Cause metrics, by contrast, refer to impacts on capitals that are upstream of those directly appropriated

TABLE 3.5 Some sustainability metrics at Cabot

Stakeholder-Driven Standards of Performance	What Cabot's Sustainability Metrics Must Measure	Type of Metric	Vital Capitals Involved*	Related Bottom Lines*
Produce Safe Food	Safety of Ingredients	Cause	H-S-C	Social
	Quality of Manufacturing	Cause	H-S-C	Social
	Safety of Finished Products	Effect	H-S-C	Social
Meet Commitments to Customers	Commercial Performance	Effect	H-S-C	Econ.
Use Water Fairly	Water Use	Effect	N-H-S-C	Soc./Env.
Limit Solid Wastes	Landfill Use	Effect	N-H-S-C	Soc./Env.
Keep Employees Safe	Employee Safety Incidents	Effect	N-H-S-C	Social
	Environmental Incidents	Effect	N-H-S-C	Env.

*Legend: N = Natural Capital, H = Human Capital, S = Social Capital, C = Constructed Capital, Soc. = Social, Econ. = Economic, and Env. = Environmental

Source: Cabot Creamery Cooperative

by stakeholders. A cause impact, for example, might be the implementation of a policy or program (social capital) intended to create the conditions required to preserve, produce and/or maintain the quality or sufficiency of some (other) vital capital more directly appropriated by stakeholders in the service of their own well-being (e.g., water resources, Earth's climate system, roads and highways, etc.). When all is said and done, then, it is the measurements taken by effect metrics that we are most interested in, since they tell us what the bottom line impacts of an organization's operations have been on vital capitals directly appropriated by stakeholders, and whether or not they meet related standards of performance for stakeholder well-being.

Having demonstrated the manner in which non-financial duties and obligations to stakeholders can be developed (again, see above and Appendix C, in particular), our next task is to explain how such norms or standards of performance can be expressed in the form of quantitative metrics. What we will be arguing for here is the use of metrics that have two variables in them: one that expresses the duties or obligations (i.e., standards of performance) we have identified, and another that expresses the corresponding, or actual, impacts on vital capitals. Indeed, we have already introduced the composition of such metrics in Chapter 2 (see again Figure 2.1), as well as a performance scale on which resulting scores can be plotted (see again Figure 2.2). Now it is time to discuss these ideas in greater detail.

As shown in Figure 2.1 (repeated here again for convenience as Figure 3.4), the particular form or construction of metric we have in mind for context-based sustainability is a numerical quotient. Thus, one of the two variables we use in our metrics is a numerator, the other is a denominator. More specifically, the denominator expresses a duty or obligation to a stakeholder, and the numerator expresses actual performance relative to the same duty. It is precisely in this way that actual impacts on vital capitals can be measured against norms or standards for what such

$$\text{Sustainability Performance*} = \frac{\text{A measure of impact on a vital capital}}{\begin{array}{c}\text{A standard or norm for what the impact}\\\text{on the same vital capital ought to be}\\\text{in order to ensure stakeholder well-being}\\\text{(i.e., for the impact to be sustainable)}\end{array}}$$

Where:

- For impacts on *natural* capital, quotient scores of ≤ 1.0 = sustainable, > 1.0 = unsustainable
- For impacts on *human, social* or *constructed* capital, quotient scores of ≥ 1.0 are sustainable, < 1.0 are unsustainable

Source: McElroy, 2008

FIGURE 3.4 Context-based sustainability metrics.

impacts ought to be in order to ensure stakeholder well-being. In other words, the measurement of actual impacts *against* normative impacts takes place when the quotient score is computed (i.e., when the numerator is divided by the denominator).

What the sustainability quotient construct we are describing here therefore amounts to is a general specification for context-based sustainability metrics. And this is precisely how we suggest the call for context in GRI's sustainability reporting guidelines should be answered. Indeed, for every quantitative metric currently featured in GRI's guidelines, there can be a corresponding duty or obligation to have impact of one kind or another on a vital capital, thereby setting up the possibility that the quantitative metrics featured in GRI's guidelines could take the form of numerators in sustainability quotients. It is for this reason that we sometimes refer to sustainability reports prepared in accordance with GRI's guidelines, and which lack context, as *numerator-only* reporting.

Given the specifics of the quotients we are proposing, it might also be useful to return to the financial measurement and reporting analogy we used before. Just as it would make no sense in the preparation of a financial report (or *income statement*) to focus only on revenues, so it makes no sense at all in sustainability (or non-financial) reporting to focus only on top-line impacts. It is not enough, for example, to know how much water an organization has used this year versus last; rather, what we need to know is how much water it has used *relative to how much water it should have used (or not used) given a specific allocation of available renewable supplies.* For sustainability measurement and reporting purposes, then, leaving standards of performance out of the picture makes about as much sense as leaving costs out of income statements.

In general, a unique sustainability quotient is required for each cause and effect metric identified in connection with duties and obligations, or standards of performance. In Table 3.5, for example, there are five standards of performance listed, but eight cause

TABLE 3.6 Formulating sustainability quotients at Cabot

Area of Performance	What Cabot's Sustainability Metrics Must Measure	Type of Metric	Denominators	Numerators
Safe Food	Safety of Ingredients	Cause	Must be 100% Safe	Actual % Safe
	Quality of Manufacturing	Cause	Must Meet Defined SQF* Scores	Actual SQF* Scores
	Safety of Products	Effect	Must be 100% Safe	Actual % Safe
Customer Commitments	Commercial Performance	Effect	Must Achieve Defined Performance Scores	Actual Scores Received
Water Use	Water Use	Effect	Must Not Exceed Defined Levels of Use	Actual Levels of Water Use
Solid Wastes	Landfill Use	Effect	Must Not Exceed Defined Limits of Use	Actual Levels of Landfill Use
Employee Safety	Employee Safety Incidents	Effect	Must Not Exceed Defined # of Incidents	Actual # of Incidents
	Environmental Incidents	Effect	Must Not Exceed Defined # of Incidents	Actual # of Incidents

*Legend: SQF = Safe Quality Food, a 3rd-party certification standard.

Source: Cabot Creamery Cooperative

and effect metrics. If Table 3.5 reflected the full scope of Cabot's sustainability landscape – which it doesn't – the CSM program at Cabot would require eight context-based metrics, or CBMs, to measure, manage and report its sustainability performance.

Taking the eight cause and effect metrics as our next point of departure, then, Table 3.6 shows how each of the cause and effect metrics included in Table 3.5 might be quantitatively expressed in terms of a sustainability quotient. Here it is important to point out that the content of the numerators and denominators shown is quantitative and numerical, and that the construction of context-based metrics must also be carried out with the following general guidelines in mind:

- Each metric must pertain to a discrete area of impact that, in turn, is tied to a single vital capital – either natural, human, social or constructed capital. It would not make sense, for example, to attempt to construct a metric that is intended to measure performance related to water use and solid waste emissions in a combined sense. Why? Because water use relates to natural capital and landfill use relates to constructed capital. Impacts on one have nothing to do with impacts on the other; thus, their metrics should be separate. Note here, as well, that even impacts on different forms of the same general type of capital (e.g., impacts on water and air quality, both of which are instances of natural capital) should not be measured by the same metrics, since, again, impacts on one have nothing to do with impacts on the other. The same can be said, too, for impacts on capitals of the same kind in cases where they are physically or socially disconnected. The sustainability of a company's water use in Vermont will have nothing to do with the sustainability of its water use in the Netherlands; thus, the metrics used to measure its impacts in either case might be the same in construction, but should be separately computed nevertheless.

- The units of measurement in sustainability quotients can be anything, as long as they are either binary or analog in form, and are consistently used for both the numerator and denominator in any one quotient. By binary or analog, we mean that (a) a binary scale can be used in cases where there are only two possible values for both the numerator and denominator, such as yes or no, black or white, satisfactory or unsatisfactory, exists or doesn't exist, meets requirements or doesn't meet requirements, passes or fails, true or false, etc. (see further discussion of how to convert non-numerical binary values to numerical forms below); or (b) an analog scale can be used in cases where there is a bounded or unbounded scale of many possible values along its axis (i.e., typically an interval or ratio scale of some kind, not a nominal or ordinal one). Thus, the key distinction between binary and analog scales, as we are using the terms, is that binary scales only have two possible values, and analog scales will have more than two, in some cases infinitely so. Examples of analog scales include temperature, length, age, brightness, performance scores, grade point averages, water consumption, etc.

In Table 3.7, three of the duties and obligations earlier shown in Tables 3.4 through 3.6 are further described in terms of whether they are binary or analog in form. Note that only the first metric shown for each of the three areas of impact is listed as binary. This is because the metrics involved are simply intended to determine whether or not a protocol (i.e., a policy, program or procedure) exists to ensure the desired performance; such a protocol either exists or doesn't exist – there is no in between. Hence, the binary nature of the metric.

TABLE 3.7 Some binary and analog metrics at Cabot

Duty or Obligation (i.e., Sustainability Performance Standard)	What Cabot's Sustainability Metrics Must Measure	Type of Metric	Binary or Analog
Produce Safe Food	Whether protocols exist to ensure production and distribution of safe food	Cause	Binary
	Quality of manufacturing facilities	Cause	Analog
	Proportion of safe ingredients used	Cause	Analog
	Proportion of safe products produced	Effect	Analog
Limit Solid Wastes	Whether protocols exist to ensure proper use of solid waste landfills	Cause	Binary
	Landfill Use	Effect	Analog
Commercial Performance	Whether protocols exist to ensure disclosure of information required by suppliers to assess commercial performance and risk	Cause	Binary
	Performance scores received on suppliers' scorecards	Effect	Analog

Source: Cabot Creamery Cooperative

- Numerators and denominators in binary metrics do not always lend themselves to numerical formulations per se, since they very often are intended to specify a condition that must be met (i.e., as stated in denominators), as well as whether or not such conditions are, in fact, being met (numerators). For example, a binary denominator for a business ethics duty owed to employees might simply state that a business ethics policy should exist. The numerator in the same quotient might then be expressed as either a *yes* or a *no*. In cases such as this, a '1' can be used as a stand-in for the standard or norm of interest, such that expressing the fact that a business ethics policy is required could be represented by a '1' in the denominator; actually having such a policy (or not) could then, in turn, be expressed in the numerator by a '1' or a '0', as in: 1 = *yes, such a policy exists,* or 0 = *no, such a policy does not exist.* This would preserve our ability to compute quotient scores in a way that is consistent with the manner in which metrics should be formulated and applied (i.e., numerically and in accordance with the sustainability performance scales we use).

In addition to the general guidelines above that apply to *both* numerators and denominators, there are some additional guidelines that apply to the construction of *only* denominators or numerators as described below in the next two sections, respectively.

Developing denominators in CBMs

In developing CBMs, denominators should logically be developed first, since they set the standards of performance that will determine whether or not an organization's impacts on vital capitals are sustainable. The units of measurement used to do so will also determine how such impacts ought to be measured when it comes to expressing actual impacts in numerators (i.e., in step 4 of the CSM cycle). Thus, once duties and obligations have been defined, it is time to express them numerically in the form of denominators (i.e., as shown in Figures 3.5 and 3.6).

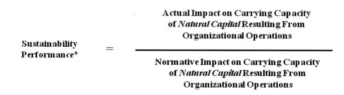

$$\text{Sustainability Performance*} = \frac{\text{Actual Impact on Carrying Capacity of } \textit{Natural Capital} \text{ Resulting From Organizational Operations}}{\text{Normative Impact on Carrying Capacity of } \textit{Natural Capital} \text{ Resulting From Organizational Operations}}$$

*Where: Scores of ≤ 1.0 = sustainable, > 1.0 = unsustainable

Source: McElroy, 2008

FIGURE 3.5 Context-based environmental metrics.

$$\text{Sustainability Performance*} = \frac{\text{Actual Impact on Carrying Capacity of } \textit{Anthro Capital} \text{ Resulting From Organizational Operations}}{\text{Normative Impact on Carrying Capacity of } \textit{Anthro Capital} \text{ Resulting From Organizational Operations}}$$

*Where: Scores of ≥ 1.0 = sustainable, < 1.0 = unsustainable

Source: McElroy, 2008

FIGURE 3.6 Context-based social and economic metrics.

For environmental metrics, denominators are defined as follows:

> Normative Impact on Carrying Capacity of *Natural Capital* Resulting from Organizational Operations

For social and economic metrics, denominators are defined as follows:

> Normative Impact on Carrying Capacity of *Anthro Capital* Resulting from Organizational Operations

Again, normative impacts must be grounded in context, which involves knowledge of the carrying capacities of vital capitals required to ensure stakeholder well-being; who the responsible human population is for producing and/or preserving them; and what an organization's own share of responsibility is for contributing to such preservation, production and/or maintenance efforts.

Specific guidelines for measuring and expressing denominator values are as follows:

- Standards for impacts on vital capitals should be confined to direct impacts only on capitals of importance to stakeholder well-being. These can be capitals that are either internal or external to an organization. By contrast, secondary or down-stream impacts of other kinds (i.e., indirect impacts on other external capitals, or of a sort that involve the well-being of stakeholders beyond the immediate effects of their appropriation, or not, of vital capitals upon which an organization has had direct impacts) should not be factored into the development of denominators; nor should any downstream effects upon the well-being or sustainability performance of non-stakeholders be considered. All such indirect impacts are at least one step removed from the boundaries of an organization's own operations and/or sphere of control, and as such fall outside the scope of its own CSM efforts. *Standards for impacts on vital capitals, therefore, should be confined to reflect only direct impacts on either internal or external capitals upon which stakeholders, themselves, directly or indirectly rely for their well-being.* Standards or norms for other, second-order-and-beyond impacts can alternatively be set using other methodologies, such as life cycle assessment (LCA), although we know of no implementations of LCA that are context-based.

- Units of measurement intended to express norms for impacts on *natural capital* (i.e., in denominators) should ideally be expressed in terms of the natural resource or ecosystem service involved. Normative impacts on water resources, for example, can be expressed in terms of *gallons per year consumed*; for waste emissions, it might be *an amount of wastes emitted that should not be exceeded.* Great care should be taken to ensure that the normative impact chosen will add up to no more than the maximum carrying capacity of the resource involved if the norm were generalized to the relevant population as a whole. When calculating a fair and equitable share of water resources, for example, the allocation made, if generalized to the population served by the resource, should not exceed the total volume of available renewable flows (i.e., its total carrying capacity), much less diminish the underlying stocks.

In cases where taking such an approach might result in levels of consumption that exceed available carrying capacity, the chosen norms should be lowered to reflect a fair and equitable share of what's actually available, and no more. Why? Because any collective use of a resource that exceeds its flows will generally lead to the degradation of the underlying stock itself, which of course is unsustainable. In cases where an organization is faced with this predicament and cannot lower its norms without putting its own viability at risk, it should be clear that the resource upon which the organization is relying for its operations may not be reliable and is itself at risk. In any case, the logic of establishing norms and defining denominators as we have explained it should be strictly adhered to.

- Units of measurement intended to express norms for impacts on *anthro capital* (i.e., in denominators) are ideally expressed in terms of the number of humans or human needs the system can or should support – such as the number of students a school system should be able to handle, or the number of beds a hospital ought to have, or the number of employees a company's safety training program should be able to handle, and so forth. After all, the purpose of anthro capital is to serve the needs of people who require its flows of goods and services in order to meet their needs, and to enable them to take effective action in their lives in their pursuit of well-being.

Thus, individual and collective appropriations of such goods and services can be seen as a volume of transactions, as it were, or at least a population of individuals who make such appropriations. This amounts to a requirement for carrying capacity, which, again for anthro capital, can be created and renewed by humans. A logical approach to specifying an organization's denominator, therefore, in cases involving impacts on anthro capital, would be to first determine what the stakeholder group needs as a whole in the particular area of interest, and then determine what the organization's fair and proportionate share of producing and/or maintaining related anthro capitals ought to be. This assumes, of course, that a duty or obligation to have impact on the anthro capitals involved has already been established.

It may also be useful, if not easier, in cases involving impacts on anthro capitals to use monetary units of measurement as proxies instead of human population counts or transaction volumes. Organizational contributions to achieving the United Nation's Millennium Development Goals (MDGs),[4] for example, might be better expressed in this way as opposed to the number of people in the world whose well-being should or might be affected by such contributions. Indeed, budgets for achieving the MDGs have already been established by the UN, so contributions made to the UN for that purpose might as well be expressed in monetary terms as well. In this case, and others, monetary units of measurement really stand for impacts on anthro capitals, since achievement of the MDGs ultimately translates into a need to create and maintain specific combinations of human, social and constructed capitals.

- Generally speaking, all denominators in analog metrics involving impacts on the carrying capacities of *natural capital* should be expressed in terms of not-to-exceed levels (e.g., a not-to-exceed level for the consumption of water resources, or the assimilative capacity of the environment to safely absorb a waste, etc.). Denominators in analog metrics involving impacts on the carrying capacities of *anthro capital*, by contrast, should be expressed in terms of not-to-fall-below levels (e.g., a minimum livable wage payable to employees, or a minimum level of investment in policies and programs for curbing greenhouse gas emissions, etc.). The difference here is due to the fact that anthro capitals are anthropogenic; natural capital is not. Thus, all duties and obligations relating to natural capital fundamentally boil down to limiting the use of it (i.e., because it is in fixed supply and must be shared with others), whereas anthro capital, by contrast, can be, and *is*, created by humans. When faced with shortages in supply, people can usually make more of it, given the will and the resources needed to do so.

- Under no circumstances should a zero value be used in a denominator of any kind, since no quotient can be calculated if the divisor is zero. In cases where the *desired* value of a denominator is, in fact, zero (e.g., *There should be no breach of business ethics in the conduct of our business*), consider turning the norm around so as to be stated in the form of a positive (e.g., *All of our employees should conduct themselves in an ethically upright fashion at all times*). The denominator in this case might be equivalent to the number of employees employed in a given time period. Assuming there are no ethical breaches during the same time period, the numerator in the same quotient would be the same number, thereby producing a score of 1.0, which would be sustainable. Alternatively, if, say, three employees were determined to have been involved in unethical behavior, then the corresponding numerator would be three less in number, thereby causing the quotient score to be less than 1.0, which is unsustainable for any metric involving impacts on anthro capital.

Incidentally, the vital capital involved in this particular example would be human capital (a form of anthro capital) held by one stakeholder or another, since

ethical entitlements are a form of human capital. It is unsustainable for an organization to undermine a stakeholder's ethical entitlements, since everyone relies
on ethical entitlements in order to take effective action in their lives, and to
ensure their own well-being.

- Another very important point should be made with respect to the specification of
denominators, and that is that universally agreed-to standards of performance
beyond those developed by an organization for its own use are emphatically *not*
required in order for context-based sustainability and the use of context-based
metrics to be meaningful. Still, the absence of such standards is sometimes raised as
an objection to CBS. *How can there be measurements against standards when there are
no universally agreed-to standards?* Our response? Again, this is a red herring. As
discussed in Chapter 2 with respect to cross-organizational comparisons, there can
indeed be measurements of non-financial performance in the absence of universally agreed-to standards in the same way as there can be – and *are* – measurements of financial performance in the absence of standards (of performance)
on *that* front, as well. Let us examine the parallels here more closely.

As earlier shown in Table 2.3, the main differences between financial performance and non-financial performance are the capitals and stakeholders involved.
Beyond that, the primary duty and obligation owed by an organization to its
stakeholders, no matter who they are, is to maintain vital capitals at whatever
levels are required to ensure their well-being. In some cases, this duty is exclusive
to the organization; in others, it is shared.

On the financial side of things, this usually translates into maximizing profitability, or at the very least not losing capital or operating at a loss. Insofar as universally agreed-to standards of performance for how much money should be spent
on salaries, rent, office supplies, equipment, travel expenses, legal fees, etc. are
concerned, there aren't any. Every organization is free to spend its money as it
sees fit. What we have in financial measurement, management and reporting,
instead, are generally accepted principles for accounting, which can be consistently
applied despite the *non*-standard ways in which organizations spend money. Note
the important difference here between *standards of performance* and *standards of
accounting*. It is important not to confuse the two. It is precisely the existence of
the latter that makes the *non*-existence of the former viable. The same principle
applies to non-financial accounting (i.e., to *sustainability* measurement and
reporting).

To be sure, there are limits to what an organization can do before its financial
performance becomes unsustainable, just as there are on the *non*-financial
front. Organizations cannot operate indefinitely at a monetary loss; there are limits
or thresholds involved. Similarly, under the context-based approach to CSM we
are advocating here, there are thresholds involved as well. They just happen to be
of a non-monetary type. Thus, instead of monetary limits, they express
minimums or maximums for such things as impacts on natural resources, contributions to organizational and social institutions, waste emissions, information
disclosures, policy and program conditions, and so forth. And just as organizations

are free to define their own standards of performance when it comes to spending, so are they free to set their own standards when it comes to their social and environmental impacts in the world. No universally accepted standards are required on either front, only rules for setting such standards and for measuring and reporting performance against them (i.e., standards of accounting, *non-financial* accounting in this case).

The absence of universally agreed-to standards of performance, then, is no basis for not establishing customized standards at the enterprise level and measuring non-financial performance against them, any more than it is on the financial side of things. Indeed, organizations must have standards of performance on both fronts, and there is no requirement whatsoever that they be identical or consistent from one organization to another in either case. In fact, how could they be? Every organization's stakeholders are different; their products are different; the communities in which they operate are different; their social, environmental and economic impacts are different; and, because of all of that, their duties and obligations to have impact on vital capitals in the world are also different. What they should have in common, however, are consistent frameworks for measuring and reporting their performance, be it their financial performance or their non-financial performance. And even though it may still be the case that accounting standards for non-financial measurement and reporting are still evolving, it is far better to be using an evolving framework than no framework at all, especially one that is context-based, as any methodology for assessing sustainability performance must be so construed in order to be meaningful.

Choosing standards for human well-being

As discussed in Chapter 1, the concept of human well-being and how to define it for purposes of setting standards of performance constitutes an important part of the system we are proposing. It comes into play in the process of defining denominators, and in determining how much of a vital capital must exist in order to ensure stakeholder well-being. Choosing a standard of well-being or a scale for expressing it, though, can be particularly challenging, especially given the inherently subjective nature of the subject. Still, choices of standards for well-being can and *must* be made in order to set standards of performance for use in denominators. The fact that there may not be universal agreement on such things does not mean that organizations can't choose or define their own standards on the basis of their own research and analysis. Here it may be helpful to consider an example.

Imagine a case in which an organization has determined that it has a duty or obligation to help create and maintain a level of healthcare facilities in the places where it does business, perhaps because of the impacts its operations have on, say, air quality. The stakeholders in such a case would be local or regional community members, and the vital capitals involved would be human, social and constructed capitals associated with the delivery of healthcare services – leaving aside, of course, other duties and obligations relating to its impacts on air quality, per se. In order to quantify what the organization's minimum impacts on the anthro capitals associated with healthcare delivery ought to be, some prior decision on what constitutes a sufficient level of human well-being would have to have been made, as well as a vision for how to operationalize it. Otherwise, it would be impossible to determine what the level of healthcare systems and services must be in order to achieve and maintain it.

This takes us squarely into the world of values and value theory, which is not the first time we've been there, since, after all, denominators are all about setting norms or standards for the way things ought to be, or for what an organization's impacts ought, or ought not, to be. The regulative ideal in play here has been all about human well-being from the start, and the level of vital capital resources required to achieve and maintain it.

Our guidance here is that organizations should do what they have always done when faced with choices: study them and make a decision. Moreover, they should forget about certainty; there isn't any to be found in anything we do, nor is there any need for it in order to take action. All that is required is that an organization research an issue and choose from among the competing ideas those propositions that best survive testing and evaluation. More importantly, organizations should always be prepared to admit error, and to modify their standards of performance in light of it. In any case, as we say, it is better to have debatable standards of performance than no standards at all.

Turning back to our example, let us imagine that there are three competing points of view about what constitutes an acceptable level of healthcare for people adversely affected by air pollution. Each would have its own levels of anthro capital required to achieve and maintain related services. And each, therefore, would carry a different implication for what the organization's impacts on such capitals ought to be. All that is required in this case is that the organization familiarize itself with the choices, and then make one. Beyond that, it should be prepared to defend its decision, and also to change its mind in the future should new information about better alternatives come to the fore. Having been through this process many times now, we can also report that the difficulty or challenge of taking this step diminishes with time. To be sure, the first round of the CSM cycle is the most difficult one, since that's when all of the initial research and weighing of alternative standards takes place. After that, things tend to become more routine and mechanical.

Defining denominators for water use at Cabot

Before moving on to step 4 of the CSM cycle, we'd like to close our discussion of step 3 and the specification of denominators by recounting in more detail the decisions made at Cabot about how to respond to the three components of context earlier discussed with respect to water use at its plant in Cabot, Vermont. Here again are the three elements of context laid out in a stepwise fashion:

1. **Carrying Capacities of Capitals**: First we identify the vital capitals (stocks) and their carrying capacities (flows) an organization is having impact on in ways that can affect stakeholder well-being, as well as capitals it *should* be having impact on in order to *ensure* stakeholder well-being.
2. **Responsible Populations**: Next we determine who the responsible populations are for ensuring the quality and sufficiency of such stocks and flows.
3. **Organizational Allocations**: And last, based on the first and second steps above, we allocate proportionate shares of available stocks and flows (in the case of natural capital) and/or burden shares for producing and/or maintaining them (in the case of anthro capital) to individual organizations.

What we want to highlight here for illustrative purposes are the decisions we made when developing the water-related metric for Cabot, and how they combined to determine the makeup of Cabot's denominator. First, as noted above, there were actually several impacts on capitals associated with water use, some of which were internal to Cabot involving impacts on anthro capitals (i.e., its organizational capacity to manage its water use), others of which dealt more directly with impacts on water resources, per se (i.e., is its water use fair and proportionate relative to the needs of others who rely on the same supplies?). The latter issue, of course, relates to impacts on natural capital, or water in this case, the context for which can be analyzed as follows:

1. **Carrying Capacities and Capitals**: The relevant carrying capacity in the case of water use is the volume of flows generated by stocks of precipitation, which are relied upon by local community members (i.e., the stakeholder group in this case) for their well-being.
2. **Responsible Populations**: The specific human population responsible for preserving and/or producing such capacities consists of the users of water resources found in a watershed.
3. **Organizational Allocations**: The organization's share of responsibility for preserving the same stocks and flows is precisely the question that must be answered in the denominator. Regarding water, the question for Cabot boiled down to determining how much of the available renewable supplies in the watershed where its plant is located should be allocated to the plant. The answer could then serve as a sustainability threshold, against which its actual levels of use could be measured.

As earlier noted, we addressed Cabot's water-related impacts using a tool called the Corporate Water Gauge® (described in Appendix D), the results of which at the Cabot plant for 2007 are shown in Appendix E. Of particular interest in that case was the manner in which the value of denominators was determined (i.e., the *organizational allocation*). In the final analysis, we chose two such values, one that was calculated on a per capita basis, and the other of which was calculated on an economic basis. This allowed us to look at the sustainability of Cabot's water use in two ways: the per capita approach allocated water on the basis of the size of the employee population at Cabot; the economic approach allocated water on the basis of the plant's contribution to GDP, and resulted in a much larger allocation than the per capita approach.

Here we want to stress the fact that the purpose of a denominator, be it for a water metric or otherwise, is to allocate a fair and proportionate share of the duty to preserve, produce and/or maintain a vital capital to an individual party. In the case of water, this would translate into a duty to use no more than a fair share of available renewable supplies, such that if all users followed the same allocation scheme, the renewable size of the stock would remain intact and would renew indefinitely. In the case of an anthro capital, by contrast, the duty has more to do with producing and/or maintaining the capitals involved at some level, such that if all members of the responsible population involved followed the same logic, the size of the related stocks would remain sufficient for purposes of ensuring human well-being indefinitely.

For the *per capita* denominator calculation at Cabot, we first computed the size of the human population in the watershed in which Cabot's operations were located. We then determined what Cabot's proportionate size of that population was by comparing its employee population size with the broader population size (i.e., in the watershed). In order to do this, we had to first express Cabot's employee size in the form of what we call a *per capita equivalent*. This was done by taking the total number of employee hours worked at the Cabot plant in the year of interest and dividing it by 8,760 (the total number of hours in a year). This allowed us to avoid overcounting the per capita headcount at Cabot, since employees in any job only spend part of their time at work. And since per capita counts always refer to people in whole person-days, if you will, we needed to express Cabot's size in like terms.

Once we had determined Cabot's per capita equivalent size, we were then able to determine what proportion of the local/watershed population its workforce represented. The same proportion of available renewable supplies could then be allocated to the plant, on the theory that people carry their entitlements to water resources with them into the workplace, and that businesses receive *their* entitlements to such resources by virtue of the same employee entitlements which are transferred to them, in a sense, to the degree that employees spend time at work. Again, this was only one of two approaches we took – a very conservative one at that, since it resulted in a comparatively low allocation of water to Cabot (i.e., when compared with the economic allocation, as further discussed below).

We should also point out that before allocating anything to Cabot or to any other user in the watershed of interest, we first decided to rely only on annual precipitation as the exclusive stock of water, and not surface or ground waters; such surface and ground water stocks were to be left intact. We then took annual precipitation levels and subtracted 45 percent for evapotranspiration. Then we allowed for another deduction of 27.5 percent for non-human ecological needs. That brought total deductions to a level of 72.5 percent. The remaining balance of 27.5 percent was then allocated for human use on a per capita basis, as described above.

The alternative approach to computing Cabot's water-related denominator was the economic one. This approach was affectionately referred to as the *Destamminator*, since it was originally formulated by Cabot's president, Dr. Richard Stammer. Dr. Stammer had expressed a concern that the per capita approach would not truly reflect the value being provided to society by the company, and that a food producer's contributions to society arguably warranted a higher share of available resources. The alternative economic approach he suggested was as follows:

1. First, start with the same original supply used for the per capita approach – annual precipitation only.
2. Then make the same deductions for evapotranspiration and ecological needs.
3. Then satisfy all household needs in the watershed of interest, using actual household consumption data supplied by an authoritative source. The number of households in the watershed and the average volume of household water use turned out to be fairly easy numbers to come by.
4. Then take the remaining water resources (again, from precipitation only) and allocate them to non-household users (i.e., businesses and other organizations or establishments) based on their proportionate contributions to GDP in the watershed of interest. Again, these numbers were fairly easy to come by.

The results of the per capita and Destamminator (economic) allocation methods at Cabot were as follows (i.e., for the Cabot plant only, in 2007):

- per capita approach: 137,074,421 gallons
- Destamminator (economic) approach: 3,004,982,852 gallons.

Despite the significant difference in the volume of water allocated to the Cabot plant under the two approaches used, its sustainability performance (relative to water use only) under both approaches was extraordinarily sustainable, since its actual use of water in the watershed of interest was only 15,647,823 gallons. When expressed in the form of quotient scores, then, the results were as follows:

- per capita approach: 0.114
- Destamminator (economic) approach: 0.005.

Both scores indicated sustainable performance because, as shown in Figure 3.5, any score of less than or equal to 1.0 where impacts on natural capital are concerned is sustainable.

The report included as Figure E.1 in Appendix E includes another measure of performance: *Intensity*. As the report indicates, Cabot's use of water per pound of product produced in 2007 (at its Cabot, Vermont plant) was only 0.131 gallons. Intensity is a measure of efficiency, or the rate at which a resource is used normalized per some other unit of interest – pounds of product produced, in this case. Here we see in graphic terms the difference between sustainability and efficiency, and the metrics involved. Both are important to understanding sustainability performance, but they are clearly not synonymous.

Step 4: Measure/assess organizational performance

Once duties and obligations have been defined and expressed in the form of numerical denominators per the guidelines set forth above, it is time to measure and express actual impacts (i.e., per the numerators shown in Figures 3.5 and 3.6). In this section, we will discuss both the measurement of actual impacts and the resulting quotient scores that follow, and also how to plot and interpret them on a sustainability performance scale. First we start with the specification of numerators.

Developing numerators in CBMs

For environmental metrics, numerators are defined as follows:

> Actual Impact on Carrying Capacity of *Natural Capital* Resulting from Organizational Operations

For social and economic metrics, numerators are defined as follows:

> Actual Impact on Carrying Capacity of *Anthro Capital* Resulting from Organizational Operations

Key guidelines for measuring and expressing numerator values are as follows:

- As in the case of denominators (see above), impacts expressed in numerators should be confined to direct impacts only on capitals of importance to stakeholder well-being. These can be capitals that are either internal or external to an organization. By contrast, secondary or downstream impacts of other kinds (i.e., indirect impacts on other external capitals, or of a sort that involve the well-being of stakeholders beyond the immediate effects of their appropriation, or not, of vital capitals upon which an organization has had direct impacts) should not be factored into the development of numerators nor should any downstream effects upon the well-being or sustainability performance of non-stakeholders be considered. All such indirect impacts are at least one step removed from the boundaries of an organization's own operations and/or sphere of control, and as such fall outside the scope of its own CSM efforts. Measures of impacts on vital capitals, therefore, should be confined to direct impacts on either internal or external capitals upon which stakeholders, in turn, directly rely for their well-being. Other, second-order-and-beyond impacts can alternatively be measured, managed and reported using other methodologies, such as life cycle assessment (LCA).
- The numerator of a quotient should express impacts on the carrying capacity of the same vital capital, and for the same period of time, referred to in the denominator of the same quotient. If the denominator expresses the normative impact Cabot's plant in Cabot, Vermont, ought to have had in 2007 on the local

watershed, the numerator, too, should express only the impact Cabot's operations *actually* had in 2007 on the same watershed – nothing else.

- The units of measurement used to express the value of a numerator should be the same as the units of measurement used to express the denominator.
- In cases where proxies are being used in denominators to express normative impacts on vital capitals, the same proxies should be used in the numerators of the same quotients. Appendix C includes an example of this approach in our discussion of the standard of performance used to measure climate change mitigation performance at Ben & Jerry's. In that case, the vital capitals of interest were a mix of internal and external human, social and constructed capitals required to ensure Ben & Jerry's contribution to climate change mitigation. But rather than directly measure investments in producing and/or maintaining the carrying capacities of related anthro capitals, we chose to use actual emissions as a proxy for determining whether or not such investments were sufficient (i.e., sustainable) based on a particular mitigation standard or scenario (again, see Appendix C for details). If actual emissions in any year were consistent with the trajectory of the standard we selected, we assumed that the underlying investments in related anthro capital were occurring at sustainable rates. Thus, both the denominator and the numerator in the quotients involved were expressed in terms of CO_2 emissions which directly affect natural capital, even though the vital capitals we were interested in looking at consisted of something else: *anthro* capital.
- As in the case of expressing denominator values for impacts on natural capital (discussed above), numerator values for impacts on natural capital are ideally expressed in terms of the natural resource or ecosystem service involved. Actual impacts on water resources, for example, should be expressed in terms of gallons of water consumed in a given time period; similarly, the emission of wastes into the environment should be expressed in terms of the volume (by weight) of wastes emitted over time.
- Regarding impacts on anthro capital, the same guidelines apply as suggested for denominators above; namely, that impacts on anthro capitals should be expressed in terms of impacts on their carrying capacities, or in the number of people and/ or transactions they can support. Alternatively, numerators can be expressed in terms of the monetary value of such impacts, but only if the denominators in the same quotients have been expressed in the same way.

Plotting and interpreting CBM scores

Once the numerator and denominator have both been specified in a quotient, the resulting score can be computed. For our purposes, all such scores should be interpreted in terms of how they compare to a score of 1.0. Why? Because given the meaning and purpose of denominators (i.e., they express standards of performance for sustainability), a score of 1.0 would mean that performance exactly matches the standard. Many, if not most, scores, however, will be more or less than 1.0.

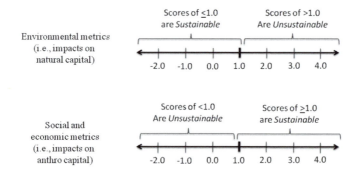

Source: McElroy, 2008

FIGURE 3.7 Sustainability performance scales.

Depending on whether the metrics involved are of an environmental or social/economic type, scores of less than or greater than 1.0 will have different meanings.

We first raised this issue and explained it in Chapter 2 (see Figure 2.2, repeated here as Figure 3.7 for convenience). What Figure 3.7 shows, then, are two instances of a sustainability performance scale with a demarcation point of 1.0 clearly indicated. The same scale is shown twice; that is, once relative to environmental scores, and a second time relative to social/economic scores. For environmental scores, any score of less than or equal to 1.0 signifies sustainable performance, because it means that an organization's impacts on natural capital are less than or equal to its fair or proportionate share of the available carrying capacity, relative to its not-to-exceed impact on the resources involved (i.e., as expressed in the denominator).

For impacts on anthro capitals, however, the logic reverses: scores of greater than or equal to 1.0 signify sustainable performance, since anthro capitals are anthropogenic, and sustainability with respect to impacts on them, therefore, is a function of the extent to which their carrying capacities are produced and/or maintained at required levels over time. Of course, organizations can also consume anthro capitals (and/or their flows), and the rate at which they do may or may not have anything to do with the normative rate at which they should separately produce and/or help maintain them. If there is, in fact, *no* duty or obligation to produce and/or maintain such anthro capitals, then the rate at which they consume them is moot. Why? Because the absence of a duty or obligation to have impact on a vital capital renders any actual impacts on the same vital capital irrelevant to CSM.

For those who may be troubled by the fact that the same score might mean two different things for two different metrics (e.g., a score of 0.8 would be sustainable for an environmental metric but unsustainable for a social metric), reversing the polarity for one or the other is always possible. If, for example, we want to favor the social convention of scoring where scores of greater than or equal to 1.0 signify sustainable performance, a score of 0.8 received for an environmental impact could be inversely expressed by simply dividing it into 1.0 (i.e., 1.0 / 0.8 = 1.25). Thus, a score of 0.8 on the environmental sustainability scale becomes 1.25 on the social/economic scale, and is thereby interpreted as sustainable, just as it should be.

Regardless of which convention is used, the distance between the scores received and 1.0 on the scale, if any, signifies the extent to which performance, per the metric involved, is either above or below the level required to achieve sustainability. Here it is interesting to observe that levels of performance greatly in excess – in a favorable sense – of those required to achieve sustainability are, strictly speaking, not required, since any score of 1.0 is sufficient for purposes of being sustainable. Indeed, it may very well be that the costs of maintaining excessively positive performance, as it were, are unwarranted and can be shifted to some other area of impact where performance is lacking.

In this regard, sustainability performance – which is a binary thing, as discussed in Chapter 2 – differs markedly from financial performance. In the case of the latter, maximizing impacts on a vital capital of interest (i.e., maximizing profits and/or the value of monetary capital) is the overarching goal; in the case of the former, however, minimally complying with normative impacts on the vital capitals of interest – no more, no less – is the norm, instead. The quality and quantity of vital capitals on the non-financial side of performance, that is, simply need to be sufficient, not excessive. To say that we need to maximize the supply of anthro capitals, for example, would be incorrect, since the excess carrying capacity involved might never be used and would be wasteful to maintain. We only need so many hospital beds, so many desks in our classrooms, so many courts in our courthouses, so many lanes on our highways, etc.

Can there be consolidated sustainability scores?

Beyond interpreting sustainability scores for individual metrics in the ways described above, sustainability performance can also be described in the aggregate, by expressing performance, for example, in a unitary or consolidated form for each of the three bottom lines, or even by reducing overall sustainability performance to a single bottom line score – much like the profitability of a company can be expressed in a single financial bottom line. Here we hasten to add that this is a unique feature of context-based sustainability and the metrics it entails, since we know of no other methodology for CSM that makes such reporting possible.

We illustrate this aspect of CBS in Table 3.8, in which nine hypothetical sustainability performance scores are shown, three for each of the three bottom lines. In the environmental bottom line category, only one metric indicates sustainable performance; in the social category, two do; and in the economic category, all three do. When consolidating scores, we do not add them up and average them, since if we did, unsustainable impacts on one form of capital might be offset by positive – even excessively positive – impacts on another. In this regard, CBS adheres to the so-called *strong* interpretation of sustainability, according to which vital capitals are not substitutable for one another and must therefore never be added to or subtracted from one another as though they are (see

Dresner, 2002, pp. 76–77, for a concise overview of the distinction between *strong* versus *weak* sustainability, and also Wackernagel and Rees, 1996, p. 37).

Instead of adding and averaging scores, then, we instead determine the proportion of all scores received that meet or exceed sustainability performance standards – a *quotient of quotients*, as it were, where a perfect score would be 100 percent. Thus, the environmental, social and economic bottom line scores shown in Table 3.8 are 0.33, 0.66 and 1.00, respectively; and the overall sustainability performance score for the hypothetical organization involved is 0.67. Notice here that if we had simply added and averaged the nine individual scores, the overall score would have been 1.1, a frankly meaningless number because of the way it mixes scores from different scales. Instead, by holding the organization accountable to sustainability standards for each of its metrics independently of the others, the score received was 0.67 on a scale of zero to one (where 1.0 is a perfect score), a truer reflection of actual sustainability performance.

TABLE 3.8 Computing sustainability bottom lines

Bottom Line	#	Area of Impact (Capital)	Score*	Sustainable?*
Environmental	1	Water (N)	0.9	Yes
	2	Toxic Air Emissions (N)	1.1	No
	3	Biodiversity (N)	1.4	No
Social	4	Climate Change Mitigation (H, S, C)	1.1	Yes
	5	Work/Life Balance (H,S)	1.0	Yes
	6	Roads and Highways (C)	0.7	No
Economic	7	Livable Wage (H)	1.5	Yes
	8	Fair Trade (H)	1.2	Yes
	9	Commercial Performance (H, S, C)	1.0	Yes
Legend: **N = Natural Capital** **H = Human Capital** **S = Social Capital** **C = Constructed Capital**		Environmental Bottom Line Score (Metrics 1-3)		0.33
		Social Bottom Line Score (Metrics 4-6)		0.66
		Economic Bottom Line Score (Metrics 7-9)		1.00
		Overall Sustainability Performance Score (Metrics 1-9)		0.67

*Sustainability performance is interpreted according to the scoring conventions shown in Figures 3.4 – 3.6.

Reporting performance

In most parts of the world, not all, sustainability or non-financial reporting is a completely voluntarily practice. To our way of thinking, however, sustainability reporting should be done by at least all publicly held companies, whether it is required or not, if only for the benefit of stakeholders whose personal well-being is no less at stake. Transparency demands it.

Notwithstanding the dictates of other, more established guidelines for sustainability reporting (e.g., GRI), here are our own thoughts on what such reporting should entail (i.e., from a CBS perspective):

- First, the scope and content of a sustainability report should be driven entirely by the results of the kind of stakeholder analysis performed in steps 2 and 3 of the CSM cycle. Here we differ somewhat from the GRI guidelines, which, although they do advocate for the inclusion of context in sustainability reports, fail to make the explicit connection between context and materiality, much less provide guidelines for how to include context. Context, from our perspective, is the primary determinant of materiality, since it leads directly to the identification of social, environmental and economic standards of performance. Nothing could be more material to a sustainability report than duties and obligations to have non-financial impacts on capitals of vital importance to stakeholder well-being.
- As indicated above, a sustainability report should identify the organization's stakeholders and the specific duties and obligations owed to each one of them to have impacts of one kind or another on vital capitals. It should then go on to explain the metrics used to measure performance against such duties, as well as the performance recorded by each of them (i.e., actual measures of performance for the period covered by the report). Here a report can utilize the quotient-based scoring system we have provided, as well as the procedure for computing blended bottom line scores. Of particular importance, of course, should be the identification of cases in which performance does not conform to standards, and analysis of the circumstances behind them. Also included should be a discussion of how the organization plans to close any related gaps. In other words, the report should include a description of the organization's intended actions, if any, in steps 5 and 6 of the CSM cycle for those areas in which its performance is deficient or unsustainable. Positive areas of performance, too, should be acknowledged and discussed, including steps, if any, the organization plans to take in order to maintain such performance or replicate it elsewhere.

We also feel compelled to comment on the growing interest in so-called integrated reporting. First let us be clear about what the term means. Eccles and Krzus (2010, pp. 10–11) explain it as follows:

> In its simplest terms, One Report [their term for the concept of an integrated report] means producing a single report that combines the financial and narrative information found in a company's annual report with the non-financial (such as on environmental, social, and governance issues) and narrative information found in a company's 'Corporate Social Responsibility' or 'Sustainability' report.
>
> … One Report has two meanings. The first and most narrow meaning is a single document, either in paper or perhaps electronically provided as a PDF file … The second and broader meaning is reporting financial and non-financial

information in such a way that shows their impact on each other. Here companies can leverage the capabilities of the Internet and its Web 2.0 tools and technologies.

In August of 2010, the Prince's Accounting for Sustainability Project[5] in the UK and GRI announced the formation of the International Integrated Reporting Committee (IIRC)[6] to create a framework or standard for integrated reporting. Since then, GRI has also announced its intent to move ahead with development of the next version of its standard (i.e., the G4, or fourth-generation version), a major difference of which, when compared with the current G3.1 version, will be the presence of guidelines of some kind for integrated reporting.

We agree that integrated reporting will be beneficial, in that it will improve the presentation of performance information to stakeholders who need it, compared with the currently fragmented and disconnected ways of doing so. We do not, however, agree that it is a priority at this time. Why not? Because it (a) pales in comparison with the urgency of incorporating context in sustainability measurement and reporting, and (b) raises the possibility that the currently prevailing context-free style of reporting will become even more established than it already is. Indeed, one could say that the only thing worse than context-free sustainability reporting is context-free *integrated* reporting.

In a very real sense, then, the investment of resources in the development of integrated reporting we see happening today amounts to a major distraction, the effects of which will only worsen the quality of sustainability reporting, not improve it, since it will mean that context will continue to be neglected even as context-free reporting becomes more and more the norm. If performance reporting becomes integrated and yet the non-financial side of reporting continues to lack context, will sustainability or performance reporting somehow be improved? Will stakeholders have access to sustainability performance information that is more meaningful? We don't think so. Indeed, how can the interrelationships between financial and non-financial performance – something that integrated reporting is supposed to reveal – be meaningful if the sustainability side of the equation is deeply flawed?

Step 5: Plan strategies and interventions

Generally speaking, the performance measures taken in step 4 will have three possible outcomes: (1) performance fails to meet sustainability standards, (2) performance exactly matches sustainability standards, or (3) performance exceeds sustainability standards. In a perfect world, performance would always exactly match sustainability standards, since it would mean that all standards are being met, but not excessively so. While excessive performance might be laudable for one reason or another, it might also mean that resources are being used or spent in ways that are not strictly required in order for performance to be sustainable. As discussed in Chapter 2, sustainability is a binary concept – all that is required to be sustainable is to meet the minimally sufficient condition.

More likely, however, in most cases is that there will be gaps in performance, both positive and negative. A positive gap is any gap that involves performance in excess of the level required to ensure stakeholder well-being. These gaps represent opportunities to shift resources from positive areas of impact to negative ones by lowering performance, so to speak, to a level that matches a standard but does not exceed it. The resources gained or recovered by such a move can then be reallocated to other areas of impact where negative gaps might exist.

A negative gap is any gap that involves performance below, or not in conformance with, a sustainability standard of performance. These are gaps, therefore, that signify unsustainable performance. The size of such gaps further signifies the magnitude of the shortfalls involved, and pertains to the carrying capacities of specific vital capitals. In other words, negative gaps in sustainability scores (i.e., greater than 1.0 for impacts on natural capital, or less than 1.0 for impacts on anthro capital) signify that either (a), in the case of impacts on natural capital, an organization is using too much of it, or (b), in the case of anthro capital, an organization is failing to produce and/or maintain enough of it.

What must be done in response to such scores is to devise strategies and interventions aimed at closing the gaps involved, so that performance will conform to sustainability standards. This requires, in turn, specific causal theories about the kinds of strategies and interventions that can lead to specific, desired outcomes or impacts on vital capitals. Mitigating CO_2 emissions, for example, can be accomplished by decreasing the use of fossil-fuel-based energy, increasing the use of renewable energy or facilitating decreases in CO_2 emissions by others (e.g., through the purchase of offsets).

Here we can see that CSM is really nothing more than the practice of identifying and attempting to close gaps in performance (i.e., gap analysis), albeit in the context of *sustainability* performance in our case. Of course the types of specific gaps that can be found and the range of possible solutions for how to close them are too numerous and complex for us to address here. Discovering, developing, testing and evaluating them is perhaps what CSM managers should be doing more than anything else, with a constant eye towards closing sustainability performance gaps in organizations. Step 5, then, represents that very process, the process by which CSM managers investigate, choose, test and evaluate promising solutions for improving the sustainability performance of their organizations.

Step 6: Implement CSM strategies and interventions

Once a CSM manager has planned a specific strategy or intervention, the solution involved can be implemented. In other words, in step 6 actions are taken to have impact on the carrying capacities of vital capitals in accordance with the strategies and interventions devised in step 5. Step 6 of the CSM cycle, then, is merely the implementation or action side of the process, a process that otherwise has three basic parts to it: plan, act and assess (see Figure 3.8). From this perspective, CSM

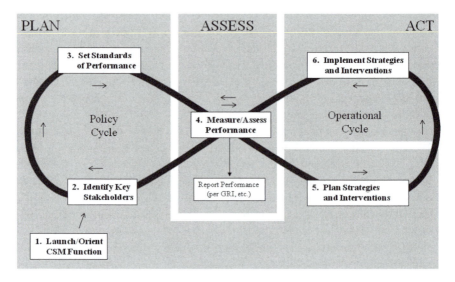

FIGURE 3.8 The (double-loop) CSM cycle (enhanced).

follows the logic of any other branch of management and can be described in that way as follows:

- In the first round of the cycle, we set goals and standards of performance. This constitutes the policy-oriented side of CSM (steps 1, 2 and 3 of the CSM cycle).
- Next we perform the first instance of measurement and (at least internal) reporting, so as to produce a baseline of performance in the areas of interest identified in steps 1, 2 and 3. This we do in step 4.
- Having identified gaps, if any, in performance, we then devise strategies and interventions aimed at closing them. This constitutes the first step on the operational side of CSM (step 5 of the CSM cycle).
- We then act in accordance with our plans (step 6 of the CSM cycle).
- Next we repeat the assessment step (step 4) in order to judge the effectiveness of our actions. To the extent that gaps still exist, we plan again, act again and assess again; from that point forward, the cycle repeats itself endlessly in a *plan–act–assess* pattern.

Stakeholder engagement

Throughout the discussion above, we have repeatedly made mention of the centrality of stakeholders to CBS and to the fact that sustainability performance is fundamentally about the impacts an organization has on capitals of vital importance to their well-being. We have not, however, had much to say about direct stakeholder involvement in the CSM cycle, or about the need for organizations to engage with stakeholders as part of the CBS methodology. Having now described the CSM cycle in its entirely, it is time to do just that.

First, we wish to be clear about our feelings that engaging with stakeholders throughout the CSM cycle is vitally important. Indeed, we see stakeholder engagement occurring in five of the six steps encompassed by the CSM cycle as follows:

Step 2: This is the step in which stakeholders are first identified. And although stakeholders themselves may or may not be directly involved in the process, they are at least engaged in the sense that their needs and existence are actively taken into account by an organization in planning its CSM program.

Step 3: It should be obvious, we think, that stakeholders have a role to play in the identification of an organization's duties and obligations to have impacts on capitals of vital importance to their well-being. That said, there is nothing wrong with an organization taking the first step to define such responsibilities in the absence of direct stakeholder participation, since such duties and obligations can certainly at least be hypothesized independent of stakeholders' involvement. Indeed, one could say that organizations are morally bound to do so. Still, stakeholders should eventually be invited to review and validate, if not modify or change, the organization's own thinking about the duties and obligations it owes to them. Exactly how to do this in cases where the stakeholders involved are numerous in quantity and/or broadly dispersed is the subject of much debate and should continue, we think, to be the focus of experimentation (e.g., using advisory boards, focus groups, surrogate NGOs, social media or what have you). Most important is that stakeholder input be factored into the development of standards of performance in step 3 (i.e., into the determination of materiality and norms for performance, as earlier discussed); exactly how that is done is of less concern to us.

Step 4: Measuring and assessing performance against standards developed in step 3 should also involve direct contact with stakeholders in order to report the results of such measures *to* them. Here again, stakeholders have an important validation role to play and are also owed the fundamental courtesy of disclosure insofar as impacts on resources important to their well-being is concerned. The primary purpose of reports produced in step 4 of the CSM cycle, then, is to disclose to stakeholders, above all others, what the sustainability performance of an organization is, or has been, for a specified period of time.

Step 5: In cases where gaps in performance are identified in step 4, stakeholders once again have a clear role to play in the formulation of strategies and interventions aimed at closing or resolving them (the gaps). The fitness or desirability of alternative solutions, for example, can be tested and evaluated with stakeholder participation prior to their implementation. Furthermore, there may be opportunities for direct stakeholder involvement in the implementation of certain alternatives in ways that can help strengthen their effectiveness and also help the organization to achieve its broader sustainability goals.

Step 6: As just noted, stakeholders may in fact have a role to play in the deployment or implementation of specific sustainability programs or solutions in ways that can enhance their effectiveness. Short of that, stakeholders may also have a role to play in helping to monitor the effectiveness of strategies or interventions, if only from the sidelines, so to speak, in ways that can later feed into and support the reassessment process afterwards (i.e., step 4).

These are just a few of the ways stakeholders can, and should, be involved in the performance of CSM. Of most importance is the need to recognize that sustainability performance is ultimately a function of impacts on not just vital capitals, but also stakeholder well-being, the circumstances of which can hardly be determined without direct stakeholder involvement. CSM programs should be structured accordingly.

Summary: how to do CSM

In this chapter, we have attempted to provide a methodology for the practice of CSM that is context-based. The purpose of CSM, as we see it, is to continuously manage the sustainability performance of an organization. This, in turn, requires continuous measurement and reporting of the social, environmental and economic impacts of an organization relative to standards of performance for what such impacts ought to be in order to ensure stakeholder well-being; and also active interventions into the business operations of organizations in order to influence and/or manage such performance. The impacts of interest to us in terms of sustainability performance, of course, are those that affect the quality and/or sufficiency of vital capitals, as such capitals may be required for stakeholder well-being.

The methodology we provided consists of a six-step cycle (i.e., the *CSM cycle*) that generally follows a pattern of trial and error aimed at achieving and maintaining sustainable levels of performance relative to standards for what such performance ought to be in order to ensure stakeholder well-being. Thus, the methodology also follows the logic of a gap analysis, according to which performance is constantly being assessed relative to targets or standards of performance. In cases where negative gaps are found, actions are subsequently taken to attempt to close them, followed by further measurements to assess the effectiveness of the actions taken. In cases where gaps still exist, further interventions are planned and implemented, followed by additional assessments, further plans, if needed, further interventions and assessments, and so on. At a high level, then, the CSM cycle can also be seen as following a general (and repetitive) pattern of *plan–act–assess; plan–act–assess; plan–act–assess*; etc. – the cycle repeats itself endlessly, as needed. This, in our view, is the best way of describing what CSM functions and their managers do, or *ought* to be doing.

The CSM cycle we described consists of the following six steps:

Step 1: Launch/orient CSM function
Step 2: Identify key stakeholders
Step 3: Set standards of performance

Step 4: Measure/assess performance
Step 5: Plan strategies and interventions
Step 6: Implement strategies and interventions

Step 1 consists of actions that must be taken in order to initialize a CSM function, and to define its scope and boundaries. Importantly, step 1 also includes the making of decisions as to what the fundamental orientation of CSM is, or should be, relative to how it should approach the subject; what the meaning of sustainability performance is; how to manage it; how to measure and assess it, etc. Here we argued for a stakeholder-centric view, according to which sustainability performance is seen as a function of what an organization's impacts are on vital capitals of importance to stakeholder well-being. This, in turn, gives rise to the context-based approach that underlies the remaining five steps of the CSM cycle, and also provides a basis for resolving the scope and boundary issues referred to above.

Step 2 consists of the process of identifying who an organization's stakeholders are. In general, this is done by category, such that the results include stakeholder groups like employees, customers, owners, communities, etc. This is a critically important step from a CBS perspective, because it sets the stage for determining standards of performance against which actual performance can be measured and managed. It is the relationships organizations have with their stakeholders, that is, that ultimately give rise to specific organizational responsibilities to have impact, or not have impact, on social, environmental and economic conditions in the world. If an impact – be it an actual or desired one – cannot be traced back to a duty or obligation owed to a legitimate stakeholder, it is, in our view, irrelevant to CSM.

Step 3 consists of the specification of detailed standards of performance, which again follow from the identification of stakeholders in step 2. In other words, the standards of performance of interest to us here are specifically those that arise from duties and obligations owed to stakeholders. Here we also made it clear that all such duties and obligations should be expressed in terms of normative impacts on vital capitals (i.e., as thresholds for impacts on natural, human, social and/or constructed capital). We further referred to human, social and constructed capitals as *anthro capital*, in the aggregate, because they are human-made; natural capital, by contrast, is not.

In our discussion of step 3, we also introduced a model for constructing context-based metrics, or CBMs. Included in our discussion of CBMs were the following key points and guidelines for how to build and use them:

- CBMs should take the form of quotients, in which denominators represent individual standards of performance as defined in step 3, and numerators represent actual performance as measured by the organization (i.e., by its CSM function).

- Both actual performance (expressed in numerators) and normative performance (expressed in denominators) should be numerical in form, and should be expressed in the same units of measurement for individual areas of impact.
- Scores produced using CBMs will be greater than, less than or equal to 1.0 and can be plotted on a common sustainability performance scale, accordingly.
- Scores of less than or equal to 1.0 for CBMs involving environmental impacts on natural capital can be seen as signifying sustainable performance, because they mean that the use of natural resources falls within an organization's fair or proportionate share of what's available; scores of *greater* than or equal to 1.0 for impacts on *anthro* capital, by contrast, can be seen as signifying sustainable performance, because they mean that an organization's contributions to the production and/or maintenance of anthropogenic resources at least conform to minimum standards for what such contributions ought to be.

In our discussion of step 3, we also described a procedure for calculating consolidated or unitary bottom lines, such as a consolidated environmental bottom line for all impacts on natural capital, or a consolidated social bottom line for all impacts on human, social and constructed capitals. The same procedure makes it possible to calculate a consolidated or blended bottom line for all non-financial impacts on all non-monetary capitals – a single sustainability bottom line, as it were – just as we commonly do in financial reporting. This is a unique feature of CBS; we know of no other methodology for measuring and reporting sustainability performance that does this.

Step 4 consists of the actual measurement of sustainability performance using the CBMs developed in step 3. This is where the gap analysis described above comes into play, since the results of step 4 include identification of specific cases in which an organization's impacts on vital capitals fail to conform to standards, meet standards or even exceed them in some cases. In principle, then, it is the results of step 4 that set the agenda for what a CSM function's priorities ought to be, since it only becomes clear in step 4 where an organization's sustainability performance is deficient. Step 4 is also the point in the cycle where sustainability reporting takes place.

Step 5 consists of the development of strategies and interventions aimed at improving and/or maintaining desired levels of sustainability performance. Once again, this will typically take the form of devising solutions for how to close negative gaps in performance (i.e., gaps in performance between actual and normative impacts on vital capitals). For gaps involving environmental impacts, this might involve reducing the levels of energy or materials consumed, or the volume of wastes emitted; for social and economic impacts, this might take the form of increasing or simply maintaining levels of contributions made towards producing and/or maintaining anthro capitals.

Step 6, the last step in the cycle – before it repeats itself, that is – is the step in which actual interventions take place. In other words, step 6 is the step in which the plans made in step 5 are implemented. The possibilities here are clearly endless, since the solutions required for achieving and maintaining sustainability performance in organizational settings are still very much in development with no end in sight. To the extent that the CSM cycle can be described as a structured process of trial and error, step 6 is where the trial takes place. The error part, if there is any, is not identified until such time as step 4 is repeated (i.e., the Measure/Assess Performance step), which immediately follows step 6 as the Operational Cycle shown in Figure 3.3 in this chapter indicates (i.e., as one moves around it in a counter-clockwise fashion).

Finally, because of the importance of stakeholders to CBS and the CSM cycle, we took steps following our description of the cycle to point out the manner in which stakeholder engagement takes place – or *should* take place – during the course of its use. Here we explained that, given the centrality of stakeholder well-being as the ultimate driver of what a CSM function's priorities ought to be, stakeholders obviously have a very important role to play throughout the CSM cycle. Of particular importance, we felt, is that stakeholders be involved in the performance of steps 2 through 6 – especially step 3, since it is in that step that duties and obligations owed to stakeholders to have impact on capitals of vital importance to their well-being are first defined.

Notes

1. Social contract theory is a political philosophy for how people in societies ought to (and demonstrably do in very many cases) willfully give up a significant part of their autonomy in deference to the authority and governance of the collective, as it were, in order to ensure their individual (and collective) well-being. The theory was most notably put forward in its initial form by Hobbes (1651), Locke (1689) and Rousseau (1762). In the corporate context, the idea of a social contract existing between an organization and the community (or society) is seen by some as the basis for, or source of, organizational legitimacy. Deegan (2007) explains this idea as follows (p. 133):

   > A central premise of legitimacy theory is that organizations can maintain their operations only to the extent that they have the support of the community. Such support is earned as a result of the organization being *perceived* by society as complying with the expectations of the society with which they interact. The expectations that society has with regards to how an entity shall act are considered to constitute the *social contract* between the organization and society. Specifically, it is considered that an organization's survival will be threatened if society perceives that the organization has breached its social contract.

2. The CSM cycle strongly resembles, and follows the logic of, a model for adaptive learning commonly found in the organizational learning literature. Argyris (1990, p. 92), for example, refers to what we portray as the *Operational Cycle* as 'single-loop learning. A thermostat [for example] is a single-loop learner. It detects when the air around it is too hot or too cold and corrects the situation by turning the heat on or off.' Double-loop learning, by contrast, devises the policies, 'governing values' or 'theor[ies]-in-use' (pp. 95–96) otherwise employed in the operational loop, or in single-loop learning. That, in turn, is what we portray as the *Policy Cycle*. Thus, the CSM cycle is essentially an organizational learning process (long established in the management and organizational learning literatures) applied to sustainability management.

3. A good example of a business-to-business sustainability scorecard can be found in the form of Walmart's Supplier Sustainability Assessment, a thorough description of which can be found here: http://walmartstores.com/sustainability/9292.aspx.
4. More information about the UN's Millennium Development Goals can be found here: http://www.un.org/millenniumgoals/.
5. More information about the Prince's Accounting for Sustainability Project can be found here: http://www.accountingforsustainability.org/home/.
6. More information about the IIRC can be found here: http://www.integratedreporting.org/.

4

SUMMARY AND CONCLUSIONS

General summary of context-based sustainability (CBS)

It has been our purpose in this book to advocate for a particular school of practice for sustainability management in organizational settings that we call context-based sustainability, or CBS. Indeed, we have taken a very strong position on the matter and have argued that it is simply not possible to effectively measure, manage or report the sustainability performance of an organization unless context is included in the mix. Context, we explained – or *sustainability context*, as GRI puts it – consists of standards or norms for what an organization's impacts on vital capitals must be in order to be sustainable and ensure stakeholder well-being. Such norms are more or less dictated by the nature of an organization's relationships with its stakeholders, and the duties or obligations it has to have impacts on related capitals of importance to their well-being (i.e., to stakeholder well-being). In taking our position, we defined stakeholders as follows:

> A stakeholder in an organization is anyone whose vital capitals – and whose interests and well-being, therefore – are affected by the organization's actions, or whose vital capitals ought to be so affected by virtue of the relationship that exists between them.

Thus, the most useful and correct interpretation of sustainability performance is one which approaches the subject from the perspective of assigning duties and obligations to organizations to have impacts (or not) on capitals of vital importance to stakeholder well-being, which duties and obligations are at least implicit in the relationships an organization has with its stakeholders. It is the existence and legitimacy of stakeholders, then, that give sustainability its relevance and importance to organizational performance, and which also provide us with guidance as to what the related standards of performance should be.

Corporate sustainability management, or CSM, therefore, is not some new, arbitrary or quixotic flight of fancy imposed on business by the liberal left, as it were, but instead is a formalized way of measuring, managing and reporting non-financial performance in accordance with duties and obligations to stakeholders that already exist. Thus, it is a way of taking responsibilities implicit in an organization's relationships with its stakeholders and making them *explicit*, and is *not* a way of imposing new duties or obligations of some discretionary or extraneous kind on organizations.

According to CBS, sustainability performance can be seen as a function of an organization's impacts on vital capitals relative to what such impacts ought to, or must, be in order to ensure stakeholder well-being. Organizational actions or behaviors that have the effect of putting stakeholder well-being at risk by damaging or failing to produce and/or maintain capital resources of vital importance to their well-being can be said to be unsustainable; actions which have the opposite effect can be said to be sustainable. Sustainability context therefore ultimately takes the form of specific duties and obligations organizations have to have impacts of one kind or another on vital capitals of importance to stakeholder well-being. These duties are, in the first instance, driven by the relationships organizations have with their stakeholders, and are determined by reference to the following three-part definition (and specification) of context:

1. **Carrying Capacities of Capitals**: First we identify the vital capitals (stocks) and their carrying capacities (flows) an organization is having impact on in ways that can affect stakeholder well-being, as well as capitals it *should* be having impact on in order to *ensure* stakeholder well-being.
2. **Responsible Populations**: Next we determine who the responsible populations are for ensuring the quality and sufficiency of such stocks and flows.
3. **Organizational Allocations**: And last, based on the first and second steps above, we allocate proportionate shares of available stocks and flows (in the case of natural capital) and/or burden shares for producing and/or maintaining them (in the case of anthro capital) to individual organizations.

It is the organizational allocations of limited natural capital and/or shares of the responsibility to produce or maintain anthro capitals, therefore, that constitute the specific non-financial duties and obligations of interest to us in CSM. And all of that, in turn, is grounded in the relationships organizations have with their stakeholders, just as the relationships they have with their shareholders give rise to financial duties and obligations.

In building our argument for context-based sustainability (CBS), we first took steps to call the reader's attention to the history and origins of the idea. In this regard, we claimed that there are actually two, not one, parallel streams of thought that eventually converged in the mid- to late twentieth century to give us the CBS approach to CSM we see before us today. The first stream was a sustainability management one, in which context, as a CSM consideration, was developed and used over time. This stream – what we can think of as the *context* stream – began with Von Carlowitz in 1713, as explained in Chapter 1.

The second stream of thought was the *capital* stream, found mostly in the economics literature. And while it is true that debate in economics over the proper meaning and interpretation of capital had long preceded the start of the twentieth century, it is Irving Fisher's handling of the subject in 1906 (Fisher, 2003[1906]), in particular, that matters most to CBS, since it was Fisher who most clearly made the all important distinction between stocks (of capital) and flows (of income, or beneficial goods and services) in terms that are still relevant today. Capitals are stocks of anything that produce beneficial flows of goods or services of vital importance to human well-being. Sustainability, in turn, is about managing impacts on vital capitals, such that the flows they produce are sufficient for human well-being.

By the mid-1960s, as clearly evidenced in the writings of Kenneth Boulding (1966), the context and capital streams had effectively converged into a distinct and integrated school of thought, according to which sustainability was – and ever since then has been – seen as a function of human impacts on vital capitals as such capitals are required for human well-being. Capital, too, was no longer confined to the economic domain, and was broadly applicable to other areas of importance to sustainability, most notably natural capital.

By 1992 the application of capital theory to sustainability had stabilized to encompass four specific capitals that are still with us today. For that we can thank Paul Ekins, whose *Four-Capital Model of Wealth Creation* (Ekins, 1992) specified (in his words) *environmental capital, human capital, physically produced capital* and *social/organizational capital.* In this book we have referred to the same four capitals (in a slightly different order) as natural capital, human capital, social capital and constructed capital, while pointing out that the last three capitals are anthropogenic or human-made; hence our reference to them collectively as *anthro* capitals.

By pointing to the intellectual history of context in sustainability management as an idea that is demonstrably 300 years old (Von Carlowitz, 1713), it has also been our intent to show that context, or CBS, is by no means a new idea, just a sorely neglected one. And nowhere is this neglect more pronounced than on the organizational or business front, especially when one considers the disproportionately high impact organizations and industry have on vital capitals in the world. Industry (including agriculture) and organizations, for example, account for at least 60 percent of all global GHG emissions, not including emissions from industry-related transport (WRI, 2005, Part 2). Similarly, industry and agriculture account for well over 95 percent of world water use (UN, 2006, p. 279, Fig. 8.3).

In light of these and other impacts businesses have on vital capitals in the world, it seems reasonable to attack the sustainability issue, so to speak, on the business and organizational front as a powerful point of leverage. Gray and Bebbington, for their part, would seem to agree (2005, p. 1):

> It seems incontrovertible that, in the absence of a fundamental change in the political will of governments (especially those of the developed world), any serious examination of sustainability and how it might be achieved must have the corporation at its heart.

We, of course, concur and have dedicated ourselves in this book to the presentation of a comprehensive set of principles and practices for exactly how to do so.

Having established the history and origins of CBS in Chapter 1, we then turned our attention in Chapter 2 to the examination of associated key issues and practice implications. Here we focused first on the question of how CBS should interact with other, better-established management and business processes already in place in most organizations, and how the two can, or should, co-exist. Of particular importance in that vein was the question of whether or not there can be, or is, a business case for CSM, and also the extent to which there should be a hierarchical relationship of some kind between commercial performance strategies and non-financial sustainability programs. On the first point, we took the position that there is always a business case to be made for the fulfillment of duties and obligations to stakeholders, and that just because such duties and obligations are in some cases non-financial is no reason to somehow discount or dismiss them.

On the second point, we took the position that CSM is really nothing more than an expansion of conventional management in its present form, in the sense that conventional management is already stakeholder-driven and capital-based. CSM simply argues that there are more than just *share*holders to take account of and, because of that, more than just monetary capital to contend with. Other than the necessity of making the monistic-to-pluralistic leap (i.e., learning to think and manage in terms of multiple stakeholders and multiple capitals, instead of just one stakeholder and one capital), therefore, non-financial management is very much like financial management in substance and form. Managers, that is, set goals for impacts on vital capitals and then manage their operations accordingly. The CBS approach to CSM simply amounts to following in the footsteps of financial management, which has always been about managing impacts on capital with stakeholder well-being in mind.

We then turned our attention to several other key issues and practice implications in the general category of sustainability measurement and reporting. Here we allowed the composition of contemporary practice and debate in the field to influence our choice of issues, so as to highlight the differences (and advantages) that context-based thinking would bring to CSM. Among our main conclusions were:

- that there is a fundamental and important difference between financial and economic bottom lines, and that the two should not be seen as synonymous;
- that there are as many non-financial bottom lines in an organization as there are discrete duties and obligations to have impacts on non-monetary capitals of vital importance to stakeholder well-being, since each such duty or obligation must be separately fulfilled independently of the others;
- that context-based metrics are nothing more than a special case of relative metrics, with factual and normative context added;
- that sustainability performance maps to a binary scale on which organizations are either sustainable or not, as opposed to a continuous or analog scale on which organizations can be more or less sustainable;

- that the adjective 'sustainable' does not apply to products or other inanimate objects, since such objects cannot be held accountable to duties or obligations. This is not to say, of course, that products cannot contribute to enhancing the sustainability performance of those who use them – indeed they can, and the more such products we have, the better. Rather, it is simply to say that the sustainability performance of a person who uses a product should not be confused with the sustainability performance of the company that produces it, much less with the product itself;
- that context-based sustainability in no way precludes cross-company comparisons of performance and instead actually enables them, since under CBS all companies' sustainability performance can be mapped to a common scale; and
- that there can be formal rules or principles for determining the social sustainability performance of organizations, just as there are for determining their environmental sustainability (i.e., analogous to Daly's rules), since anthro capitals must always be produced and/or maintained at levels required to ensure stakeholder well-being.

We next turned our attention at the end of Chapter 2 to the issue of GRI, and how CBS stacks up against it and vice versa. And while we found that CBS and GRI are philosophically compatible insofar as they both subscribe to the concept of context as a first principle in sustainability measurement, management and reporting, we were fairly critical of GRI's failure to operationalize, much less enforce, the concept in its own guidelines and policies.[1] The result, we think, is that quite possibly no – or at most very few – corporate sustainability reports ever prepared in accordance with GRI have actually included context of a materially relevant kind (i.e., involving performance compared with normative impacts on vital capitals needed to ensure stakeholder well-being), thereby making it impossible for their readers to comprehend the true sustainability performance of the organizations they describe. We ourselves have never seen one that does.

How, then, should organizations measure, manage and report their sustainability performance *in context*? This is the question we took up in Chapter 3, the specific answer to which took the form of a six-step CSM cycle, within which context-based metrics are systematically developed and applied to an organization's own operations. Determining the proper scope of a CSM program, however, must come first, and for that we turned to stakeholders, or more specifically to the relationships organizations have with them and the non-financial duties and obligations involved. Once an organization's non-financial duties and obligations to stakeholders have been identified, metrics for measuring actual performance against them can be developed and deployed. In cases where negative gaps are found, strategies and interventions can be devised to help close them. As earlier pointed out, this is substantially identical to the manner in which financial management has always been done. Thus, the CSM cycle we described is nothing but a tried-and-true methodology applied to a broader set of stakeholders and capitals.

Of further significance in the CSM cycle we described is the manner in which its focus on duties and obligations owed to stakeholders has a very beneficial boundary-setting effect on CSM programs. Indeed, one of the various criticisms sometimes made of CSM is that it goes too far in its reach and is too unreasonable in its expectations; that businesses cannot solve all of the world's problems, nor should they be expected to; and that businesses exist for other reasons, profit-making reasons. On this point we agree, while also taking the position that businesses in fact have stakeholders of *many* kinds, not just shareholders, and that the relationships they have with their stakeholders very often include non-financial duties and obligations that are just as legitimate as the financial ones they have.

We can easily conclude, therefore, that it is a mistake to expect organizations to apply themselves to improving the well-being of constituencies other than their own stakeholders; but it is just as much a mistake to assume that the monetary well-being of shareholders is the only legitimate duty or obligation an organization has – indeed it is not. To the extent that an organization has non-shareholder stakeholders, the fact that they even exist necessarily means that there are other legitimate non-financial duties and obligations that must also be attended to. And it is precisely the scope of such non-financial duties and obligations that should determine the content and boundaries of a CSM program – no more, no less.

Mini-cases of CBS in action

In addition to the case study involving Cabot Creamery highlighted in Chapter 3, we thought it might be useful to provide readers with some additional (and fictitious) examples of how CBS might shake out, so to speak, in several different scenarios. Tables 4.1a and 4.1b have been constructed accordingly, but they are by no means

TABLE 4.1A Mini-cases of CBS in action

Enterprise Type	Stakeholders	Duties and Obligations (Primary Type of Capital Involved)
Hospital	• Patients • Community	• Safeguard patient health (human) • Enforce best practices (social) • Maintain clean facilities (constructed) • Manage solid (medical) waste safely (constructed)
Energy Production Plant	• Customers • Community	• Supply energy (constructed) • Mitigate greenhouse gas emissions (natural)
Airport	• Travelers • Community	• Maintain safe operations (constructed) • Noise abatement (natural)
Candy Store	• Customers	• Ensure product safety (human)
Professional Soccer Club	• Fans • Players	• Provide collective leisure time (social) • Ensure player safety (human)

TABLE 4.1B Mini-cases of CBS in action

Enterprise Type	Stakeholders	Duties and Obligations (Primary Types of Capital Involved)
City Hall	• Tax Payers • Employees	• Provide government services (social) • Maintain safe working conditions (constructed) • Pay fair/livable wage (human)
University	• Students • Faculty	• Deliver quality education (human) • Maintain creative environments (social) • Maintain fair tenure system (human)
Automobile Manufacturer	• Customers • Employees • Community	• Provide transportation solutions (constructed) • Maintain safe working conditions (human) • Use water resources responsibly (natural) • Mitigate greenhouse gas emissions (natural)
Political Party	• Members • Society	• Ensure ethical behavior (social) • Act for social good (social) • Act for environmental good (natural)

comprehensive in scope and are merely intended to be illustrative. In reviewing these examples, certain key points should be borne in mind:

- The stakeholders of an organization will almost always include customers or direct constituents of some kind, as well as employees and communities.
- The fulfillment of specific duties and obligations will very often include not only direct impacts on the vital capitals involved (e.g., a manufacturer's obligation to use water resources responsibly or to mitigate its greenhouse gas emissions – two cases involving impacts on natural capital), but also impacts on other capitals of a less direct kind. In order to use water responsibly, for example, a company needs to invest in building the individual and collective capacity of its employees to manage water use effectively (human and social capital, respectively), and also acquire and maintain whatever equipment and/or technologies may be required to minimize water use or treat wastewater effluents (constructed capital). Thus, the sustainability of a company's impacts on water resources will very likely be a function of its impacts on relevant (and internal) anthro capitals, and not just directly on natural capital itself (i.e., water in this case).
- It will almost always be the case that an organization's sustainability performance in the areas pertaining to its primary business or reason for being will be extraordinarily high or sustainable, assuming its primary business also relates to a duty or obligation owed to a stakeholder group. The per capita duty or obligation for anyone in society to provide a proportionate share of the healthcare services required by a population, for example – if the burden of doing so were spread out that way – would be well below the levels actually being provided by employees in a hospital. Thus, if we were to allocate the burden of producing and maintaining healthcare-related vital capitals to a hospital on that

basis, we would undoubtedly find that the per capita and enterprise-wide performance relative to that allocation or standard of performance would be significantly in excess of levels required to achieve sustainability. On the other hand, the same organizations might be having some other entirely unsustainable effects on, say, the quality or sufficiency of natural capital, in which case their overall performance would be sustainable in one area but unsustainable in another. What's required in the final analysis, of course, is sustainable performance on all fronts, not just the one that happens to correspond to an organization's primary business.

General conclusions

Several important conclusions can be drawn from what we have said in this book, of which some are practical, on the one hand, and some scientific or theoretical, on the other. Our main practical conclusions are as follows:

- Most of what passes for mainstream sustainability measurement, management and reporting is arguably ineffective because of the absence of context in related methodologies. Here a distinction can be made between (1) management efforts that recognize and aim towards falling on the sustainable side of social and environmental thresholds, and (2) management efforts that merely work towards achieving marginal improvements in performance. On the environmental front, for example, we can see that most corporate sustainability efforts are really aimed at improving the efficiency with which resources are used, whether the resulting performance also happens to be sustainable or not. To say, for example, that a company's use of water resources has decreased by 10 percent is not to say that its decreased use of water is sustainable – rather, it is to beg the question.
- Leading standards in use and/or development for sustainability measurement, management and reporting also fail to take context fully into account, and for that reason are ineffective insofar as their stated purpose and goals are concerned (i.e., to facilitate sustainability measurement, management and reporting). There simply can be no genuine or literal sustainability measurement, management or reporting in the absence of context as we have defined it in this book. Because of this, and despite its open advocacy for the inclusion of context in sustainability measurement and reporting, even the Global Reporting Initiative (GRI) fails to achieve its intended goal – to make sustainability measurement and reporting possible. A better name for reports prepared in accordance with GRI might be *Triple Top Line Reporting – Guidelines for Reporting the Marginal Social and Environmental Impacts of a Company.*
- Many other standards and methods frequently used with the intent of performing sustainability analyses – such as life cycle assessments, the Greenhouse Gas Protocol, the AASHE (Association for the Advancement of Sustainability in Higher Education) STARS (Sustainability Tracking Assessment and Rating System) program in the United States[2] and various supplier and/or supply chain scorecards

(e.g., Walmart's)[3] – also suffer from a lack of context and, therefore, like GRI, do not, in any strict sense of the term, address sustainability performance per se. Thus, it may be possible to fully comply with the policies of a standard (such as a call for lower levels of water consumption or mitigated greenhouse gas emissions) and thereby ostensibly show 'positive' patterns of performance, when, in fact, the performance involved is empirically unsustainable. Whenever that is the case, the standards involved should be rejected as *sustainability* standards – indeed they are not. They may be standards of some other kind, perhaps, but they are not sustainability standards.

- It is, in fact, possible to measure, manage and report the sustainability, or non-financial, performance of organizations in an empirically rigorous way, just as it is possible to measure, manage and report their financial performance in like terms. The manner in which this can be done is to measure an organization's impacts on vital capitals relative to levels of what such impacts ought to be in order to be sustainable and ensure stakeholder well-being. And since all of this can be expressed in a quantitative fashion, empirical assessments of the sustainability performance of organizations are now possible, as are cross-organizational comparisons of such performance. In short, it is now possible to fully operationalize the triple bottom line.

- It should be separately stated, perhaps, that because we have found a way to empirically measure, manage and report the sustainability performance of organizations in a context-based fashion, we have at the same time found a way to operationalize GRI's principle of *sustainability context*. To do this, we had to formulate, test and evaluate a measurement model (i.e., context-based metrics). As our case studies involving Cabot Creamery and Ben & Jerry's clearly show, the resulting methodology is practical in form and can be applied at the organizational level with relative ease.

Our main scientific or theoretical conclusions are as follows:

- The concept of sustainability is fundamentally grounded in capital theory, the substance of which is well documented in the economics literature. In the mid- to late twentieth century, key elements of capital theory were formally taken up by leading sustainability theorists – some of whom were economists and are still living today – in order to sharpen and better define the subject (of sustainability). Of particular note in this regard was the concept of *natural capital*, and also the application of capital theory to other forms of vital resources (i.e., *human capital*, *social capital* and *constructed*, or *built*, *capital*). In recent years, the literature on these various forms of capital has become broad and deep, and is the subject of much scientific research, testing and evaluation, not to mention Nobel prize awards in economics: Gary Becker in 1992 (human capital) and Elinor Ostrom in 2009 (social capital).

  So fundamental was, and is, capital theory to the concept of sustainability that we find no other competing or alternative theoretical bases or foundations to the subject that are logically consistent (i.e., which, if applied, do not result in, or tolerate, unsustainable behaviors in the plain or empirical sense of the term). Eco-efficiency doctrines, for example, that treat marginal improvements in environmental impacts as sustainable, or *more sustainable*, do not preclude the possibility of natural resource depletion and widespread human suffering; instead, they merely slow things down.

- The capital basis of sustainability theory and practice is also tightly coupled to the concept of human well-being. Human well-being, that is, is utterly contingent upon the availability of vital capitals in the world, the quality and sufficiency of which must be maintained in order to ensure it. And while it is true that there are competing points of view on what constitutes an adequate level of human well-being, how to define it, and how to measure it, such disagreements do not change the fact that human well-being, however it is defined and measured, is at least in part dependent upon the availability of critical resources in the world at some level (e.g., environmental resources, knowledge, social structures and the world of human-made material things). The fact that there may be disagreements over how to define and measure human well-being does not undermine the validity of the capital/well-being thesis put forward on these pages; instead it simply tells us that there is more work to be done in terms of developing human well-being theory, or in choosing one or more variants of that theory for application in CSM. Nonetheless, we think we have succeeded in providing a rendition of CBS that is theoretically compatible with *all* forms of human well-being theory, no matter what their differences might be.

- Of additional importance to CBS is recognition of the fact that capitals vary in terms of their origins insofar as whether or not they are anthropogenic. Natural capital, of course, is not human made; human, social and constructed capitals, however, are. This has major implications when it comes to measuring the sustainability performance of organizations, since in some cases (i.e., cases involving impacts on natural capital) sustainability is a function of not exceeding normative levels of natural resource use, while in others (i.e., cases involving impacts on human, social and constructed capitals) sustainability is a function of not failing to produce and/or maintain such capitals, again at normative levels.

- The application of CBS to the organizational level of analysis has not been without its challenges. Since organizations are only individual actors in a world that is otherwise full of many such actors, the greatest challenge has been how to set organization-level standards of performance against which actual impacts on vital capitals can be measured in a way that is fair and proportionate. Thus, the first move, as we have explained, was to determine that sustainability is a function of impacts on vital capitals; this we learned from the economics literature in the twentieth century, and the manner in which capital theory has been applied to the sustainability domain by early theorists in the field.

The solution for how best to allocate levels of responsibility for preserving, producing and/or maintaining vital capitals to individual organizations, however, was found in another, entirely different body of thought: epistemology. There – and in particular in the literature of ethics, morality and value theory – can be found a basis for determining the duties and obligations owed by individual actors to do anything, including to have impact on vital capitals in the world. Of most importance in this regard was Immanuel Kant's development of the *categorical imperative* (CI) in 1785 (Kant, 1785), which we alluded to in Chapter 3 as the *what if everybody did it* principle of establishing sustainability standards of performance. In Kant's (translated) words, the CI reads as follows (Kant, 1785, p. 46):

> There is therefore but one categorical imperative, namely, this: Act only on that maxim whereby thou canst at the same time will that it should become a universal law.

In other words, the correct moral course of action is the one which, if everybody did it, would lead to a fair, just and equitable world – or to a sustainable world, in the case of our subject. Others in the sustainability arena have also relied upon the CI, or at least the same basic idea, as a basis for making their own arguments, including Daly (1996) who wrote as follows (p. 106):

> [A]n overdeveloped country might be defined as one whose level of per capita resource consumption is such that if generalized to all countries [i.e., as a *maxim*, to use Kant's term] could not be sustained indefinitely; correspondingly an underdeveloped country would be one whose per capita resource consumption is less than what could be sustained indefinitely if all the world consumed at that level [or, in other words, *if everybody did it*].

The *Ecological Footprint*, too, is arguably predicated upon the same *what if everybody did it* ethic to the extent that it measures and reports national impacts on natural capital in terms that are generalized to the world as a way of determining whether or not such impacts are sustainable, and, if not, by how much. From this perspective, we can say that sustainability is the subject of a social science that studies, and strives to manage, human impacts on vital capitals relative to norms or standards for what such impacts ought to be in order to ensure human well-being.

At the end of the day, then, sustainability is fundamentally a normative affair aimed at ensuring human well-being, the basis of which is capital theory and propositions for what our impacts on related resources *ought to be* in order to achieve a *valued* end. Statements about *oughts* and *values* are creatures of value theory, and value theory is a branch of epistemology. This is why in our CBS scheme of things, value claims, or standards of performance, play such an important role. Indeed, it is precisely why the denominators in our sustainability quotients exist, since without them (such standards, that is) meaningful sustainability measurement, management and reporting could not be done.

- We have also taken the position that insofar as standards of performance are concerned as a basis for measuring, managing and reporting sustainability, there is no need for consensus, much less certainty, about any of that in order for related efforts to be meaningful. Here again one can find a long tradition, or at least a debate, in epistemology about the role of consensus in the production of knowledge claims, including the view that consensus is no guarantor of truth and in fact can mask it. If consensus exists relative to the volume of water individual organizations should be permitted to use, for example, or the greenhouse gases they should be permitted to emit, or the livable wages they should be expected to pay, can we be certain in such cases that the consensus view is necessarily correct? In other words, can claims that we make be justified purely by virtue of the consensus or unanimity that stands behind them? We think not.

Justification, or truth by consensus, therefore, is a red herring in business, just as it is in science, since consensus is no guarantor of truth. Thus, every organization should feel entirely free to formulate its own claims about what its social and environmental impacts in the world ought to be in order to ensure stakeholder well-being, and to move ahead with and act upon them as it sees fit, so long as it holds itself – and its claims – open to criticism, and, yes, change. And if we can say, then, that there are competing points of view between and across organizations as to what their standards of performance should be in order to achieve sustainability, then let the competing ideas compete. It is precisely such competition over time that results in the production of new or better knowledge, including – for those who care about such things – knowledge that may, in fact, be accompanied by a consensus.

- In addition to relying on well-established concepts in economics (capital theory) and epistemology (value theory) for our thesis, we have also turned to another source for determining what the boundaries or constraints of a CSM program should be: stakeholder theory. Here again, we find that the literature and science involved are extensive, and that much has come before us in terms of the ideas we are using here. Based largely on the work of Freeman et al., we have defined stakeholders as follows:

> A stakeholder in an organization is anyone whose vital capitals – and whose interests and well-being, therefore – are affected by the organization's actions, or whose vital capitals ought to be so affected by virtue of the relationship that exists between them.

Stakeholder theory, for us, provides a ready-made solution for what may be described as the *boundary problem* in CSM. The boundary problem in CSM is the problem of determining how far to go in terms of addressing the world's social, environmental and economic problems when formulating the content of a CSM program. As Porter and Kramer put it (2006, p. 92): 'Corporations are not responsible for all the world's problems, nor do they have the resources to solve them all.' For Porter and Kramer, then, the solution to the boundary problem in CSM is to define the scope of a CSM program opportunistically, such that only initiatives that also happen to benefit the organization in some instrumental way are included. We disagree.

Our problem with the solution proposed by Porter and Kramer is that it is not stakeholder-driven, and because of that fails to address the interests of stakeholders in any sort of intentional or comprehensive way. Thus, it leaves open the question of whether or not a company has taken steps to manage its impacts on vital capitals of importance to its stakeholders, and whether or not, therefore, a company has fulfilled its non-financial duties and obligations to them, which is what CSM is arguably all about.

Stakeholder theory, by contrast, provides us with the solution we need not only to properly address the legitimate interests of stakeholders, but also to put boundaries around the content of CSM programs in a logical, responsible and systematic way (i.e., to determine materiality). At the same time, it in no way imposes extraneous or supererogatory duties or obligations on organizations that were not already there before (i.e., there as a consequence of stakeholder relationships that may already exist). CSM simply helps to reveal them in ways that enhance an organization's ability to effectively act upon them in response – or at least the *CBS approach* to CSM does.

- Of additional importance in our research and development is our conclusion that although our own particular focus has mainly been on the application of our ideas to organizations per se, the same principles, methods and metrics are just as applicable to human social systems or collectives of other kinds (e.g., professional networks, communities, regions, nations and humanity at large). Thus, measuring, managing, reporting and improving sustainability in the conduct of human affairs at any level of analysis arguably boils down to – if not *requires* – application of the same context-based *CSM cycle* methodology we described in Chapter 3, as well as the kind of context-based metrics also described therein. Indeed, we are quite convinced that sustainability at any scale must be context-based in order to be effective, and that the kind of context-based approach we have articulated for organizational use can also serve as a model for what must be done at any other level of analysis if progress in the general sustainability of human activity on Earth is to be achieved.

Looking ahead

In this final section of Chapter 4, we turn our attention to the future of CBS – where it goes from here, and what the obstacles might be to its success. All told, there are five key issues to contend with, each of which requires further research, development and practical application before we can expect CSM to fully mature, much less evolve into the context-based form we have described here. The five issues we have in mind are: standards, accounting, assurance, organizations and the capital markets. Our discussion in that order follows below.

- The first question to consider when contemplating the future of CBS is: *will there ever be a formal standard for sustainability measurement and reporting that is context-based? And if not, why not?* As we have tried to show in the first three chapters of this book, the necessity of including context in related efforts is already advocated by many, including the leading sustainability standard in the world (GRI), even as the frequent absence of context is widely lamented by others. The contradiction here is palpable and simply cannot continue without putting the credibility of the standards-making bodies at risk – not to mention the viability of our leading economies, whose impacts on vital capitals in the world are still not being properly taken account of. Listen again to how Gray and Bebbington put it (2007, pp. 386–87):

> Within those reports identified as 'sustainability reports' … even those that are 'in conformance with' the *Global Reporting Initiative Sustainability Reporting Guidelines* provide only the most superficial data on the extent of the organization's sustainability or otherwise. Indeed, sustainability is much more likely to be entirely ignored; it is rare to see any corporation address it all. No reasonable person could make any sensible judgement on the basis of an organization's reporting in their 'Sustainability Reports' on whether or not the organization was [sustainable or] un-sustainable.

In our view, it is incumbent upon GRI, having declared the importance of context to sustainability measurement and reporting many years ago, to follow through with an actual implementation of the idea, be it completely consistent with our own or not.

In order to be credible, though, the implementation of context in measurement and reporting must be reflective of the role vital capitals play as critical resources for human well-being, as well as the impacts organizations can, do and should have upon them. In order to be credible, then, any context-based approach to CSM must address three things at a minimum: (1) the identification of organizational stakeholders, (2) duties and obligations owed to stakeholders to have impacts on vital capitals of importance to their well-being, and (3) organizational allocations of such duties that can be generalized to the population as a whole, without unfairly or disproportionately favoring individual organizations, much less putting the sufficiency of vital capitals at risk.

We also find it useful to distinguish between standards of four different kinds in sustainability: (1) measurement and reporting, (2) management, (3) performance and (4) assurance. GRI, for example, is primarily a measurement and reporting standard, not a management or performance one. It is not a management standard because it does not specify standards for managing sustainability (e.g., programs or policies that should be in place, or specific methodologies for managing sustainability performance). It is not a performance standard either, because it does not specify target levels of sustainability performance that should be achieved and/or maintained. Instead, with respect to management and performance, it simply specifies measurement and reporting guidelines for how to measure and report them, although not in a context-based fashion, as we have already discussed at length. (GRI's treatment of assurance, and assurance standards in general, will be further discussed below.)

Interestingly, other standards, such as ULE ISR 880, constitute a mix of measurement and reporting, management and performance guidelines, since, in addition to including metrics and standards for measurement and reporting, they include standards for management polices and programs that should be in place, and also standards for performance or outcomes. The ULE ISR 880 standard, for example, requires that year-over-year reductions in water use and greenhouse gas emissions be achieved, which clearly goes beyond measurement, reporting and management and crosses over into performance.

Here it should be clear that standards for sustainability in the future can, and will, comprise a mixture of measurement and reporting, management and performance types, and that the principle of context can, and should, be applied to all three. What this means, then, is that not only measurement and reporting standards, such as GRI, should be context-based in their orientation, so should standards related to management and performance.

This is not to say that management and performance standards should necessarily be too prescriptive in terms of what management methods should consist of, or what the outcomes should be; rather, they should simply require that management be oriented to CBS in ways that make it possible to manage and measure impacts on vital capitals of importance to stakeholder well-being, and that performance be similarly conceived, such that performance standards are expressed in terms of actual impacts on the carrying capacities of vital capitals relative to levels required to ensure stakeholder well-being.

Here one could say that *if you're not managing, or setting targets for, performance relative to impacts on vital capitals, as such capitals are required to ensure stakeholder well-being, you're not managing, much less talking about, sustainability performance at all.*

- While standards are certainly important, they should be reflective of the most appropriate or useful way of doing things. That, in a sense, is a matter that should precede the development of standards, not the reverse. Here we can raise the question of whether or not *sustainability accounting* as a management discipline has been sufficiently defined, much less standardized, and whether or not formal standards for measuring and reporting sustainability performance, therefore, are appropriate at this time.

In our view, deep divisions currently exist within the field of sustainability accounting, if only between those who feel that context-free measurement and reporting is acceptable and those who don't – in the latter of which we ourselves are included. This, to our way of thinking, is an untenable situation and amounts to a crisis in CSM, for how can standards for measurement and reporting exist if the underlying accounting principles on which they supposedly sit are the subject of such fundamental disagreement and controversy? And if all of that were not enough, we also have a situation where the leading measurement and reporting standard in the world (GRI) effectively straddles the fence on the issue (of context) by strongly advocating for its treatment on the one hand, while failing to define and enforce it on the other, thereby taking a perfectly ambiguous stand on the subject.[4]

Assuming standards for sustainability measurement and reporting – not to mention management, performance and assurance – must be predicated on some common understanding of how to account for sustainability performance in the first place, the resolution of the divisions we speak of and the establishment of what could be thought of as *GAAP for non-financial accounting* should be accorded the highest level of priority on the CSM agenda. What the world desperately needs, perhaps, is a kind of *Manhattan Project* for sustainability accounting, the results of which can be used as a basis for mainstream measurement/reporting, management, performance and assurance, instead of the other way around or instead of no standards for accounting at all, as if we didn't need them – *which we do.*

That all said, many efforts to develop so-called sustainability accounting methods have been in progress for years, as the literature clearly shows.[5] One particular survey of the (sustainability accounting) literature (Thomson, 2007), for example, identified more than seven hundred articles on the subject dating back to the early 1970s. Still, we know of no specific attempts – other than our own – to formulate a context-based approach to sustainability accounting at the organizational level (i.e., in which organization-specific duties and obligations are defined) that are expressed in terms of impacts on the carrying capacities of vital capitals, as such capitals may be required to ensure stakeholder well-being. Instead, what we tend to see more often are measurement methods that focus only on marginal impacts, or other methods that set out to somehow monetize the social and/or environmental performance of organizations.

This latter approach to sustainability accounting (the monetization approach) strikes us as deeply misguided, since it (a) constitutes a mixing of impacts on vital capitals in cases where such impacts, and capitals, are in fact not substitutable for one another or commensurable in that regard, (b) fails to take the carrying capacities of vital capitals explicitly into account, and (c) fails to measure impacts on natural and anthro capitals relative to allocations of resources or burden shares to produce and/or maintain them to specific organizations. What does the theoretical monetary cost of unwanted impacts on water resources, for example, have to do with their environmental or empirical sustainability? If the organizations responsible for such impacts account for them in some monetary way in their financial statements, are they somehow absolved of the impacts they're having? Do their environmentally unsustainable impacts somehow become any less unsustainable? We don't think so, nor do we think sustainability accounting should have anything to do with monetization.

Indeed, sustainability performance is *non-financial* performance, and for that reason shouldn't be expressed in terms of financial units of measurement. What's required, instead, are *carrying capacity* units of measurement, which, as we indicated earlier, are best expressed in terms of the number of humans and/or human transactions that can be supported by the flows of vital capitals. *That*, then, is where we think sustainability accounting needs to go; and *that* is where we ourselves are attempting to take it.

- Above we claimed that there are four main areas of standards, including measurement and reporting, management and performance. The fourth area, assurance, differs from the other three in that it is not as directly applicable to organizations and CSM as it is to *third-party evaluators and evaluations* of CSM. Still, the assurance of corporate sustainability reports is a key issue in CSM and is no less relevant to the CBS agenda, insofar as it is connected to sustainability measurement/reporting, management and performance. All of these aspects of CSM programs are potentially scrutinized and judged by assurance functions, and so assurance must be sensitized to, if not fundamentally grounded in, CBS as well.

Standards and methodologies for assurance, however, are just as logically downstream from the science of sustainability accounting as standards in the other three areas discussed above are. It is for that reason, perhaps, that standards and methodologies for the performance of assurance engagements are just as fragmented and unsettled at this time as standards in the other three areas are. How can we have a standard for assuring sustainability reports when a standard for sustainability accounting itself does not yet exist? Still, consistency in at least some areas of enormous importance to CBS is starting to appear, most notably in the areas of materiality and stakeholder considerations in some leading assurance standards. Two divergent orientations to assurance, however, can be seen, as Owen (2007, pp. 172, 173 and 175) explains:

> [E]xtant guidelines for providing assurance for corporate sustainability reports fall into two distinct categories. Firstly, we have the somewhat cautious 'accountancy'-based approach of FEE[6] and the GRI[7] which is largely concerned with attesting to the accuracy of published data, rather than the relevance of such data for external stakeholder groups …
>
> The contrasting approach adopted by assurance providers applying the AA1000 Assurance Standard[8] … [is more concerned with] core issues of completeness, materiality and responsiveness viewed from a stakeholder perspective …
>
> The evaluative approach adopted here can certainly be argued to 'add value' from the perspective of external stakeholder groups in terms of imparting a far fuller appreciation of the strengths and weaknesses of the sustainability performance of the reporting organization.

Clearly, the latter, stakeholder-oriented approach to assurance is more compatible with CBS. The AA1000AS (AccountAbility, 2008b) standard, in particular, is of great interest to us. That said, we do not think it, or any other assurance standard, yet goes far enough in terms of the treatment of stakeholder interests, since it fails to take impacts on vital capitals specifically into account. A corporate report that commits the same mistake could still, therefore, be subjected to an AA1000AS review and fare relatively well, even though it might tell us nothing about the actual sustainability performance of the organization in those terms, thanks to its lack of context. Here it may be helpful to examine exactly how AA1000AS handles sustainability performance more closely, in order to see where problems can occur. In the parlance of AA1000AS, the more thorough forms of assurance efforts are known as Type 2 engagements. AA1000AS defines Type 2 engagements as follows (AccountAbility, 2008b, pp. 9–10):

> Type 2 – Accountability Principles and Performance Information
> The assurance provider shall evaluate the nature and extent of the organization's adherence to the AA1000 Accountancy Principles, as for Type 1. When conducting a Type 2 engagement, the assurance provider shall also evaluate the reliability of specified sustainability performance information. Specified sustainability performance information is the information the assurance provider and the reporting organization agree to include in the scope of the assurance engagement. Specified information is selected based on the materiality determination and needs to be meaningful to the intended users of the assurance statement. An assurance engagement that only includes an evaluation of the reliability of specified publicly disclosed sustainability performance information is not in accordance with the AA1000AS.

Materiality, according to the *AA1000 Accountability Principles Standard* (AccountAbility, 2008a, p. 12), is, in turn, defined as follows:

> Materiality is determining the relevance and significance of an issue to an organization and its stakeholders.
> A material issue is an issue that will influence the decisions, actions and performance of an organization or its stakeholders.

And finally, 'sustainability performance information' is defined in the AA1000AS standard as follows (AccountAbility, 2008b, p. 24):

> Performance statements or data about sustainability issues or processes that have been included in the scope of a Type 2 assurance engagement.

The first thing to notice about all this, as we have already noted, is that AA1000AS is deeply committed, like us, to a stakeholder-centric orientation to the subject – so far, so good. Next is that the standard defines sustainability performance a bit differently than we do. In our three-category perspective on standards briefly described above, performance pertains to actual impacts in the world, or sustainability outcomes, if you like. For AA1000AS, by contrast, performance is about 'statements or data about sustainability issues or processes'. From our perspective, this points to the management of performance – as in the policies and actions an organization takes with certain intended outcomes in mind – as opposed to sustainability performance (or outcomes) itself (themselves). In other words, management is upstream of performance, and performance is downstream of management.

Nonetheless, we can still hold management accountable to a CBS standard of *management performance*, if you like, or to a standard of management that is itself context-based. Nowhere in the AA1000AS materials, however, are context, capitals or their carrying capacities mentioned. Instead, the indication from the excerpts above is that all that is required for an organization to fare well on a Type 2 AA1000AS review, insofar as the issue of performance disclosure is concerned, is for the reporting organization and the assurance provider to have agreed beforehand on the information to be included in the scope of the assurance engagement, *even if that information has nothing to do with the carrying capacities of vital capitals, or the related allocations of duties and obligations organizations have to have impact on them in order to ensure stakeholder well-being.*

Here it should be clear, once again, that just as we saw in the case of measurement/reporting, management and performance standards, assurance standards suffer from the shortcomings of sustainability accounting in the sense that context is missing from their scope. But this stands to reason, doesn't it? If there is no need to address context in sustainability accounting, why should there be any need to address it in sustainability measurement and reporting, management, performance or assurance? To the extent that it is missing from sustainability accounting at all, it will necessarily be missing from everything else, since everything else is logically downstream of sustainability accounting and is, therefore, largely determined by it.

Our conclusions? Just as we have been heartened by the explicit mention of context in GRI, so are we heartened by the commitment to stakeholders in the AS1000AS standard and the supporting documentation. There is a glimmer of hope for CBS on both fronts. Both standards, however, still need to take the next steps in the direction of CBS, by (a) operationalizing the *sustainability context* principle, in the case of GRI, according to the criteria we have suggested above, and (b) including in assurance engagements, in the case of AA1000AS (or other assurance standards), a requirement that sustainability reports include evidence of their producers having actually engaged in sustainability management, measurement and reporting (i.e., CBS), as opposed to some pseudo form of it. Assurance standards for CSM measurement and reporting have made impressive gains over the years, but they still have some way to go before genuine sustainability reporting is being assured in any sort of rigorous, literal or meaningful way. CBS can help them get there.

- Of central importance to our look ahead, of course, is the organizational setting, which is where most of what we have had to say in this book applies. It should go without saying, then, that where we think organizations need to go in terms of their CSM programs is in the direction of context, or CBS. No need to repeat what we have already said about that here.

We do have some additional thoughts to offer, however, on the sequence and pace at which CBS should enter into the enterprise domain. Given the magnitude of the differences between conventional CSM and the context-based approach we have described, it would be too much to ask, we think, that organizations summarily put the old methods aside in favor of the new ones in one fell swoop – all of a sudden, as it were. Instead, a period of transition is needed. That transition, we think, should be tailored to each organization individually, although the steps involved can be the same.

What we have in mind, then, is a simple two-step progression. The first step can be a transition step, in which CBS is applied in a purely experimental way, in a testing, evaluation and development mode, in parallel with the continued practice of conventional CSM. The second step is the conversion step, in which CBS is more fully deployed on a production basis, if you like, and the older, more conventional methods are discarded.

Under this approach, actual sustainability performance can be of little or no concern in the first step – old or pre-existing performance is grandfathered, no matter what it is. More important is the fact that the CSM function is applying a context-based approach to some degree, if only in the form of a small pilot. Over time, the scope of pilots can be expanded until the organization is ready to take the final plunge. For some organizations, this will take months, for others it will be years. Either way, the most important thing is that initial steps be taken by all organizations, and that the methodology we described in Chapter 3 be learned and implemented, if only on a limited or experimental basis. This will allow CSM practitioners to gain some much-needed, hands-on experience in the practice of CBS, and to see, too, how well it performs in revealing the sustainability performance of their organizations and in enhancing their ability to manage it. At the same time, it will make it possible to at least begin the process of base-lining organizational performance for future reference, a step that is just as important to the CBS approach as it is to the conventional one.

- Turning finally to the capital markets – the final frontier, if you will, and perhaps the most challenging one to crack – we begin by acknowledging the growing interest in (and market response to) investment opportunities in companies whose performance is sustainable, or at least *less unsustainable* than that of their peers. This trend was reported by the Social Investment Forum in its *2010 Report on Socially Responsible Investing Trends in the United States* as follows (2010, p. 8):

> Sustainable and socially responsible investing (SRI) in the United States has continued to grow at a faster pace than the broader universe of conventional investment assets under professional management. At the start of 2010, professionally managed assets following SRI strategies stood at $3.07 trillion, a rise of more than 380 percent from $639 billion in 1995, the year of the Social Investment Forum Foundation's first Trends Report. Over the same period, the broader universe of assets under professional management increased only 260 percent from $7 trillion to $25.2 trillion. During the most recent financial crisis, from 2007 to 2010, the overall universe of professionally managed assets has remained roughly flat while SRI assets, as documented in this report, have enjoyed healthy growth.

The report goes on to explain that 'nearly one out of every eight dollars under professional management in the United States today – 12.2 percent of the $25.2 trillion in total assets under management tracked by Thomson Reuters Nelson – is involved in some strategy of socially responsible investing' (p. 8).

Despite these impressive figures, not one of the dozens (if not hundreds) of socially responsible investment funds, rating systems or indexes found in the capital markets today is context-based.[9] None of them, therefore, actually succeed in achieving their stated goals – when expressed in terms of sustainability performance, that is – which is to somehow report, indicate, rate and/or rank the sustainability performance of publicly-traded companies. Indeed, since most organizations do not themselves measure, manage or report their sustainability performance in a context-based fashion, how could they?

Two things come quickly to mind here. First is that it is, in fact, possible to create an index, or ranking, of the sustainability performance of publicly-traded companies from the sidelines, as it were, without having to rely on such companies to measure and report their performance in context-based terms themselves. This can be done by using context-free data that organizations very often *do* report (e.g., in their GRI reports or what have you) and by adding context to it, the substance of which can be obtained from other sources (e.g., water resource data, poverty levels, etc., as such data may be tracked and reported by government agencies, NGOs or others).

In the language of context-based metrics described in Chapter 3, company data published in such cases can be used to populate *numerators*, while contextual information from other sources can be used to populate *denominators*. A limited set of context-based indicators can then be used to profile the true sustainability performance of publicly-traded companies, albeit with greater levels of effort being required to do so in some cases. An experimental prototype of exactly that kind of context-based index (i.e., one created for application in the capital markets by analysts on the sidelines, so to speak) is currently in development. Known as the True Sustainability Index®[10] the model being developed, if successful, will make it possible to rate and rank publicly-traded assets according to the *true* or context-based sustainability performance of the companies involved.

Our second thought regarding the absence of context-based metrics and indexes in the capital markets is that, apart from indexes per se, whole trading exchanges predicated on the importance of context-based measurement, management and reporting are beginning to appear. One new stock exchange in particular, the Bright Exchange®[11] in the Netherlands, is taking steps to explicitly embrace context-based sustainability by only listing companies and projects that have at least started to use CBS methods on a pilot or experimental basis to some degree. This is consistent with the two-step approach to implementation of CBS at the organizational level discussed above and would provide investors – including impact investors – with unprecedented assurance that the companies whose shares they are buying are at least practicing CBS to some degree, and are thereby making genuine sustainability measurement, management and reporting possible.

In time, such practices will also make sustainability *performance* in the positive sense possible within their own operations. That, at least, is our hope.

It may also be useful to point out here again – this time in the context of capital markets instead of the organizational context, per se – that the same lengthier planning horizons that make sense at the organizational level for purposes of managing sustainability performance also make sense at the *capital market* level of analysis. Sustainability performance, that is, is a multi-year phenomenon, not a monthly or quarterly one. Non-financial capitals simply do not respond as readily or as quickly to management interventions as financial or monetary capitals do. Sustainability performance measurement, rating and ranking systems in use in the capital markets should be oriented accordingly.

Similarly, it should be clear that just as non-financial management has taken – or at least *can* take, under our method – a page out of the financial management playbook and measures, manages and reports performance in terms of impacts on capitals relative to levels of such capitals required for stakeholder well-being, so the same thing can be done in the capital markets, too. In other words, just as the capital markets interpret and assess financial performance in terms of impacts on capital (monetary capital) with stakeholder (shareholder) well-being in mind, so, too, can they interpret and assess non-financial performance in terms of impacts on other *non*-monetary capitals and with other *non*-shareholder stakeholders in mind. So far as we know, no capital market on Earth does this, and yet the need for it is acute.

Some closing words

As enthusiastic as we are about the approach to CSM put forward in these pages, we hold no illusions as to how quickly, or even if, it will be taken up by business on a widespread basis in the years ahead. Management in most organizations tends to focus only on what they have to do in order to (a) maximize profits – in the case of commercial organizations (nothing wrong with that, of course) – and (b) comply with regulations (nothing wrong with that either). Indeed, as earlier noted, sustainability measurement and reporting, be it context-based or not, is simply not yet required in most countries in the world. Doing it at all, therefore, is a largely voluntary thing. Why, then, should any company adopt CBS?

First, as we have already explained at length, a company should adopt CSM, be it context-based or not, because of the duties and obligations it has to non-shareholder stakeholders. Unless a company can show that it has no other stakeholders than shareholders, it clearly has non-financial duties and obligations to other parties that must be attended to. At the very least, its failure to take them seriously generates risk, and risk is bad for business. Indeed, depending on the severity of the neglect, stakeholders might simply not stand for it, and bad things can happen in such cases.

Second, once a company has come to understand that CSM is logically entailed in the very existence of stakeholder relationships, a fork in the road suddenly appears: to take the context-based route or not? It should be clear from what we have said in this book that if a company is serious about measuring, managing and reporting its sustainability performance, it must take the CBS path. Why? Because to take a context-free path while still cloaking itself in the language and accoutrements of sustainability is to take an intellectually dishonest path, which again stakeholders may not accept, thereby leading to more risk.

Finally, there is a clear and compelling first-mover advantage to be gained by embracing not only CSM but the CBS approach to it, since CBS is arguably the most genuine, effective and powerful approach for measuring, managing and reporting the sustainability performance of an organization. Context is so fundamental to the process, true or authentic CSM cannot be done without it. Organizations that take the high road, as it were, while calling attention to the commitment they've made to real sustainability, are entitled to some serious bragging rights for having done so, the availability of which can bestow a competitive advantage on them, especially in cases where the pressures to improve the social and/or environmental performance of an organization (or industry) are truly challenging and already a factor of competition.

What's more, beyond receiving the credit due for having adopted CBS, and the reputational and competitive advantages that come with it, organizations that decide to take a context-based approach to CSM are much more likely to actually achieve sustainability in their operations. Imagine a company whose sustainability performance is, in fact, positive on all social, environmental and economic fronts, and whose reputation, costs and risk profile have been optimized because of it. Now ask yourself if it would have been possible for that company to have achieved such performance – much less measure and report it – without the aid of context-based tools and methods. We don't think so.

Positive sustainability performance, that is, cannot be achieved, much less maintained, without the use of context-based frameworks; nor can businesses, or the modern economy as a whole, carry on in the years ahead unless they are sustainable – truly so, in a literal sense. What businesses desperately need, therefore, is a context-based solution to CSM, and CBS is here to provide it. By all means use it!

Notes

1. See note 3 in Chapter 1.
2. More information about AASHE (Association for the Advancement of Sustainability in Higher Education) and its STARS (Sustainability Tracking Assessment and Rating System) program can be found here: http://www.aashe.org/.
3. See, for example, Walmart's Supplier Sustainability Assessment/Index, which is context-free: http://walmartstores.com/Sustainability/9292.aspx.
4. See note 3 in Chapter 1.
5. See, for example, the Centre for Social and Environmental Accounting at the University of St. Andrews in Scotland: http://www.st-andrews.ac.uk/~csearweb/index.html, and also Unerman et al.'s (2007) account of the subject. See also the journals *Accounting for the Environment* and *Social and Environmental Accounting* for related research and development.
6. More information about the FEE (Federation of European Accountants) and its perspectives on assurance of sustainability reports can be found here: http://www.fee.be/.

7. Although GRI is primarily a standard for measuring and reporting sustainability performance, it also includes some guidelines for external assurance.
8. More information about the AA1000 Assurance Standard and other related standards can be found here: http://www.accountability.org/.
9. See, for example, the Dow Jones Sustainability Indexes[SM] described here: http://www.djindexes.com/sustainability/, and also the FTSE4Good Index Series described here: http://www.ftse.com/Indices/FTSE4Good_Index_Series/index.jsp.
10. More information about the True Sustainability Index[®] can be found by visiting the Center for Sustainable Organizations' website at: www.sustainableorganizations.org.
11. More information about the Bright Exchange[®] can be found here: http://www.bright-exchange.com/.

Appendix A
CABOT CREAMERY COOPERATIVE'S APPROACH TO SUSTAINABILITY

Cabot's approach to sustainability is systematic, disciplined and pragmatic.

We start with a careful review of how sustainability should be defined and then address how it should be implemented. We have chosen a branch of sustainability practice known as *context-based sustainability*, and the remainder of this report is an explanation of what that is and how we are applying it at Cabot.

Context and capitals – the basis of our approach

'Context' and the role it plays in sustainability measurement, management and reporting are at the core of Cabot's approach to sustainability. Here's what *we* mean by context in our formulation of sustainability.

Context for Cabot means:

- Sustainability performance is based on Cabot's specific environment, not on broadly defined standards meant to cover a wide range of organizations. One size does not fit all, and our approach is customized to our circumstances.
- The key to sustainability reporting is to measure how Cabot affects economic, environmental and social conditions as required for stakeholder well-being.
- Simply reporting on trends in performance such as lower water usage or fewer miles traveled is insufficient. We need to know whether or not we are meeting specifically defined standards.
- Stakeholders are considered in all facets of our business, and the term is defined later.

Sustainability reporting is often referred to as *non-financial reporting* and is divided into three primary areas. These three areas of performance are called the 'triple bottom line':

- economic performance
- environmental performance
- social performance.

Note that 'economic performance' does not refer to Cabot's financial health. It refers instead to Cabot's broader economic impact on and benefit to the economy where we operate.

For this approach to work, we must first establish standards of performance and then measure actual performance against them in each of these three areas. We must be able to definitively say whether or not our activities and impacts are sustainable. To do this, we need to determine what Cabot's impacts on economic, environmental and social conditions ought to be in order for them to be sustainable.

So, what kind of economic, environmental and social impacts are we talking about, and how do we know if they are sustainable? This question is at the very heart of context-based sustainability.

The conditions most important to sustainability measurement and reporting are known as *vital capitals*. These are resources that people rely on for their well-being. As it turns out, there is already a long tradition in the sustainability field addressing *natural capital* in particular.

Natural capital

Natural capital is defined as natural resources and ecosystem services that are vitally important to human well-being. Any impact on natural capital that diminishes its quality or sufficiency below levels required to ensure human well-being is unsustainable. Sustainability management at Cabot therefore focuses on controlling, measuring and reporting our impact on natural capital so that we don't reduce resources below levels required to ensure stakeholder well-being.

Establishing the quality and sufficiency of natural capital is the first step in assessing Cabot's sustainability performance. We then need to extend the vital capital concept into the economic and social arenas as well.

In addition to natural capital, there are three other forms of vital capital that social scientists have long recognized as critical to human well-being.

Human capital: Human capital consists of *individual* knowledge, skills, experience, health and ethical entitlements that enhance the potential for effective individual action and human well-being.

Social capital: Social capital consists of *shared* knowledge and organizational resources (e.g., networks of people committed to achieving common goals) that enhance the potential for effective individual and collective action and human well-being.

Constructed capital: Constructed capital consists of *material objects and physical systems or infrastructure* created by humans for human benefit and use. It is the material world of human artifacts.

These forms of capital are much like natural capital in that they produce goods and services required for human well-being; they differ from natural capital in that they are exclusively human-made. In other words, they are anthropogenic, so we refer to them as *anthro* capital.

Taken as a whole, Cabot's sustainability program can be seen as an attempt to manage our impacts on vital capitals relative to specific standards of performance grounded in human well-being. When added to financial management, each of the resulting four bottom lines (i.e., social, economic, environmental and financial) can be tied to at least one form of vital capital as shown in Figure A.1. This is the capital-based theory of sustainability, the technical centerpiece of context-based sustainability.

	Social Bottom Line	Economic Bottom Line	Environmental Bottom Line	Financial Bottom Line
Natural Capital			✓	
Human Capital	✓	✓		
Social Capital	✓	✓		
Constructed Capital	✓	✓		
Monetary Capital				✓

FIGURE A.1 The four bottom lines and their capitals.

Adding stakeholders to the formula

Cabot has many stakeholders with economic, environmental or social interests in what we are doing. These stakeholders expect us to act in their best interests or at least to refrain from harming them.

Stated in the affirmative, the purpose of sustainability management is to:

(a) acknowledge that we have non-financial impacts in the world and that those impacts matter; and
(b) make it possible to measure, manage and report those impacts *relative to the interests of our stakeholders*. For example, a company with manufacturing facilities whose operations impact shared water resources has a de facto relationship with the surrounding community. The well-being of both depends on the quality and sufficiency of water resources.

This determines the relevant scope of Cabot's sustainability management efforts since we confine our focus only to those impacts that affect stakeholder well-being.

A good first step in implementing a context-based sustainability program, then, is to define who our stakeholders are. We include the following:

- owners/farmers
- customers – those stores that sell our products
- consumers – those individuals who buy our products
- people in our local/regional/global communities where we have impacts
- employees
- suppliers and other trading partners.

To the extent that Cabot's performance can be assessed in non-financial terms, the standards of performance that should apply are those that:

(a) pertain to relationships we already have with existing or prospective stakeholders, and
(b) involve economic, environmental or social impacts on vital capitals that matter to their well-being.

Non-financial obligations

The next step in our context-based approach to sustainability is to define our specific obligations to each stakeholder group; these must be defined separately for each group because the interests of various constituencies may differ. Our impact on water resources, for example, is typically limited to local or regional communities.

In determining Cabot's specific non-financial obligations, we are guided by the capital-based perspective discussed above. For each stakeholder group, we systematically ask ourselves the following question:

> What are our obligations concerning vital capitals important to this stakeholder group's well-being?

We further differentiate between impacts on natural capital and those on the three anthro capitals. This lets us distinguish between environmental bottom line performance, which impacts natural capital only, and economic and/or social bottom line performance, which impacts anthro capitals only. This way we can put the triple bottom line into operation by correlating the impacts on specific capitals to each of the three bottom lines (see Figure A.1).

In addition to correlating our impact on capitals with the non-financial bottom lines, we also correlate our impacts with specific stakeholder needs. Vital capital resources are not just created and maintained for their own sake. Rather, the goods and services they help produce are consumed by stakeholders to meet their own needs. The food we produce, for example, is a type of constructed capital (i.e., we source, process and package it), and the human need it addresses is the need for nutrition. For an obligation to be legitimate, it must be possible to associate related impacts to specific stakeholder needs in this way.

It is worth underscoring that the economic bottom line we rely on is different from the company's financial health. We view economic performance as a narrow form of social performance. In other words, the economic bottom line is a type of social bottom line since the economy is a subset of society – a particular domain of social interaction. This is why the capitals involved in the economic bottom line are the same as those involved with the social bottom line; they just differ in context.

An example may be helpful

All our relationships with suppliers and other trading partners are fundamentally economic in form. The relevant form of stakeholder well-being in this case is our trading partners' ability to prosper in business as a result of their dealings with us. Our ability to fill orders, for example, requires us to hire, train and maintain staffing (human and social capital) and facilities and equipment (constructed capital) required to produce, store and deliver our products. These investments in anthro capital are distinctly different from, say, separate investments to support a local clinic in a community where we do business. The latter would pertain to the social bottom line, not the economic bottom line.

Once we have identified each of the specific obligations on vital capitals important to our stakeholders, we can then associate each one with its corresponding bottom line. All obligations related to natural capital, for example, pertain to the environmental bottom line. All obligations on anthro capitals of an economic kind pertain to the economic bottom line. And all other obligations related to anthro capitals of a social kind pertain to the social bottom line. This lets us build a highly customized, stakeholder-driven, sustainability management program consistent with our stakeholder relationships.

Context-based metrics, measurement and reporting

Once we have successfully …

(a) identified our stakeholder groups,
(b) defined our obligations to each stakeholder group, and
(c) determined and correlated our impact on vital capitals with the three non-financial bottom lines,

… we are ready to define metrics.

These three steps prepare us to measure and report our performance in numerical terms. We can then quantify our performance for each of the three non-financial bottom lines, which tells us whether or not we are performing sustainably.

Our approach to metrics is again context-based. Unlike most of what passes for mainstream sustainability measurement, which often amounts to little more than reporting on trends in performance, context-based metrics allow us to quantify our impacts on specific vital capitals by comparing such impacts against specific standards. We refer to these standards of performance as *normative impacts*. Their source? The very same obligations discussed above, all of which are grounded in our stakeholder relationships.

In the context-based approach we use, we rely on the basic formula:

$$S = A/N$$

where:
S = sustainability performance
A = actual impact on a vital capital
N = normative impact on a vital capital.

We can illustrate this with a specific example involving how we measure our use of water resources in the vicinity of our manufacturing plants. In measuring the sustainability of our water use, we must first determine the volume of local supplies. We use data provided by government agencies that give us annual precipitation levels, watershed sizes and configurations, and other factors involving the climate and ecology. We then determine the needs of the local community with whom we are sharing water resources.

Having determined local conditions – based mainly on the volume of available renewable supplies and the size of the population that uses them – we then allocate a proportionate share of this resource to Cabot. In the case of water, this takes the form of a not-to-exceed threshold, which essentially amounts to a self-imposed limit on how much water we can use in our manufacturing plants. This limit serves as a standard of performance against which we measure our actual use. Thus the amount of water we are allowed to use is represented by 'N' in the equation above; the water we actually use is represented by 'A'.

Under this approach, our usage should produce a score less than (or, at most, equal to) 1.0. Why? Because any score less than or equal to 1.0 means we do not exceed our threshold. Likewise, any score of greater than 1.0 would mean an unsustainable level of water use. This would be true for impacts on any other form of natural capital as well.

Interestingly, this is not the case for anthro capitals. Why? Because, unlike natural capital, anthro capitals are human-made. When we run short, we can usually make more of them. Thus, instead of standards of performance being expressed in the form of maximums, standards for impacts on anthro capitals are expressed in terms of minimums. The volume of food we produce that meets our standards of quality, for example, should be *no less* than a certain level, not *no more* than a certain level. Scores for impacts on anthro capitals, therefore, should be greater than or equal to 1.0, not less than 1.0.

In either case, then, a score derived from context-based metrics will show:

(a) whether our impacts on vital capitals are sustainable, and
(b) if not, what the size of the gap is.

This information is critical since it identifies where we need to change course, and it further shows the size of the problem. It helps us establish priorities and allocate resources to improve performance. Without this information, sustainability managers are tracking meaningless trends whose impacts have no bearing on a true measurement of sustainability.

There is one other distinction we use in our approach to metrics, and that is to measure cause versus effect. Cause metrics measure policies or programs intended to produce a sustainable outcome. Effect metrics, by contrast, measure actual sustainability outcomes. A cause metric for water, for example, might measure how well water conservation programs are being used at a specific plant. The corresponding effect metric would measure how sustainable water usage actually is at the same plant.

Finally, since we are able to measure and report our non-financial sustainability performance in quantitative terms, we can roll up all of our individual CBM scores into one single score for the environmental, economic and social bottom lines. We can do this by determining the proportion of scores that meet or exceed our sustainability standards in each case. When we do this, a perfect score would be 100 percent, in which case we could say that all of our individual sustainability scores meet or exceed our standards for impacts on vital capitals.

Summary

In a very real sense, all of the key principles that underlie our sustainability program can be expressed in the following simple credo:

Living within Our Means and Ensuring the Means to Live

We recognize environmental limits and work to stay within them; for social and economic impacts, we recognize broader human needs and strive to fulfill them. We do all of this with stakeholder well-being in mind and always with Cabot's context sharply in focus. In short, we set explicit standards of performance for ourselves, and we work to meet them.

Appendix B
AREAS OF IMPACT CHECKLIST

Below we revisit the definitions of the four non-financial capitals of vital importance to stakeholder well-being (i.e., as earlier defined in Chapter 3). Next, the definitions are re-cast in terms of the *internal* versus *external* capitals distinction we can make, so as to be able to differentiate between impacts on internal vital capitals and those on external vital capitals – internal versus external to an organization, that is. Finally, we have compiled lists of representative areas of impact (by capital type) that correspond to human needs and well-being. These lists are purely illustrative and can be used to help determine what an organization's stakeholder-related duties and obligations are to have impact (or not) on vital capitals, as required in step 3 of the CSM cycle.

Vital capitals of importance to stakeholder well-being

Natural capital: Natural capital consists of natural resources, living organisms and ecosystem services that humans and non-humans alike rely on in order to take effective action and for their physical well-being.

Human capital: Human capital consists of *individual* knowledge, skills, experience, health and ethical entitlements that enhance the potential for effective individual action and human well-being.

Social capital: Social capital consists of *shared* knowledge and organizational resources (e.g., formal or informal networks of people committed to achieving common goals) that enhance the potential for effective individual and collective action and human well-being.

Constructed capital: Constructed capital (or built capital) consists of *material objects and/or physical systems or infrastructures* created by humans. It is the material world of human artifacts in which human knowledge is also embedded, and which humans use in order to take effective action.

Vital capitals differentiated by internal versus external areas of impact

Internal areas of impact (on vital capitals)

- *Natural capital*: These are impacts on natural resources, living organisms and ecosystem services internal to an organization's own facilities and/or operations.
- *Human capital*: These are impacts on individuals internal to an organization in ways that affect individual well-being (e.g., employee well-being).
- *Social capital*: These are impacts on programs and institutions internal to an organization, which in turn constitute, or have impact on, shared social capital resources and services (e.g., standardized business processes, safety programs, etc.).
- *Constructed capital*: These are impacts on human-made infrastructures and/or material goods internal to an organization (e.g., workplace facilities).

External areas of impact (on vital capitals)

- *Natural capital*: These are impacts on natural resources, living organisms and ecosystem services external to an organization's own facilities and/or operations.
- *Human capital*: These are impacts on individuals external to an organization in ways that affect individual well-being (e.g., consumer well-being).
- *Social capital*: These are impacts on programs and institutions external to an organization, which in turn constitute, or have impact on, shared social capital resources and services (e.g., schools, hospitals, etc.).
- *Constructed capital*: These are impacts on human-made infrastructures and/or material goods external to an organization (e.g., roads and highways, transportation facilities, etc.).

Illustrations of internal vital capitals and the basic human needs they relate to

Natural capital

- Clean/uncontaminated land and workplaces
- Clean/uncontaminated air
- Clean/uncontaminated water
- Natural resources
- Ecosystem services (including climate system)
- Biodiversity

Human capital

- Food, water and nutrition
- Health
  - via in-kind and supportive monetary means

- – via direct impacts of products and/or services when produced or used
- Child care
- Education (individual training and personal enrichment)
- Exercise and physical recreation
- Housing
- Material necessities
- Jobs at livable wage
- Justice and rule of law
- Ethical entitlements
  - – human rights
  - – labor rights
  - – anti-corruption
  - – transparency
  - – stakeholder inclusiveness
  - – gender equality and empowerment
  - – diversity
- work/family balance
- Information
- Safety and security
- Aesthetics
- Religion and spirituality

Social capital

- Food, water and nutrition
- Health
- Child care
- Education (including organizational learning and innovation)
- Exercise and physical recreation
- Housing
- Justice and rule of law (policies and programs)
- Ethical entitlements (policies and programs)
  - – human rights
  - – labor rights
  - – anti-corruption
  - – transparency
  - – stakeholder inclusiveness
  - – gender equality and empowerment
  - – diversity
  - – work/family balance
- Information
- Safety and security
- Aesthetics
- Religion and spirituality

Constructed capital

- Material goods and technologies
- Infrastructure
  - power
  - water
  - sanitation
  - roads
  - transport services
  - telecommunications
  - life safety

Illustrations of external vital capitals and the basic human needs they relate to

Natural capital

- Clean/uncontaminated land and habitat
- Clean/uncontaminated air
- Clean/uncontaminated water
- Natural resources
- Ecosystem services (including climate system)
- Biodiversity

Human capital

- Food, water, and nutrition
- Health
  - via in-kind and supportive monetary means
  - via direct product and/or service impacts when used
- Child care
- Education and personal enrichment
- Exercise and physical recreation
- Housing
- Material necessities
- Jobs at livable wage
- Ethical entitlements
  - human rights
  - labor rights
  - anti-corruption
  - transparency
  - stakeholder inclusiveness
  - gender equality and empowerment
  - diversity
  - work/family balance

Social capital

- Food, water, and nutrition
- Health
    - via in-kind and supportive monetary means
    - via indirect product and/or service impacts when consumed
- Child care
- Education
- Exercise and physical recreation
- Clean environment
- Housing
- Material necessities
- Infrastructure
    - power
    - water
    - sanitation
    - roads
    - transport services
    - telecommunications
- Jobs at livable wage
    - workers at other firms
- Commerce and trade
    - impact on local/regional businesses
    - impact on minority/women-owned businesses (mwobs)
    - commerce with fair trade suppliers
- Bank services and credit
- Safety and security
    - local
    - national
    - global
- Government
    - social services administration
    - trade regulation
- Justice and rule of law
- Ethics
    - human rights
    - labor rights
    - anti-corruption
    - transparency
    - stakeholder inclusiveness
    - gender equality and empowerment
    - diversity
    - work/family balance
- Information

- Aesthetics
- Religion and spirituality

Constructed capital (impacts on social resources)

- Material goods
- Infrastructure
  - power
  - water
  - sanitation
  - roads
  - transport services
  - telecommunications
  - life safety

Appendix C
FORMULATING DUTIES AND OBLIGATIONS AT CABOT CREAMERY COOPERATIVE

(Including an important anecdote from Ben & Jerry's)

In this appendix, we want to explain the logic and thinking that went into the identification of each of the ten duties and obligations shown in Table 3.4 at Cabot and the five further elaborated upon in Table 3.5 (see Chapter 3), and what step 3 of the CSM cycle looks like in practice. What follows below, then, are ten brief explanations of the content shown in Tables 3.4 and 3.5. Included in each explanation will be discussion of the stakeholder group to which a duty or obligation (D/O) is owed, the nature of the duty owed, the types of capitals and carrying capacities involved, and the types of metrics required to track and assess performance. Each of the ten summaries will also include an explanation of how the D/O was interpreted in terms of the three elements of sustainability context earlier summarized as follows:

1. **Carrying Capacities of Capitals**: First we identify the vital capitals (stocks) and their carrying capacities (flows) an organization is having impact on in ways that can affect stakeholder well-being, as well as capitals it *should* be having impact on in order to *ensure* stakeholder well-being.
2. **Responsible Populations**: Next we determine who the responsible populations are for ensuring the quality and sufficiency of such stocks and flows.
3. **Organizational Allocations**: And last, based on the first and second steps above, we allocate proportionate shares of available stocks and flows (in the case of natural capital) and/or burden shares for producing and/or maintaining them (in the case of anthro capital) to individual organizations.

Here, then, is our discussion of Tables 3.4 and 3.5, organized under ten subheadings corresponding to the ten duties and obligations shown in Table 3.4.

1. Consumers: produce safe food

Consumers of Cabot's products are clearly stakeholders of theirs because Cabot has an impact on a vital capital of importance to their well-being – namely, their food, which, in turn, affects their physical health. And because its products are intended to be consumed by people, Cabot owes those people a duty to produce them in such a way that their consumption is safe. Here in its own words is how Cabot explains this duty (Cabot Creamery Cooperative, 2009):

> This duty or obligation (D/O) is predicated on the view that human well-being is, in part, a function of having access to safe food. Consumers must therefore be able to trust and rely upon producers as having sufficient quality control procedures in place to safeguard their products against contamination or other risks to human health. To fulfill this D/O, Cabot must invest in the development and use of human and social capital consisting of the knowledge and skills required to produce safe products, and constructed capital consisting of ingredients, technology, equipment, and facilities needed to produce and deliver safe products.

Thus, in order to fulfill this duty, Cabot must not only ensure that the product itself (a form of constructed capital) is safe; it must also take steps to ensure that its own equipment and facilities for producing, packaging and shipping products are clean and safe (more constructed capital); that it has appropriately trained employees on hand who know how to ensure product safety (human capital); and that shared programs and processes for ensuring food safety are also in place (social capital). In this particular case, all of the capitals involved are internal to Cabot, including the products themselves until such time, that is, as they leave Cabot's custody.

The sustainability of Cabot's operations therefore includes consideration of whether or not its products are safe to consume. And since the products themselves are a form of vital capital that consumers, in this case, rely on for their well-being, consumers constitute a stakeholder group to whom Cabot owes a duty or obligation to produce safe food, the performance of which requires that it adhere to certain standards of performance insofar as its impacts on a set of related vital capitals are concerned. Those capitals, as we explained, certainly include the food products themselves, but they also include other capitals germane to their production. Understanding how Cabot performs relative to these standards, then, is clearly material to their sustainability performance and to the focus of their CSM program.

With respect to the three-part definition of sustainability context we are using, this D/O can be interpreted as follows:

1. **Carrying Capacities of Capitals**: Consumers of Cabot's products are stakeholders with standing, since Cabot produces food products that they consume. The food it produces must therefore not compromise – and, instead, should enhance – the carrying capacity of human capital held by consumers (i.e., their

individual health). Fulfillment of this D/O also requires that the carrying capacity of Cabot's own operations – a separate blend of human, social and constructed capitals – and their sufficiency for purposes of managing the safety of their products, be maintained at whatever levels are required to ensure safe food.

2. **Responsible Populations**: Cabot is exclusively responsible for the safety of its products.

3. **Organizational Allocations**: Cabot's share of responsibility for ensuring the safety of its products, and the carrying capacity of its operations insofar as the safety of its products is concerned, is absolute.

In terms of metrics, the most obvious one to use in this case is a metric that measures the safety of Cabot's finished products. The standard of performance here, in turn, is *100 percent safe products* – that is, all products produced by Cabot should be completely safe for consumption by consumers. In order to meet that standard, Cabot must invest in creating and maintaining appropriate human, social and constructed capitals internally, so that it can take whatever steps are required to produce and deliver safe food. The degree to which safe food is, in fact, produced and delivered then serves as a kind of proxy measure for whether or not the company's efforts to create and maintain these capitals are sufficient.

This reliance upon outcomes as compared to direct measures of investments made in preserving, producing and/or maintaining the underlying capitals is quite common in context-based sustainability. Why trouble ourselves with the complexity of measuring the quality or sufficiency of vital capitals when we can more easily measure, instead, the quality or sufficiency of the outcomes from the flows they produce? If the outcomes are sufficient, then the capital stocks and flows that preserve or produce them must also be sufficient – unless of course the flows consist, in part, of the capital stocks themselves, in which case the stocks are being depleted. That, of course, would be unsustainable, just as it would be unsustainable if the flows alone were inadequate.

In this case, the outcomes of interest to us are not so much the products themselves as their safety. As long as product safety is as high or as comprehensive as it should be, the quality and sufficiency of safety-related capital stocks and flows must also be sufficient.

Regarding the vital capitals involved in producing safe food, it may also be helpful here, and for the other dimensions of sustainability performance discussed below where internal vital capitals are involved, to refer back to Figure 1.1, where we first made the connections between vital capitals and human (stakeholder) well-being (see Chapter 1). In the case of safe food, the party involved in making the appropriations shown on the right-hand side of the figure is a consumer. The goods and services being appropriated are (1) food products themselves and their safety, and (2) the actions and outcomes associated with the people, processes and programs Cabot has in place to ensure food quality. The vital capitals that produce such valuable goods and services are a particular mix of those indicated in Table 3.4 (human, social and constructed); for that reason, performance on the safe food front, so to speak, accrues to the social bottom line, not the environmental or economic one. Why? Because food safety is a personal health issue, not an environmental or (directly) economic one, and the capitals involved point to it, as earlier indicated in Table 2.2 (see Chapter 2).

In addition to the effect metric described above, two other cause metrics were identified by Cabot as being of importance to safe food (see explanation of *cause* versus *effect* metrics in Chapter 3). One was a measure of the safety of the ingredients used in producing its products, and the other was a measure of the quality and cleanliness of its manufacturing processes and facilities. Here we found that several quality control processes and metrics already in place could be harnessed in the service of the company's CSM program, since the quality of ingredients and the quality and cleanliness of its manufacturing processes and facilities were already being actively managed, measured and reported.

Of particular relevance in this case was a food quality certification program known as *Safe Quality Food* (SQF), which is administered by an independent third party called the Safe Quality Food Institute.[1] As it turns out, the SQF program already in place at Cabot had certain standards of performance that, by any other description, pertain to vital capitals at Cabot in the form of its manufacturing processes (social capital) and the facilities used to produce its products (constructed capital). Thus, we were very easily able to incorporate the SQF standards (and metrics) into the CSM program at Cabot; here again, the metrics involved were assigned to the social bottom line.

2. Consumers: provide information

Another duty owed to consumers of Cabot's products is the requirement that information be provided about the products themselves. This is a duty to be transparent, and to respect the needs of consumers, who in order to manage their own diets effectively need access to information about the content of Cabot's products, how they are produced, and which, if any, certification standards they conform to. Cabot describes this duty as follows (Cabot Creamery Cooperative, 2009):

> This duty or obligation (D/O) is predicated on the view that human well-being is, in part, a function of good dietary management. Any company involved in food production is therefore duty-bound to make its best efforts to be transparent and truthful in all disclosures about its products, including ingredients, production methods, nutritional content, certifications, etc. To fulfill this D/O, Cabot must invest in internal human, social and constructed capital, so as to create individual and shared knowledge about its products, which can then be disseminated to, and appropriated by, consumers.

As was the case for the safe food duty earlier discussed, this duty pertains to a consumer's need for nutrition in order to ensure his or her own well-being, and to be able to safely and knowledgeably obtain it. As a provider of related products, Cabot has a corresponding duty to provide related information, which in turn means it must invest in and maintain associated forms of vital capital. Human and social capital, in particular, are required here, since it is individuals and teams within Cabot that must research, compile and publish the information in question. Constructed capital also comes into play in the sense that material goods are required to research (i.e., by using computers and telecommunications systems) and publish (i.e., on product labels and its website) the information to be disclosed to consumers. And all of this again points to the social bottom line as the category to which performance on this front should be assigned.

With respect to the three-part definition of sustainability context we are using, this D/O can be interpreted as follows:

1. **Carrying Capacities of Capitals**: Consumers of Cabot's products are stakeholders with standing, since Cabot produces food products that they consume. The carrying capacity of Cabot's own operations, therefore – a blend of human, social and constructed capitals – and their sufficiency for purposes of managing their own information disclosures, must be maintained at whatever levels are required to ensure that information about its products is fully and reliably disclosed at all times.
2. **Responsible Populations**: Cabot is exclusively responsible for maintaining whatever resources are required to fully and reliably disclose information about its products.
3. **Organizational Allocations**: Cabot's share of responsibility for ensuring the disclosure of information about its products is absolute.

The effect metric in this case is simply a measure of the extent to which Cabot discloses the information its consumers require relative to a standard that it do so comprehensively – which is, again, a proxy measure of the sufficiency of investments being made in preserving and/or producing the underlying vital capitals. The cause metrics we identified were twofold: one, that a policy or protocol be in place requiring disclosure of regulated/mandatory information; and two, that a similar policy or protocol be in place that requires disclosure of discretionary/non-mandatory information, such as whether a product is kosher.

3. Customers: meet commitments

Strictly speaking, most of Cabot's sales are made to retailers, such as Walmart, Publix and others, who in turn sell them to consumers. Cabot's customers, therefore, are mostly retailers, not end-users or consumers of their products. As buyers and resellers of Cabot's products, however, its customers clearly have a stake in Cabot's operations and are affected by its actions. This includes, in particular, its actions relative to day-to-day commercial performance and the effects such actions have on vital capitals of importance to their (the customers') economic well-being. This gives rise to a duty or obligation on Cabot's part to meet its commercial commitments to customers in non-financial ways, not just financial ways. Here is how Cabot describes this duty (Cabot Creamery Cooperative, 2009):

This duty or obligation (D/O) is predicated on the view that human well-being is, in part, a function of being free from economic conflicts or risks. Parties to commercial transactions therefore have a moral obligation to conduct themselves in such a way as to not expose their trading partners to such conflicts or risks. Cabot should therefore truthfully and transparently disclose all material information its customers might need to independently determine whether or not its products and operations pose legal or commercial risks of any kind. Cabot must also perform according to customer expectations, contractual and otherwise. To fulfill this D/O, Cabot must invest in internal human, social and constructed capital, so as to create individual and shared knowledge about its products and operations, which can then be disseminated to, and appropriated by, Cabot's own employees as well as Cabot's customers.

As indicated in Table 3.5, Cabot's sustainability performance relative to this duty and obligation takes the form of a measure of *commercial performance*. Of particular novelty in this case was the fact that many buyers and resellers of consumer products, such as Walmart and others, already measure and report the commercial performance of their suppliers and then share the resulting information with them. Indeed, not surprisingly, suppliers are held accountable to certain commercial standards of performance (e.g., turnaround time on order fulfillment, etc.), the thresholds for which are also useful for CSM purposes (i.e., as a basis for setting non-financial standards of performance).

In the case of Cabot, five such customer scorecards were in use at the time of our investigation. What we ultimately decided to do was create a composite scorecard of sorts that would be fed by the measures otherwise reported on the individual scorecards, and which would be blended in such a way that transaction performance, as opposed to other dimensions of performance, was highlighted. This took the form of turning mainly to performance data related to (1) the accuracy of orders, (2) the efficiency of order deliveries and (3) the incidence of damages and returns.

With respect to the three-part definition of sustainability context we are using, this D/O can be interpreted as follows:

1. **Carrying Capacities of Capitals**: Customers of Cabot's are stakeholders with standing, since Cabot produces food products that they buy and resell. The carrying capacity of Cabot's own operations, therefore – again, a blend of human, social and constructed capitals – and their sufficiency for purposes of managing their own commercial performance, must be maintained at whatever levels are required to meet its commercial transaction commitments at all times.
2. **Responsible Populations**: Cabot is exclusively responsible for meeting its own commercial transaction commitments.
3. **Organizational Allocations**: Cabot's share of responsibility for meeting its commercial transaction commitments is absolute.

Once again, specific standards of performance for the metrics involved here were sourced from customers themselves. In cases where there were competing standards for the same measures of performance, the higher standards were used as a basis for Cabot's metrics. In its final form, this metric was composed of roughly a dozen individual measures of performance in the three categories noted above (i.e., accuracy, efficiency and damages/returns). For consolidated reporting purposes, we simply determined the proportion of all measures of commercial performance that met or exceeded standards, and reported that figure as the single, unitary commercial performance score for a given period of time (see related box in Chapter 3).

Regarding the vital capitals involved in commercial performance, here again they are composed of a particular mix of human, social and constructed capitals as already indicated above. But because what we are talking about in this case is economic well-being, not just general well-being or well-being of another kind, performance on this front – the commercial performance front – accrues to the economic bottom line.

4. Customers: keep employees safe

Just as any company has an obligation to safeguard the physical well-being of its employees from possible hazards in the workplace, so does a company have a similar duty or obligation to safeguard the employees of its customers to the extent that the company is interacting with them on the customers' premises. The shipping and delivery of products by a company to its customers' premises, in particular, comes quickly to mind here. Here is how Cabot describes this duty in its own case (Cabot Creamery Cooperative, 2009):

> This duty or obligation (D/O) is predicated on the view that human well-being is, in part, a function of being free from physical danger or risk. Parties to commercial transactions therefore have a moral obligation to conduct themselves in such a way as to not expose their trading partners' employees to such dangers or risks. Cabot should therefore take steps to ensure that its own employees do not in any way put the safety of customer employees at risk. To fulfil this D/O, Cabot should invest in measures aimed at enhancing internal human and social capital, so as to create individual and shared knowledge about how to avoid putting trading partner safety at risk, and constructed capital intended to enhance the safety of its operations (e.g., safety features on trucks used to deliver products to customer sites).

Here again we have a case of a stakeholder group (customers, or their employees, more specifically) that is relying on a supplier's (Cabot's) investments in creating and maintaining vital capitals so as to ensure its own well-being. And whereas this and the other areas of impact so far discussed involve the production and maintenance of human, social and constructed capitals at appropriate levels, this D/O also involves impacts on natural capital, in the sense that employee safety depends, in part, on having access to a clean working environment (e.g., clean space, air and water) and a safe workplace in general. A supplier therefore has a duty to refrain from putting customer well-being at risk by compromising environmental conditions on customers' premises through actions of its own, or by causing any other adverse effects to natural resources or ecosystem services that customer personnel come into contact with.

With respect to the three-part definition of sustainability context we are using, this D/O can be interpreted as follows:

1. **Carrying Capacities of Capitals**: Customers of Cabot's are stakeholders with standing, since Cabot produces food products that they buy and resell and which are delivered to their facilities. The carrying capacity of Cabot's own operations, therefore – a blend of human, social and constructed capitals – and their sufficiency for purposes of not impairing the environmental quality of its customers' facilities (i.e., on the carrying capacity of related natural capital), must be maintained at whatever levels are required to avoid diminishing the physical and environmental safety of its customers' places of work.
2. **Responsible Populations**: Cabot is exclusively responsible for managing the effects of its own operations on customer premises.
3. **Organizational Allocations**: Cabot's share of responsibility for managing the effects of its own operations on customer premises is absolute.

In this case, then, we have one part of performance that ties to the social bottom line and another part that ties to the environmental bottom line. The social bottom line part involves impacts on the human, social and constructed capitals required to maintain customer employee safety (i.e., internal human, social and constructed capitals that pertain to safety). The environmental bottom line part, in turn, involves impacts on natural resources and ecosystem services, also for ensuring customer employee safety (i.e., external natural capital at the customers' places of work).

Notice, as well, that the standard of performance for the social bottom line part requires that investments in related capitals not fall below certain levels (i.e., so that the flows of related goods and services remain sufficient), while the standard of performance on the environmental side is to have no impacts at all – none of an adverse kind, that is. So, in the first case, the operable standard calls for the ongoing production and maintenance of (anthro) capitals; in the second, it calls for the preservation of natural ones.

5. Employees: keep employees safe

Just as any company has an obligation to safeguard the physical well-being of its customers' employees, so does it have an obligation to ensure the well-being of its own employees. Here is how Cabot describes this duty (Cabot Creamery Cooperative, 2009):

> This duty or obligation (D/O) is predicated on the view that human well-being is, in part, a function of being free from physical danger or risk.

Organizations therefore have a moral obligation to conduct themselves in such a way as to not expose their employees to such dangers or risks. Cabot should therefore take steps to ensure that it does not in any way put the safety of employees at risk. To fulfill this D/O, Cabot should invest in measures aimed at ensuring the quality and safety of natural capital (i.e., not polluting the workplace environment), enhancing internal human and social capital, so as to create individual and shared knowledge about how to avoid putting employee safety at risk, and constructed capital intended to enhance the safety of its operations.

The situation regarding duties to have impacts on vital capitals related to employee safety, then, is exactly parallel to that just discussed regarding the safety of customer employees. Namely, an organization must produce and maintain related human, social and constructed capitals of whatever sort are required to ensure employee well-being, and it must also take steps to safeguard the quality of natural capital in the workplace (i.e., to ensure air and water quality and to guard against direct contact with harmful materials or exposure to other dangers from equipment, manufacturing processes, etc.). Once such capitals are preserved (natural capital), produced and/or maintained (anthro capital), employees are then able to appropriate beneficial goods and services from their flows every day, from one minute to the next – be it in the form of breathing clean air, drinking clean water, being free from toxic exposures, or by following safety related procedures developed by their employers.

With respect to the three-part definition of sustainability context we are using, this D/O can be interpreted as follows:

1. **Carrying Capacities of Capitals**: Employees of Cabot's are stakeholders with standing, since Cabot employs them and controls their working environment in most respects. The carrying capacity of Cabot's own operations, therefore – which is, again, a blend of human, social and constructed capitals – and their sufficiency for purposes of managing the environmental quality of its own facilities – a mix of natural capitals – must be maintained at whatever levels are required to ensure the physical and environmental safety of its own places of work.
2. **Responsible Populations**: Cabot is exclusively responsible for managing the safety of its own operations on its own premises.
3. **Organizational Allocations**: Cabot's share of responsibility for managing the safety of its own operations on its own premises is absolute.

Metrics for measuring performance in this area of impact are also exactly parallel to those required for customer employee safety, except that they, of course, are internally focused. Pre-existing safety records can be of particular value here, as can records regarding environmental and facility management. As always, though, data regarding past performance, incident tracking, etc. must be reported against standards and not just in the form of top-line historical records or year-to-year trends. It is up to each organization to establish its own standards of performance, ideally by turning to outside/independent third parties who may have developed industry standards or targets that can be internally adopted.

Metrics for performance in this area tie to both the social and the environmental bottom lines, since some of the impacts pertain to human, social and constructed capital (social bottom line), while others pertain to natural capital (environmental bottom line).

6. Visitors: keep visitors safe

Here again we have another personal safety duty, this time involving visitors to Cabot's facilities. Cabot receives visitors, periodically, at each of its four plants, one of which in Cabot, VT is also a Visitor Center per se. In addition, Cabot owns and operates two retail stores, one in Quechee, VT, and the other in Waterbury, VT. In order to be sustainable, then, Cabot must take steps to preserve and produce vital capitals related to ensuring visitor well-being in cases where visitors are, in fact, spending time at Cabot's facilities. Here is how Cabot describes this duty (Cabot Creamery Cooperative, 2009):

> This duty or obligation (D/O) is predicated on the view that human well-being is, in part, a function of being free from physical danger or risk. Organizations that host and interact with the public therefore have a moral obligation to conduct themselves and manage their facilities in such a way as to not expose visitors to such dangers or risks. Cabot should therefore take steps to ensure that its own employees do not in any way put the safety of visitors at risk. To fulfill this D/O, Cabot should invest in measures aimed at ensuring the quality and safety of natural capital (i.e., the workplace or visitor environment), enhancing internal human and social capital, so as to create individual and shared knowledge about how to avoid putting visitor safety at risk, and constructed capital intended to enhance the safety of its operations and facilities.

With respect to the three-part definition of sustainability context we are using, this D/O can be interpreted as follows:

1. **Carrying Capacities of Capitals**: Visitors of Cabot's are stakeholders with standing, since Cabot actively hosts them at its own facilities. The carrying capacity of Cabot's own operations, therefore – once again, a blend of human, social and constructed capitals – and their sufficiency for purposes of managing and ensuring the environmental quality of its own facilities (i.e., for ensuring the carrying capacity of related natural capital), must be maintained at whatever levels are required to ensure the physical and environmental safety of its own places of work.
2. **Responsible Populations**: Cabot is exclusively responsible for managing the effects of its own operations on its own premises.

3. **Organizational Allocations**: Cabot's share of responsibility for managing the effects of its own operations on its own premises is absolute.

As for the other two categories of human safety discussed above, the capitals involved here are human, social, constructed and natural. The metrics required to measure performance in this area are therefore analogous to those required for the other two cases, and can also involve the use of separate records already in use for measuring, managing and reporting environment, health and safety performance. Metrics, too, for performance in this area tie to both the social and the environmental bottom lines, since some of the impacts pertain to human, social and constructed capital (social bottom line), and others pertain to natural capital (environmental bottom line).

7. Community (local): use water fairly

Turning to the communities in which Cabot does business as a separate class of stakeholders, another important area of sustainability performance involves water use. Indeed, since water resources are shared by the inhabitants of a community or region, individual users must be careful not to overuse or jeopardize in any way the quality or sufficiency of related stocks. Here is how Cabot describes this duty (Cabot Creamery Cooperative, 2009):

> This duty or obligation (D/O) is predicated on the view that human well-being is, in part, a function of having access to sufficient supplies of freshwater resources on Earth. Since Cabot's operations have impact on related natural capital (i.e., on surface and ground water supplies), it has a D/O to manage its impacts accordingly, such that they are fair and equitable and do not put other people's access to water resources at risk. To fulfill this D/O, Cabot should manage its freshwater intake and wastewater outflows such that it does not either exceed its proportionate share of related resources or deprive others of theirs (either through overuse or contamination). Internally, investments in human, social and constructed capital will be needed to fulfill this D/O, the effects of which will contribute to impacts had on natural capital, namely water.

As the narrative above states, fulfillment of this duty requires that Cabot take steps to produce and maintain vital anthro capitals (human, social and constructed) of whatever types are needed to ensure that its impacts on water resources are fair, just and appropriate, and also that its more direct impacts on water resources themselves do not in any way put the quality or sufficiency of related stocks at risk insofar as stakeholder well-being is concerned. Its more direct impacts on water resources through use of them, of course, must also be managed within the bounds of sustainability (i.e., within their respective carrying capacities).

With respect to the three-part definition of sustainability context we are using, this D/O can be interpreted as follows:

1. **Carrying Capacities of Capitals**: Neighbors of Cabot's in the places where it does business are stakeholders with standing, since Cabot shares water resources with them. The carrying capacity of Cabot's own operations, therefore – here again, a blend of human, social and constructed capitals – and their sufficiency for purposes of managing their impacts on the carrying capacity of locally available water supplies (a form of shared natural capital), must be maintained at whatever levels are required to ensure that their use of water resources is fair, just and sustainable.

2. **Responsible Populations**: Regarding its impacts on the carrying capacities of its own human, social and constructed capitals in order to regulate and control its own use of water, Cabot is the exclusively responsible population. Regarding its impacts on natural capital (water in this case), however, Cabot is only one of many parties who have such impacts in the communities where it does business. Thus, Cabot shares the responsibility to manage impacts on water resources with the other members of the communities in which it does business.

3. **Organizational Allocations**: Cabot's share of responsibility for managing its impacts on the carrying capacities of its own human, social and constructed capitals as required to regulate and control its own use of water is absolute. Its share of responsibility for managing the quality and sufficiency of the carrying capacity of water resources in the places where it does business, however, is proportionate to (a) its size relative to the total number of users (and uses) in the community, and (b) the volume of available renewable supplies. Its responsibility for having impact on the carrying capacity of water resources should therefore take the form of a proportionate, not-to-exceed allocation of available renewable supplies that is separately calculated for each of its facilities.

Regarding metrics for assessing the sustainability of Cabot's water use, a combination of related cause and effect metrics were specified: cause metrics to determine whether or not appropriate policies, programs and technologies are in place to help guide and manage its impacts on water, and effect metrics to determine whether or not its actual impacts on water resources are sustainable. Of particular significance here was the decision to use an effect metric that would make it possible for Cabot to measure its water use at each of its locations against a context-based allocation of available renewable supplies. The measurement model, or metric, selected for this purpose was the *Corporate Water Gauge* (described in Appendix D), the results of which at one of Cabot's plants are provided in Appendix E.

Here again, metrics for performance in this area tie to both the social and environmental bottom lines, since some of the impacts pertain to human, social and constructed capitals (social bottom line), while others pertain to natural capital (environmental bottom line).

8. Community (regional): limit solid wastes

Another classification of the communities in which Cabot does business is the broader regional one. This orientation to community is arguably applicable in terms of the impacts Cabot has on solid waste facilities, since landfill facilities are often designed to serve large regions. In the state of Vermont, for example, there are only two landfills in place to serve the entire state. With few exceptions, businesses and residents anywhere in Vermont are permitted to send their solid wastes to either of these facilities, which Cabot does, in fact, do. Thus, Cabot must share the existing – and limited – solid waste facilities with everyone else in the state in a way that is fair and equitable. Here is how Cabot describes this duty (Cabot Creamery Cooperative, 2009):

> This D/O is predicated on the view that human well-being is, in part, a function of having access to properly designed and managed solid waste facilities. Since Cabot's operations have impact on related facilities (i.e., on regional solid waste facilities), it has a D/O to manage its impacts accordingly, such that they are fair and equitable and do not put other people's entitlements to the same resources at risk. To fulfill this D/O, Cabot should manage its solid waste emissions such that it does not either exceed its proportionate share of related resources or deprive others of theirs. Internally, investments in human, social and constructed capital will be needed to fulfill this D/O, the effects of which will contribute to impacts had on constructed capital, namely landfill facilities, and also natural capital, since solid wastes, if not properly managed, can contaminate the environment.

This is a surprisingly complex area of CSM, if only because many believe the very practice of emitting solid wastes into the environment is unsustainable to begin with. From a purely environmental perspective, this view would seem to hold up, as Herman Daly's third rule would suggest: 'waste emission rates should equal [or not exceed] the natural assimilative capacities of the ecosystems into which the wastes are emitted' (Daly, 1990, p. 2). Depending on how one defines assimilative capacities or chooses to allow for time as a variable, emitting solid wastes into landfills, by conventional standards, might or might not be seen as complying with Daly's rule.

Here we should also acknowledge the fact that, regardless of how solid waste, per se, fares under Daly's rule, the illegal emission of toxic or other illicit wastes of one kind or another into conventional landfills might very easily fail to comply with his rule, since many such substances cannot be assimilated by the environment at all, at least not in the time frames of interest to us (i.e., within human time scales, as opposed to geological ones).

That all said, separate sustainability issues of a non-ecological kind remain to be considered as well, since landfills constitute a form of constructed capital that people create and share in order to meet their needs. Such sharing must therefore be fair and equitable. As a user of landfill facilities, then, Cabot has a duty and obligation to use them in a way that does not deprive others of their own fair shares of the same facilities. In order to fulfill this duty, Cabot needs to invest in creating knowledge about how to use landfills and manage its own emissions (human capital); it similarly needs to create policies, procedures and programs that its employees can turn to in their collective attempts to manage their solid wastes, including guidance on what constitutes legal versus illegal emissions for solid waste facilities (social capital); and it must invest in equipment and facilities required to physically handle its wastes (constructed capital).

With respect to the three-part definition of sustainability context we are using, this D/O can be interpreted as follows:

1. **Carrying Capacities of Capitals**: All regional residents and businesses with whom Cabot shares access to landfills are stakeholders with standing, since Cabot shares landfill facilities with them. The carrying capacity of Cabot's own operations, therefore – here again, a blend of human, social and constructed capitals – and their sufficiency for purposes of managing their impacts on the carrying capacity of regionally available landfill facilities (a form of shared constructed capital), must be maintained at whatever levels are required to ensure that their use of related landfill facilities is fair, just and equitable. Separately, Cabot's use of such facilities also constitutes a direct impact on external natural capital.

2. **Responsible Populations**: Regarding its impacts on the carrying capacities of its own human, social and constructed capitals in order to regulate and control its own solid waste emissions, Cabot is the exclusively responsible population. Regarding its impacts on external constructed capital (landfills, in this case), however, Cabot is only one of many parties that have such impacts in the regions where it does business; thus, Cabot shares the responsibility to manage impacts on landfill facilities with the other members of the regions in which it does business. Regarding its impacts on natural capital (i.e., on the natural environment in which landfills are located), once again Cabot is only one of many parties who have such impacts in the regions where it does business. Thus, Cabot shares the responsibility to manage impacts on the environment with the others in the regions in which it does business (i.e., to not contaminate the environment in ways that violate landfill laws and regulations).

3. **Organizational Allocations**: Cabot's share of responsibility for managing its impacts on the carrying capacities of its own human, social and constructed capitals as required to regulate and control its own solid waste emissions is absolute. Its share of responsibility for managing its impacts on the carrying capacity of landfills in the regions where it does business, however, is proportionate to (a) its size relative to the total number of users (and uses) of the same facilities in the region, and (b) the volume of available constructed supplies. Its responsibility for having impact on the carrying capacity of landfills will therefore take the form of a proportionate, not-to-exceed allocation of available capacity (usually expressed in terms of weight or tonnage). Separately, its responsibility to refrain from contaminating landfills with toxic or other illicit emissions is shared with all other

users of the same facilities, although its responsibility to refrain from violating related laws and regulations with respect to its own emissions is absolute.

Regarding metrics for assessing the sustainability of Cabot's solid waste emissions, a combination of related cause and effect metrics were specified: cause metrics to determine whether or not appropriate policies, programs and technologies are in place to help guide and manage its impacts, and effect metrics to determine whether or not its actual impacts on landfills are sustainable. The effect metric we used simply measured the volume of Cabot's emissions against a context-based allocation of available constructed supplies (i.e., available landfill capacities). Cause metrics related to investments in the kinds of internal human, social and constructed capitals required to manage its own solid waste emissions were not developed by Cabot, since the effect metric used can serve as a proxy for them (i.e., if solid waste emissions are sustainable in terms of the effect metric, then the investments being made in the cause metrics must also be sustainable).

This is also true for the requirement that impacts on the natural environment at the landfill locations Cabot uses be sustainable (the measure of which would call for another effect metric), since, in the case of Cabot, the quality of emissions in terms of their compliance with associated laws and regulations was otherwise incorporated into the capacity-oriented effect metric discussed above (i.e., the one that measures the volume of Cabot's emissions against an allocation of available capacity, in the sense that all such emissions must be quality-compliant, so to speak – or compliant with regulations).

As in some other cases, metrics for performance in this area tie to both the social and the environmental bottom lines, since some of the impacts pertain to human, social and constructed capital (social bottom line), while others pertain to natural capital (environmental bottom line).

9. Community (global): limit GHG wastes

A third classification of the communities in which Cabot does business is the global one. This orientation to community is arguably applicable in cases where Cabot is having impacts on vital capitals of importance to people anywhere in the world – an admittedly rare event, but certainly applicable in the case of greenhouse gas (GHG) emissions, as it is for any other emitter. The solution to climate change brought on by excessive GHG emissions – or so the scientists tell us – is relatively simple in theory but extraordinarily difficult and problematic to achieve in practice: *humans must dramatically reduce their GHG emissions*. This applies to every one of us in everything we do, including, most especially, our business lives.

Because of the complexity and the implications of making major emission reductions in the short term (i.e., doing so can constrain the growth of a business or its ability to keep up with demand, not to mention lower its profits), Cabot, like many companies, is weighing its options. Indeed, at the time of writing, management there has not yet put a stake in the ground in terms of what its reduction targets should be, and over what period of time. Among the options being considered are three of emblematic value insofar as our own purposes here are concerned: (1) an overall industry-level reduction target of 25 percent by 2020 (from 2007 levels) proposed by Dairy Management, Inc. (DMI),[2] a non-profit dairy industry association in Chicago funded by dairy farmers throughout the U.S.; (2) a GHG-intensity goal that Cabot would devise for itself, according to which GHG emissions per, say, pound of product produced would be lowered over time; and (3) a more context-based reduction plan that would be tied to a specific CO_2 stabilization scenario, according to which emissions would be gradually reduced over time until a specific concentration of CO_2 in the Earth's atmosphere is achieved at a stable (and safe) level. Each of these options is more fully discussed below; first, here is how Cabot describes this duty (Cabot Creamery Cooperative, 2009):

> This D/O is predicated on the view that human well-being is, in part, a function of being able to live in a safe and properly functioning climate system on Earth. Since Cabot's operations have impact on related natural capital (i.e., on the global climate control system), it has a D/O to manage its emissions accordingly. To fulfill this D/O, Cabot should not only manage its emissions relative to ecological limits, but should also invest in human, social, and constructed capitals required to devise and implement solutions for climate change mitigation. Here the standard of performance is a social one, not an environmental one (i.e., the standard calls for making improvements in human, social, and constructed capital in order to achieve climate change mitigation). Such impacts on anthro capital can either be internal to an organization, or external.

The first thing to say about this particular formulation of what a standard of performance for GHG emissions ought to be is that it ties to the social bottom line, not the environmental one. Indeed, it has more to do with contributions of a social kind to *climate change mitigation* than with contributions of an ecological kind to *global warming*. The reasoning here is subtle, but all-important:

- From a purely ecological perspective, all GHG emissions – even reduced ones – are unsustainable. Why? Because according to climate science, anthropogenic GHG emissions have already interfered with the Earth's capacity to assimilate them at levels that put human well-being at risk. Thus, under Daly's third rule – which, again, reads 'waste emission rates should equal [or not exceed] the natural assimilative capacities of the ecosystems into which the wastes are emitted' (Daly, 1990, p. 2) – all current GHG emissions are unsustainable and should be stopped immediately.
- Since the immediate cessation of all anthropogenic emissions of GHGs on Earth is unlikely to happen anytime soon, our focus should shift to mitigation – and also to adaptation, which goes beyond the scope of this book. Climate change mitigation, then, assuming anthropogenic climate change is real, is one place where we must focus our efforts. Four alternative ways of reducing fossil fuel emissions

come quickly to mind here: (1) energy conservation, (2) increased use of renewable energy (i.e., non-fossil fuels), (3) carbon capture and sequestration, and (4) geoengineering. Certainly other options may exist, or will exist, but the key point here is that every one of these mitigation solutions calls for investments in anthro capital so that people will know how to implement them (human capital), can implement them together (social capital), and can have access to supporting technologies (constructed capital).

Any measure of progress towards achievement of climate change mitigation therefore requires a focus on building and maintaining related anthro capitals, not natural capital. It is already trivially the case, as explained above, that the anthropogenic emission of GHG gases is ecologically unsustainable. The more pertinent and important question is: *what steps are we taking to develop and operationalize the kind of human, social and constructed capitals we need to mitigate our emissions?* In response, we believe standards of performance for impacts on anthro capitals required to push ahead with climate change mitigation can be defined, even at the organizational level, and be used as a basis for measuring sustainability performance insofar as climate change mitigation is concerned. What this means is that even as a company's GHG emissions might be ecologically unsustainable − which, again, all GHG emissions arguably are today − its impacts on vital capitals required to make progress on climate change mitigation can be sustainable − one measures impacts on natural capital, the other measures impacts on anthro capital.

With this background in mind, let us return to the three options Cabot is considering to see how they compare.

The first option under consideration at Cabot is the DMI one: reduce emissions by 25 percent by 2020 using 2007 emissions as a baseline. By most standards, this is a rather challenging and ambitious goal, although not impossible to achieve. DMI itself, with the support of many dairy industry participants, has identified a dozen or so specific opportunities to reduce emissions by at least half that amount. Still, the manner in which the goal has been expressed makes it difficult to operationalize at an organizational level. Why? Because it fails to take flux in the industry (or even within individual enterprises) into account in a way that would make it possible for an individual company (e.g., Cabot) to embrace it.

Consider, for example, what would happen if Cabot doubled in size between now and 2020, and yet its emissions per pound of product fell by 25 percent during the same period. In that case, its overall emissions as a company would have increased by 50 percent even though its emissions per pound of product compared with the baseline year would have declined at the very rate called for by the DMI goal. How, then, should its performance against the goal be judged? On target, or above target? Without explicit guidance, it is impossible to say. Indeed, goals expressed at the level of an industry cannot be operationalized or embraced at the level of an individual enterprise unless such questions are explicitly addressed in advance − which, unfortunately, has not been done in the case of the DMI goal.

The second option identified as a possible basis for reducing GHG emissions at Cabot was to do so at a per-unit-of-production level, such as *per pound of cheese produced*. This has the advantage of measuring performance in a way that is not distorted by growth, while also providing management with an operational measure of efficiency in ways that tie to cost (i.e., lower GHG emissions per unit of product produced may very well also translate into lower costs for energy). On the downside, as discussed mainly in Chapter 2, managing for eco-efficiency is not the same as managing for sustainability. The latter is context-based; the former is not. And so even if a GHG intensity metric is used at Cabot (i.e., one that measures GHG emissions per unit of production), it would still leave open the question of how best to set a context-based target for climate change mitigation at the company, and how best to measure performance against it.

Turning to the third option, it should first be made clear that neither of the preceding two options – not only the second one, that is – is context-based, at least not explicitly so. Indeed, the DMI target is not grounded in context either (i.e., in the *climate change stabilization* sense of the term). Rather, it is simply a target for reducing emissions by a specified amount by 2020 – nothing more, nothing less. By the same token, the eco-efficiency approach is arguably even less closely connected to a defined climate change outcome, since even if its *emissions per unit of production* targets are met, overall GHG emissions could still very well increase, not decrease. Unlike the first two, though, the third option is context-based and is explicitly tied to a greenhouse-gas stabilization scenario, which if achieved (at least according to a specific, peer-reviewed climate model) would result in lower, safe and stabilized GHG concentrations in the atmosphere and the reversal of climate change.

Piloting a context-based climate change mitigation metric at Ben & Jerry's

While it is true that Cabot had not yet made a decision regarding its GHG emission goals at the time of writing, many other organizations of course have, including Ben & Jerry's Homemade, Inc. in South Burlington, Vermont, a wholly owned subsidiary of Unilever. In 2005, Ben & Jerry's participated with us in piloting exactly the kind of context-based climate change mitigation metric under consideration at Cabot (i.e., one of at least three possible metrics there). Referred to by Ben & Jerry's at the time as the *Global Warming Social Footprint*[3] (see McElroy, 2008 for a more complete case study), the approach we took was first to choose a credible climate change mitigation scenario, which ultimately took the form of a model developed by Tom Wigley, Richard Richels and James Edmonds known as the WRE350 scenario (for a full description of this and other so-called WRE scenarios, see Wigley, 2000).

The WRE350 scenario is an attempt to specify a pattern of CO_2 emissions that, if followed, will lead to a reduction of CO_2 concentrations in the

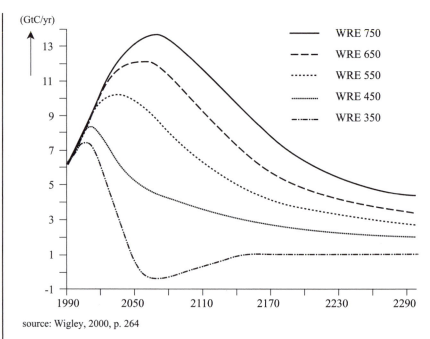

source: Wigley, 2000, p. 264

FIGURE C.1 WRE profiles of industrial CO_2 emissions.

atmosphere to a stabilized level of 350 parts per million by the year 2150. The pattern of emissions it describes is therefore a prescriptive or normative one. Of course WRE350 is just a model, but the thinking behind it is grounded in world-class science and economics. What it provides, then, is a blueprint of sorts that anyone, or any organization, on Earth can embrace as a guideline for how their own CO_2 emissions should be modified, starting from a baseline year of, say, 2000. If everyone, and every organization, adhered to the same trajectory of emissions specified in WRE350 (see Figure C.1), the goal would be achieved by 2150 (see Figure C.2) – assuming the model is correct, that is. In Figures C.1 and C.2, several other WRE scenarios are also shown, all of which result in higher concentrations of CO_2 in the atmosphere by 2150 than the WRE350 scenario entails.

Notwithstanding the fact that, as some people say, all models are wrong, WRE350 is at least a credible attempt to specify a climate change mitigation scenario that is context-based. It is context-based in the sense that it satisfies our definition of context as follows (i.e., only applicable to companies that actually emit CO_2):

1. **Carrying Capacities of Capitals**: All people on Earth with whom a company shares a properly functioning climate system – wherein a company also emits greenhouse gases, or GHGs – are stakeholders with standing, since the company has impact on the Earth's climate system. The

carrying capacity of a company's own operations, therefore – a blend of human, social and constructed capitals – and their sufficiency for purposes of managing their own CO_2 emissions, must be maintained at whatever levels are required to ensure that their emissions are mitigated in accordance with a credible CO_2 stabilization scenario.

2. **Responsible Populations**: Regarding its impacts on the carrying capacities of its own human, social and constructed capitals in order to regulate and control its own CO_2 emissions in accordance with a credible CO_2 stabilization scenario, the company is the exclusively responsible population.

3. **Organizational Allocations**: Each company is responsible for mitigating its own CO_2 emissions in accordance with (a) a credible CO_2 stabilization scenario, and (b) the proportion of global emissions it was responsible for emitting in the baseline year (i.e., its required emissions reductions under the scenario must be relative to the volume of whatever its emissions were in the baseline year). In this way, assuming everyone follows the same guidelines, the mitigation scenario will be collectively achieved. And even if not universally followed, the scenario still provides a standard of performance for climate change mitigation that can be applied at the level of individual organizations.

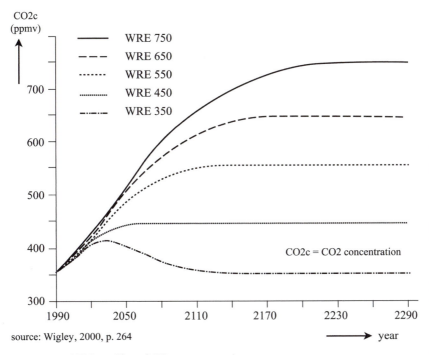

source: Wigley, 2000, p. 264

FIGURE C.2 WRE profiles of CO_2 concentrations.

> Although originally conceived and developed by the Center for Sustainable Organizations in the U.S., this particular approach to climate change mitigation at the level of individual organizations was first piloted in production, as it were, by Ben & Jerry's in 2007. The standard of performance used was, in fact, the WRE350 scenario, and the baseline year chosen was 2000. Among other things, the WRE350 scenario has the advantage of being interpretable at the level of individual years, so that prescribed changes in emissions for each year following the baseline year are specified and can be used as a standard of performance by any organization on an annual basis thereafter (i.e., assuming it has knowledge of its emissions in 2000 and beyond). Subsequent years can also be used as a baseline with the WRE scenarios, although there are limitations.

Of the three options for reducing GHG emissions at Cabot, it should be clear that, in all three cases, the metrics involved point to the social bottom line, not the environmental one, because in no case is performance being measured against the assimilative capacity of the environment per se. Instead, each of the three examples expresses targets of performance in terms of a mitigation goal, the achievement of which requires investments in anthro capital. This is why, in the case of the WRE350 scenario utilized by Ben & Jerry's (see box), the method used was referred to as the Global Warming *Social* Footprint (emphasis added).

That said, it should also be clear that, unlike the other two alternatives, the stabilization scenario approach to climate change mitigation is deeply grounded in an assessment of the Earth's capacity to absorb CO_2 emissions, which includes consideration of current concentration levels and other ecological factors. Indeed, the prescribed reductions in any such model are based explicitly on considerations of that kind. To that extent, then, performance measured against related targets at least indirectly ties to the environmental bottom line. More importantly, however, it ties to the *social* bottom line, since it tells us the extent to which an organization is investing in vital anthro capitals at whatever levels are required to achieve climate change mitigation, at least according to a defined and peer-reviewed scenario of some kind.

10. Farmer/owners: promote industry

Because Cabot is a cooperative, its owners or shareholders are the farmers whose milk products it processes into cheese and other dairy products. Cabot, the dairy food production and wholesaling company – not to be confused with the farmers themselves – therefore has a number of financial duties to its farmers, but also some non-financial ones. Chief among them is to advocate for their economic interests in the marketplace by actively participating in dairy industry organizations and other economic forums. Here is how Cabot describes this duty (Cabot Creamery Cooperative, 2009):

> This D/O is predicated on the view that human well-being is, in part, a function of having access to a strong and healthy market for one's products or

services. Since Cabot represents the interests of its farmer/owners in the marketplace, it has a duty to do whatever it can to support and participate in industry-level efforts aimed at strengthening the dairy industry, and increasing demand for Cabot's products. To fulfill this D/O, Cabot should invest in creating and maintaining sufficient levels of internal human and social capital as are required to act effectively on behalf of its farmer-owners, and to similarly invest in external human and social capital, which may take the form of industry associations such as DMI, etc. This duty also requires investments in constructed capital, such as in products and other materials, as may be required to promote Cabot in the marketplace.

Cabot's efforts in this area are extensive, including the degree to which it actively participates in the sustainability initiatives of the dairy industry at a national level. The DMI program previously mentioned constitutes one such initiative, as do a number of others at a more local or regional level. Beyond its participation in sustainability initiatives, Cabot also regularly promotes and showcases its products at various industry events, including a number of high-profile product competitions. Indeed, it has accumulated an impressive array of blue ribbons and other such awards for its products, some of which (products) are reputed to be the *World's Best Cheddar!*

With respect to the three-part definition of sustainability context we are using, this D/O can be interpreted as follows:

1. **Carrying Capacities of Capitals**: All farmer/owners of Cabot's cooperative are stakeholders with standing, since they are owners of the Cabot cooperative. The carrying capacity of Cabot's own operations, therefore – once again, a blend of human, social and constructed capitals – and their sufficiency for purposes of promoting the economic interests of their farmer/owners, must be maintained at whatever levels are required to ensure that their farmer/owners' economic interests in the marketplace are, in fact, being met.
2. **Responsible Populations**: Regarding its impacts on the carrying capacities of its own human, social and constructed capitals in order to promote the economic interests of its farmer/owners, Cabot is the exclusively responsible population.
3. **Organizational Allocations:** Cabot's share of responsibility for managing its impacts on the carrying capacities of its own human, social and constructed capitals in order to promote the economic interests of its farmer/owners is absolute.

Regarding metrics for assessing the sustainability of Cabot's industry promotion efforts, a combination of cause and effect metrics may be used: cause metrics to gauge the sufficiency of the company's promotional staff, budget and other resources, and effect metrics to gauge the quality and effectiveness of outcomes (e.g., the degree of participation in, and influence on, industry sustainability goals and standards, number of product awards won, etc.).

Because of the manner in which outcomes in this area have impact on farmer/owner well-being, performance here ties to the economic bottom line. Once again, the capitals involved in the social and economic bottom lines are identical (human, social and constructed); the application of those capitals will vary, however, such that in some cases they are being created and maintained in order to serve a stakeholder's *economic* interests as opposed to some other human or social need. In such cases, we attribute impacts on the capitals involved to the economic bottom line.

Notes

1. More information about the Safe Quality Food Institute and the SQF standard can be found here: http://www.sqfi.com.
2. More information about DMI's research and development efforts aimed at improving the sustainability performance of the dairy industry in the U.S. can be found here: http://www.usdairy.com/Pages/Home.aspx.
3. More information about Ben & Jerry's efforts to pilot a context-based climate change mitigation metric (referred to at the time as the *Global Warming Social Footprint*) can be found in their Social and Environmental Assessment Reports (SEAR reports), starting with the 2006 SEAR report: http://www.benjerrys.com/company/sear/2006/sear06_6.2.6.cfm?mid=menu6–2.

Appendix D

CORPORATE WATER GAUGE®

Corporate Water Gauge®

A Context-Based Solution for Measuring the Sustainability of Organizational Water Use

Developed by Mark W. McElroy, Ph.D. and
Heather A. Carlos, Acer GeoAnalytics

Introduction

- A new metric for measuring the ecological sustainability of an organization's water use
- Based on the 'quotients approach' to sustainability measurement and reporting developed by the *Center for Sustainable Organizations* (www.sustainableorganizations.org)
  - *Rate of use* measured against *rate of renewable supply* determines sustainability performance
- A watershed–centric approach
- Technology–enabled
  - GIS for spatial analysis

A 4–Step Method

1. Identify relevant watershed(s)

2. Determine net renewable water supplies in watershed(s) of interest, and allocate proportionate share to facilities

3. Determine net water use by facilities in watershed(s) of interest

4. Populate *Corporate Water Gauge®* quotient with data developed in steps 1 through 3 above, and compute sustainability scores, accordingly

GIS functionality
used to
determine
levels of
precipitation
in watersheds
of interest*

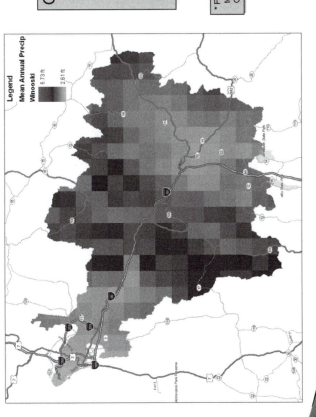

Legend
Mean Annual Precip
Winooski
■ 5.73 ft
■ 2.61 ft

* For U.S. sites, includes reference
to data provided by the PRISM
Group at Oregon State University.

4

Corporate
Water Gauge™

GIS functionality also used in combination with census data to determine human populations in watersheds

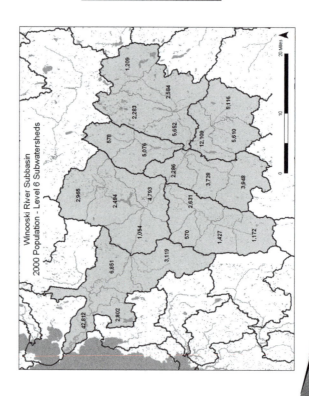

Winooski River Subbasin
2000 Population - Level 6 Subwatersheds

GIS functionality then used to determine per capita levels of available renewable water resources per watershed

Winooski River Subbasin
Gal per Capita - Level 6 Subwatersheds
(50% precip / 2000 Pop)

353,181

12,357,923

2,931,723

8,169,724

20,654,098

13,619,697

11,134,405

13,937,330

8,367,387

10,007,173

3,320,876

7,212,426

3,618,925

4,910,597

23,680,277

3,356,513

5,168,663

1,968,054

630,823

1,592,210

8,308,758

8,660,536

3,296,762

15,609,402

20 Miles
0   5   10

6

Key Principles

- Sustainability of water use should be grounded in knowledge of site-specific precipitation levels

- Renewable supplies should be determined by reference to associated watershed boundaries

- Stocks of surface and groundwater resources should be preserved and not drawn down

- Human use of water resources should be balanced with ecological needs

- Water use should be measured against available renewable supplies that are allocated to individual facilities using per capita and/or economic criteria

Advantages Over Other Tools

▶ Measures sustainability performance with local context taken fully into account

　○ Assesses water use in terms of local renewable water resource levels, which are allocated to a facility in per capita terms and/or as a function of economic impacts

　○ Makes it possible to score sustainability performance at a local, regional, national, global, and enterprise-wide level, with local contexts taken fully into account

▶ Makes use of advanced GIS tools in combination with site-specific datasets

▶ Results in measures that are fully compliant with GRI (i.e., includes 'sustainability context')

Appendix E
2007 WATER SUSTAINABILITY REPORT AT THE CABOT CREAMERY

Background and scope

Like most companies involved in manufacturing, water plays a vitally important role at Cabot. This is true, of course, on the farm as well as in our manufacturing plants. At Cabot we have two plants in Vermont, one in Massachusetts and one in upstate New York.

Since water resources are locally and unevenly distributed, the sustainability of water use should be examined individually for each facility. Our first analysis focused on our plant in Cabot, VT, where we examined the sustainability of that plant's water use in 2007. This report contains the results of that analysis.

Context-based sustainability

At Cabot our entire sustainability program is referred to as context-based sustainability (CBS). This approach to sustainability management measures, manages and reports sustainability performance in terms of our actual impacts on vital capital resources relative to what those impacts ought to be in order to ensure stakeholder well-being.

This means that water use, for example, is always measured, managed and reported in the context of locally available water supplies and never in isolation from them. Social impacts, in turn, are viewed from the perspective of demographically relevant social conditions and needs. This also applies to economic impacts such as wages paid versus norms for livable wages.

Our adoption of CBS as an organizing framework for sustainability management logically leads to the use of context-based metrics (CBMs) for measurement and reporting. All of the metrics and measurements featured in this report, therefore, are based on actual conditions found in Cabot's local environment.

Methodology

Working with the Center for Sustainable Organizations and Acer GeoAnalytics, both in Vermont, we decided to utilize a context-based tool for measuring the sustainability of water use, called the Corporate Water Gauge (CWG). Unlike most tools and methods for measuring water use at individual facilities, the CWG measures use against specific allocations of locally available supplies (i.e., it measures water use *in context*).

Thus, our goal was to hold ourselves accountable to a standard of performance for water use which if adhered to by all users of water in the watershed would fall well within total available renewable supplies. By taking this position, none of the locally available surface and ground waters would be touched, since, by definition, *locally available renewable water supplies* consist only of precipitation volumes in a given watershed. In this regard, the CWG takes a very conservative stance on resources deemed available for human use versus resources that should be left alone.

How we measure our sustainability performance

Our commitment to context-based sustainability gives rise to the use of context-based metrics (CBMs) as a tool for measuring sustainability performance. CBMs are generally constructed in the form of numerical quotients, where numerators represent an organization's impacts on a vital resource (e.g., water), and denominators represent a threshold for what those impacts ought to be in order for them to be sustainable.

Denominators in CBMs pertaining to environmental impacts generally express *ceiling* thresholds in a not-to-exceed sense of the term. Denominators that pertain to social or economic impacts, however, express thresholds in a *floor* or not-to-fall-below sense of the term. In either case, denominators express standards of performance that we should conform to.

For environmental measures, any score of ≤ 1.0 signifies sustainable performance since it shows that we are living within our environmental means. For social or economic measures, the opposite is true. Here any score of ≥ 1.0 signifies sustainable performance since it means that we are at least keeping up with our obligations to produce and/or maintain some vital (and non-environmental) resource important to stakeholder well-being.

The process we followed in using the CWG at our Cabot plant is summarized as follows:

1. We first determined the geography of the watershed where our Cabot plant is located by referring to USGS data sources.
2. We then computed the volume of precipitation that occurs in our watershed and established the size of the human population there. We arrived at these figures by

referring to various federal agencies and other third parties, as well as through the use of a geographic information system (GIS).

3. Next we determined the size of GDP in our watershed, and we used this figure to establish how much of the available renewable water could be allocated to the Cabot plant versus how much to other users in the same watershed. This was one of two ways we approached the allocation issue (described more fully below).

4. Having obtained the information above, we then measured the volume of water actually used by our plant in 2007. We did this by focusing on water sources, which in this case consisted of two on-site wells and a small supply piped in from the local municipality. Since all these supplies came from the same watershed where the Cabot plant is located, we knew that the watershed boundaries we had identified earlier were appropriate. If any water had come from sources beyond our watershed, we would have broadened the geographic scope of our analysis.

In measuring the volume of water consumed by our plant, we differentiated between water resources embedded in fluid milk received from our farmers versus water resources obtained from local supplies. While water resources embedded in incoming fluid milk are handled and processed by the plant, our farmers draw these supplies from their own local watersheds, and they, not the plant, must therefore account for them.

That said, all wastewater discharged by the plant back to the local watershed is accounted for as an offset to water withdrawals (by the plant), including wastewater originally embedded in milk. This is only true for legally permitted and benign discharges, which for our Cabot plant applies to all of our discharges.

5. Having calculated the net volume of water used at our Cabot plant (i.e., water withdrawals from the local watershed minus wastewater discharged back into it), we then turned our attention to what our water use should be. In other words, we defined a not-to-exceed threshold for water use.

We did this by first determining how much renewable water is available for all needs and users in the watershed (human and non-human alike), and then we allocated a proportionate or fair share to the Cabot plant. We did this in two ways.

The first way was to allocate water on a per capita basis. The logic of this approach is that organizations can be viewed as collectives of individuals entitled to no more natural resource use than their employees bring with them into the workplace in the form of their own entitlements. This is a conservative approach, which usually results in a lower allocation of resources when compared with other approaches.

In order to avoid double counting of people in their work lives versus their non-work lives, we use a measure called the *per capita equivalent* (PCE), which adds up total employee hours and then divides the sum by the total number of hours in a year (8,760). For example, a headcount of 1,000 employees will typically result in an adjusted per capita equivalent of 240 people, since most people only spend about 24 percent of their lives at work.

Having calculated the per capita equivalent size of our Cabot plant, we then allocated a proportionate volume of available renewable water supplies in the watershed to the plant. We based this on our PCE size relative to the total population of the watershed where the plant is located. This established a threshold or *standard of performance* for how much water could be used by the plant. Any usage beyond that threshold would be disproportionate and therefore unsustainable if it were generalized to the population as a whole.

In establishing this threshold, we also accounted for the volume of precipitation that is lost to evapotranspiration (ET). In Vermont that figure is around 45 percent.

We further allocated a share of available renewable water to non-human, ecological needs by assigning half the remaining supplies (55 percent of total precipitation, or 27.5 percent) to that purpose. The remaining 27.5 percent was then treated in our calculations as available for human use.

All in all, then, we subtracted 72.5 percent of annual precipitation levels in the Cabot watershed before allocating anything to human use (including our own plant). In addition to defining a threshold (i.e., denominator value) under the per capita allocation method, we also defined an alternative threshold using a method that considers the value of the economic contribution a business makes to society instead of merely its headcount. After all, businesses arguably need more than a per-capita-based share of resources in order to do what they do. And assuming we want them to make products and provide jobs, it is important to allocate resources accordingly.

We refer to this second approach for allocating resources as the *economic approach*. Under the economic approach, we first make all the same deductions for evapotranspiration and non-human needs described above for the per capita equivalent approach. From there we proceed a bit differently. First, we allocate as much of the remaining resources as are needed to satisfy household needs in the watershed, and then we distribute the remaining balance to organizations according to their respective contributions to GDP (i.e., in the same watershed).

Here we should point out that there is nothing hard and fast about how allocations are made in studies like this. Rather, it is simply the case that, in context-based sustainability, allocations of some kind must be made. In our case, we have developed two alternative ways of doing this. Other approaches are certainly possible, and the ones we have used might be imperfect.

6. Finally, in addition to measuring water use against sustainability standards for what such use ought to be, we then decided to measure the intensity of our water use at the Cabot plant in terms of water used per unit of production. The unit of production we selected was 'pounds of product handled or processed' at the plant. The resulting metric was: *gallons of water consumed per pound of product handled or processed.*

Here it should be clear that water intensity is not a measure of sustainability, but of eco-efficiency. Still, it is an important measure of water use, since improvements in efficiency can contribute to improvements in sustainability.

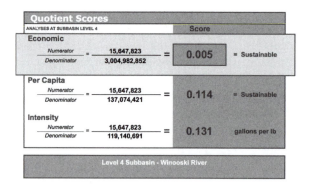

FIGURE E.1 Results of water analysis at Cabot plant (2007).

Results

The results of our analysis using the two allocation methods described above are shown in Figure E.1. The highlights are as follows:

1. First, the watershed system we decided to focus on is known as the Winooski River Subbasin (see Figure E.2). Since watersheds are actually nested within each other in a hierarchical fashion, this was an important choice. We could have chosen a watershed at a higher or lower level of analysis, but we ultimately settled on a mid-level watershed (referred to by the USGS as HUC Level 4) so as not to be too local or too global (geographically) in our approach.

2. Next, we determined that the net volume of water used at the Cabot plant in 2007 was 15,647,823 gallons. This is reflected in all three quotients shown in Figure E.1, and it includes consideration of water resources returned to the Winooski River Subbasin.

3. In terms of the sustainability measures taken for 2007, the results differed for each of the two allocation methods. This was expected. Starting with the economic allocation, the volume of available renewable water allocable to the Cabot plant was quite high: 3,004,982,852 gallons. For the per capita method, water resources allocable to the Cabot plant were about 22 times less: 137,074,421 gallons. Either way, both figures far exceeded the volume of water actually used by the plant in 2007, which again was 15,647,823 gallons. This resulted in the superb sustainability performance scores shown in Figure E.1.

   Under either allocation method, then, water use at our Cabot plant in 2007 can be described as *sustainable*. Indeed, if all users of water resources in the Winooski River Subbasin consumed water at the same rate as the Cabot plant that year – assuming either of the same two allocation methods was used – the collective use of available renewable water resources in the subbasin would be well below levels that are naturally regenerated through annual precipitation.

4. Lastly, the intensity or eco-efficiency of water use at our Cabot plant in 2007 came in at 0.131 gallons of water per pound of product handled or processed. For our purposes, this figure will be used as a baseline for future management and comparison purposes, since this is the first time we have made such a measurement at the Cabot plant.

Summary and conclusions

The water sustainability analysis performed (2007) for the plant in Cabot, VT, was one of the first experiences we had in using context-based metrics. Not only did we prove the viability of the use of such metrics, but the results of this particular study were strikingly positive. Few people may realize or appreciate just how fortunate we are in the northeast to have as much fresh water at our disposal as we do.

Indeed, as a result of the enormous volumes of renewable water resources found in this region, both of the allocation methods yielded extraordinary results. Scores in both cases were well below 1.0, indicating that our use of water resources at the Cabot plant by either measure was well within our fair share of available renewable supplies.

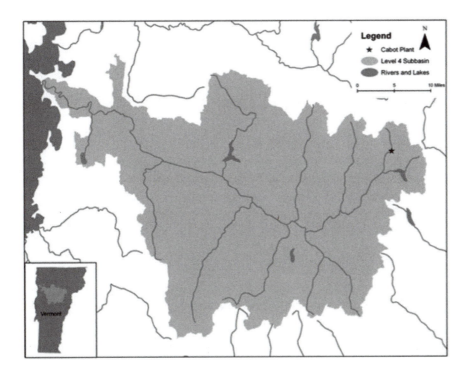

FIGURE E.2 Winooski River Subbasin.

GLOSSARY

Anthro capital

Anthro capital is a category of non-natural, vital capitals consisting of a mix of human capital, social capital and constructed (or built) capital. All three are human-made, or anthropogenic, hence the term we use.

Capital

Capital is a stock of anything that yields a flow of beneficial goods or services into the future – beneficial to humans and/or non-humans, that is.

Carbon footprint

A carbon footprint is a measure of a human collective's (i.e., an organization's) emissions of carbon dioxide or, more broadly, greenhouse gases. Such emissions can be calculated in at least four different ways: (1) *numerator-only* (see below), (2) *full-quotient-based* (see below) with denominators consisting of financial or economic values (i.e., resulting in so-called carbon *intensity* measures), (3) *full-quotient-based* with denominators consisting of ecological norms or thresholds (i.e., similar to the *Ecological Footprint Method*), or (4) *full-quotient-based* with denominators consisting of social norms or thresholds (i.e., similar to the *Social Footprint Method*).

Carrying capacity

Carrying capacity is a measure of a vital capital's ability to satisfy the basic needs of those who rely on it for their well-being (humans and/or non-humans) and is often expressed in terms of the size of the population it can support.

Cause metrics

A type of metric that is used to measure the level or condition of a factor that contributes in some causal way to a sustainability performance outcome or state of affairs involving one or more vital capitals. Contrasts with *effect metrics*.

Constructed (or built) capital

Constructed capital (or built capital) consists of *material objects and/or physical systems or infrastructures* created by humans. It is the material world of human artifacts in which human knowledge is also embedded, and which humans use in order to take effective action.

Context

Same as *sustainability context* below. In corporate sustainability management, context, or sustainability context, refers to specific thresholds for human impacts on vital capitals, conformance to which must be maintained in order for human activity to be sustainable.

Context-based metrics (CBMs)

A class or type of metrics used for measuring the sustainability performance of a human collective or organization that expresses impacts relative to specific thresholds for human impacts on vital capitals, conformance to which must be maintained in order for human activity to be sustainable.

Context-based sustainability (CBS)

A distinct branch or school of corporate sustainability management that measures, manages and reports sustainability performance relative to specific thresholds for human impacts on vital capitals, conformance to which must be maintained in order for human activity to be sustainable.

Corporate social responsibility (CSR)

A term defined by the World Business Council for Sustainable Development (WBCSD, 1999, p. 3) as follows: 'Corporate social responsibility is the continuing commitment by business to behave ethically and contribute to economic development while improving the quality of life of the workforce and their families as well as of the local community and society at large.'

Corporate sustainability management (CSM)

A management discipline that focuses on measuring, managing and reporting the (non-financial) sustainability performance of a company.

Denominator-based sustainability measurement and reporting

Same as *full-quotient-based sustainability measurement and reporting* below.

Eco-efficiency

An alternative, numerator-only approach to sustainability defined by the World Business Council for Sustainable Development in 1992 (Schmidheiny and WBCSD, 1992, p. 10) as follows: 'Industry is moving toward "demanufacturing" and "remanufacturing" – that is, recycling the materials in their products and thus limiting the use of raw materials and of energy to convert those raw materials ... That this is technically feasible is encouraging; that it can be done profitably is more encouraging. It is the more competitive and successful companies that are at the forefront of what we call "eco-efficiency".' The eco-efficiency of an organization or product is sometimes referred to as the intensity of natural resource use.

Ecological capital

Same as *natural capital*.

Ecological Footprint Method

The Ecological Footprint Method is a full-quotient-based approach for measuring and reporting the ecological impacts of a human collective (on natural capital), developed by Mathis Wackernagel and William Rees (1996).

Economic bottom line

A component of the so-called triple bottom line that businesses must attend to if they are to be sustainable, this is a measure of the economic sustainability performance of a company. Sometimes confused with the financial bottom line of a company, the economic bottom line is more a measure of a company's impacts on the general economic conditions of the communities in which it operates. The *Social Footprint Method* was designed to measure this bottom line.

Effect metrics

A type of metric that is used to measure the level or condition of a sustainability performance outcome or state of affairs involving one or more vital capitals. Contrasts with *cause metrics*.

Environmental (or ecological) bottom line

A component of the so-called triple bottom line that businesses must attend to if they are to be sustainable, this is a measure of the environmental (or ecological) sustainability performance of a company. The *Ecological Footprint Method* was designed to measure this bottom line, although it can also be measured by using other types of context-based metrics.

Financial bottom line

A measure of the financial performance of an organization expressed in terms of its impacts on monetary capital, usually as either profits or losses.

Financial measurement and reporting

Performance measurement and reporting that deals with human or organizational impacts on monetary capital and/or the monetary value of other types of assets. Contrasts with *non-financial measurement and reporting*, which deals only with impacts on natural capital, human capital, social capital and constructed capital.

Financial performance

Financial performance is a type of performance that involves impacts on financial or monetary capital. It is the complement to non-financial performance, which involves impacts on natural, human, social and constructed (or built) capitals.

Full-quotient-based sustainability measurement and reporting

An approach to measuring and reporting the sustainability performance of an organization that measures impacts (quantified in numerators) against standards of performance for such impacts (quantified in denominators). The Social and Ecological Footprint Methods, and some but not all carbon footprint methods, are examples of this.

Geographic information system (GIS)

A geographic information system (GIS) is any system that captures, stores, analyzes, manages and presents data that are linked to location(s). In the simplest terms, GIS is the merging of cartography, statistical analysis and database technology (source: Wikipedia).

Human capital

Human capital consists of *individual* knowledge, skills, experience, health and ethical entitlements that enhance the potential for effective individual action and human well-being.

Intensity

Same as *eco-efficiency*.

Life cycle assessment (LCA)

A life cycle assessment or LCA (also known as a 'life cycle analysis', 'eco-balance', 'cradle-to-grave-analysis', etc.) is the investigation and valuation of the environmental impact of a given product or service caused or necessitated by its existence. It is a variant of input–output analysis that focuses on physical rather than monetary flows (source: Wikipedia).

Metric

A standard of measurement. In corporate sustainability management (CSM), metrics can be numerator-only in form, denominator-based in form, or full-quotient in form. In CSM, a distinction can also be made between cause metrics and effect metrics (see above), either of which can be numerator-only, denominator-based or full-quotient in form.

Monetary capital

Monetary capital consists of money and/or the pecuniary value of other assets.

Natural capital

Natural capital is defined by Hawken et al. (1999, p. 151) as: 'the sum total of the ecological systems [including life itself] that support life, different from human-made capital in that natural capital cannot be produced by human activity'. It is the stock of environmental resources on Earth that yields the flow of natural resource goods and ecosystem services.

Non-financial measurement and reporting

Non-financial measurement and reporting is a type of performance measurement and reporting that deals with human or organizational impacts on natural capital, human capital, social capital and constructed capital. Contrasts with *financial measurement and reporting*, which deals only with impacts on monetary capital and/or the monetary value of other types of assets.

Non-financial performance

Non-financial performance is a type of performance that involves impacts on natural, human, social and constructed (or built) capitals. It is the complement to financial performance, which involves impacts on financial or monetary capital.

Numerator-only sustainability measurement and reporting

An approach to measuring and reporting the sustainability performance of a human collective (e.g., an organization) that is not context-based, and which therefore fails to take sustainability thresholds into account. Eco-efficiency as an approach to corporate sustainability management is one such example.

Per capita equivalent (PCE)

A nuanced per capita metric that is used to convert the employee size of an organization from a population of part-time workers (i.e., even full-time workers only work 8 hours a day) to their true full-time equivalent (i.e., to what the size of a workforce would be if its workers worked 24 hours a day, but no more in total hours than they already do in a year). This is computed by taking total employee hours worked in a year and then dividing it by 8,760 hours, which is the total number of hours in a year. The resulting number is the per capita equivalent, or PCE, size of an organization.

Quotient-based sustainability measurement and reporting

Same as *full-quotient-based sustainability measurement and reporting*.

Social bottom line

A component of the so-called triple bottom line that businesses should attend to if they are to be sustainable. It is a measure of the social sustainability performance of a company, and one of the things the *Social Footprint Method* was designed to measure.

Social capital

Social capital consists of *shared* knowledge and organizational resources (e.g., formal or informal networks of people committed to achieving common goals) that enhance the potential for effective individual and collective action and human well-being.

Social Footprint Method

A context-based approach for measuring and reporting the social sustainability performance of an organization, developed by Mark W. McElroy and the Center for Sustainable Organizations (McElroy, 2008).

Stakeholder

A stakeholder in an organization is anyone whose vital capitals – and whose interests and well-being, therefore – are affected by the organization's actions, or whose vital capitals ought to be so affected by virtue of the relationship that exists between them.

Sustainability

The subject of a social and/or management science that studies the impacts of human activity on the carrying capacities of vital capitals – usually accomplished by measuring such impacts against standards of performance, or norms, for what they ought to be in order to ensure human and/or non-human well-being.

Sustainability context

Same as *context* above. In corporate sustainability management, context, or sustainability context, refers to specific thresholds for human impacts on vital capitals, conformance to which must be maintained in order for human activity to be sustainable.

Sustainability performance

A measure of the sustainability of an organization's (or human collective's) activities as a function of their impacts on vital capitals.

Sustainable

A description of human activity indicating that the impacts of such activity on vital capitals are consistent with related standards of performance, or norms, for what such impacts ought to be in order to ensure human and/or non-human well-being.

Triple bottom line (TBL)

An organizing principle (and term) coined by John Elkington (Elkington, 1997), which refers to the measurement, management and reporting of corporate sustainability performance in terms of a social bottom line, an environmental bottom line and an economic bottom line. According to TBL theory, the overall performance of an organization must be judged in terms of all three areas of impact, and not just in terms of financial impacts.

Vital capitals

Types of capital required for basic human and/or non-human well-being, the absence of which can put such well-being at risk. In sustainability theory and practice, such capitals generally consist of natural (or ecological) capital and anthro capital (i.e., human, social and constructed capital).

REFERENCES

AccountAbility (2008a) *AA1000 Accountability Principles Standard 2008 (AA1000APS)*, http://www.accountability.org/about-us/publications/aa1000.html, accessed January 27, 2011.

——(2008b) *AA1000 Assurance Standard 2008 (AA1000AS)*, http://www.accountability.org/standards/aa1000as/index.html, accessed January 27, 2011.

Argyle, M. (1987) *The Psychology of Happiness*, Routledge, London.

Argyris, C. (1990) *Overcoming Organizational Defenses*, Prentice Hall, Upper Saddle River, NJ.

B Lab (2010) 'Maryland first state in union to pass benefit corporation legislation', www.csrwire.com/press_releases/29332-Maryland-First-State-in-Union-to-Pass-Benefit-Corporation-Legislation, accessed October 5, 2010.

Bakan, J. (2004) *The Corporation – The Pathological Pursuit of Profit and Power*, Free Press, New York.

Black, J., Hashimzade, N. and Myles, G. (2009) *Oxford Dictionary of Economics*, Oxford University Press, Oxford.

Becker, G. (1993[1964]) *Human Capital*, University of Chicago Press, Chicago, IL.

Begon, M., Harper, J. and Townsend, C. (1996) *Ecology*, Blackwell Science, Oxford.

Boulding, K. (1949) 'Income or welfare', *The Review of Economic Studies*, vol. 17, no. 2, pp. 77–86.

——(1966) 'The economics of the coming spaceship earth', in H. Jarrett (ed.) *Environmental Quality in a Growing Economy*, Johns Hopkins University Press, Baltimore, MD.

Cabot Creamery Cooperative (2009) *Sustainability Scope Documentation v10.0*, Unpublished Internal Documentation, Montpelier, VT.

Cavaleri, S., Firestone, J. and Hadders, H. (2011) 'Measuring organizational sustainability performance: the adaptive quadruple bottom line scorecard', *Dimensions, International Management Journal of IBS Mumbai*, vol. 2, no. 1, pp. 1–8.

Cavaleri, S. and Seivert, S. (2005) *Knowledge Leadership: The Art and Science of the Knowledge-Based Organization*, Butterworth-Heinemann, Boston, MA.

Cherchye, L. and Kuosmanen, T. (2006) 'Benchmarking sustainable development: a synthetic meta-index approach', in M. McGillivray and M. Clarke (eds) *Understanding Human Well-Being*, United Nations University Press, Tokyo.

Costanza, R. and Daly, H. (1992) 'Natural capital and sustainable development', *Conservation Biology*, vol. 6, no. 1, pp. 37–46.

Daily, G. (1997) 'Introduction – what are ecosystem services?', in G. Daily (ed.) *Nature's Services – Societal Dependence on Natural Ecosystems*, Island Press, Washington, DC.

Daly, H. (1977) *Steady-State Economics*, Freeman, San Francisco, CA.

——(1990) 'Toward some operational principles of sustainable development', *Ecological Economics*, vol. 2, pp. 1–6.

——(1996) *Beyond Growth*, Beacon, Boston, MA.

Dasgupta, P. (2001) *Human Well-Being and the Natural Environment*, Oxford University Press, Oxford.

Davis, K. and Blomstrom, R. (1975) *Business and Society: Environment and Responsibility*, McGraw-Hill, New York.

Deegan, C. (2007) 'Organizational legitimacy as a motive for sustainability reporting', in J. Unerman, J. Bebbington and B. O'Dwyer (eds) *Sustainability Accounting and Accountability*, Routledge, New York.

Diener, E. (1984) 'Subjective well-being', *Psychological Bulletin*, vol. 95, pp. 542–75.

Diener, E. and Larsen, R.J. (1993) 'The experience of emotional well-being', in M. Lewis and J.M. Haviland (eds) *Handbook of Emotions*, Guilford, New York.

Doyal, L. and Gough, I. (1991) *A Theory of Need*, Macmillan, London.

Dresner, S. (2002) *The Principles of Sustainability*, Earthscan, London.

Eccles, R. and Krzus, M. (2010) *One Report – Integrated Reporting for a Sustainable Strategy*, Wiley, Hoboken, NJ.

Edinger, R. and Kaul, S. (2003) *Sustainable Mobility*, Praeger Publishers, Westport, CT.

Eid, M. and Diener, E. (2003) 'Global judgements of subjective well-being: situational variability and long-term stability', *Social Indicators Research*, vol. 65, pp. 245–77.

Ekins, P. (1992) 'A four-capital model of wealth creation', in P. Ekins and M. Max-Neef (eds) *Real-Life Economics*, Routledge, London.

Elkington, J. (1997) *Cannibals with Forks – The Triple Bottom Line of 21st Century Business*, Capstone, Oxford.

Faber, N. (2006) 'Knowledge in sustainable behavior – using knowledge-based decision support systems for the improvement of sustainability', PhD thesis, University of Groningen, the Netherlands, Labyrint Publications, Ridderkerk.

Faber, N., Jorna, R. and van Engelen, J. (2005) 'The sustainability of "sustainability" – a study into the conceptual foundations of the notion of "sustainability"', *Journal of Environmental Policy and Assessment Management*, vol. 7, no. 1, pp. 1–33.

Firestone, J. and McElroy, M. (2003) *Key Issues in the New Knowledge Management*, Butterworth-Heinemann, Burlington, MA.

——(2005) 'Doing knowledge management', *The Learning Organization*, vol. 12, no. 2, pp. 189–212.

Fisher, I. (2003[1906]) *The Nature of Capital and Income*, Simon Publications, San Diego, CA.

Forrester, J. (1961) *Industrial Dynamics*, MIT Press, Cambridge, MA.

——(1969) *Urban Dynamics*, Pegasus Communications, Waltham, MA.

——(1971) *World Dynamics*, Pegasus Communications, Waltham, MA.

Freeman, E. (1984) *Strategic Management: A Stakeholder Approach*, Pitman, Boston, MA.

Freeman, E., Harrison, J., Wicks, A., Parmar, B. and de Colle, S. (2010) *Stakeholder Theory: The State of the Art*, Cambridge University Press, Cambridge.

Freeman, E. and Reed, D. (1983) 'Stockholders and stakeholders: a new perspective on corporate governance', in C. Huizinga (ed.) *Corporate Governance: A Definitive Exploration of the Issues*, University Press, Los Angeles, CA.

Friedman, M. (1970) 'The social responsibility of business is to increase its profits', *The New York Times Magazine*, September 13, 1970 (available online at: http://www.colorado.edu/stu dentgroups/libertarians/issues/friedman-soc-resp-business.html, accessed February 25, 2011).

Gleick, P., Cooley, H., Cohen, M., Morikawa, M. and Palaniappan, M. (2009) *The World's Water*, Island Press, Washington, DC.

Global Reporting Initiative (GRI) (2011) *Sustainability Reporting Guidelines*, Global Reporting Initiative, Amsterdam.

Gray, R. and Bebbington, J. (2005) 'Corporate sustainability: accountability or impossible dream?', http://www.st-andrews.ac.uk/~csearweb/researchresources/dps-sustain-handcorp. html, accessed January 20, 2011.

——(2007) 'Corporate sustainability: accountability or impossible dream?', in G. Atkinson, S. Dietz and E. Neumayer (eds) *Handbook of Sustainable Development*, Edward Elgar Publishing Limited, Cheltenham.

Gray, R. and Milne, M. (2002) 'Sustainability reporting: who's kidding whom?', *Chartered Accountants Journal of New Zealand*, vol. 81, no. 6, pp. 66–70.

——(2004) 'Towards reporting on the triple bottom line: mirages, methods and myths', in A. Henriques and J. Richardson (eds) *The Triple Bottom Line – Does It All Add Up?*, Earthscan, London.

Greenfield, K. (2006) *The Failure of Corporate Law – Fundamental Flaws and Progressive Possibilities*, University of Chicago Press, Chicago, IL.

Hawken, P., Lovins, A. and Lovins, L. (1999) *Natural Capitalism – Creating the Next Industrial Revolution*, Little, Brown & Co., New York.

Hicks, J. (1939) *Value and Capital*, Oxford University Press, London.

——(1974) 'Capital controversies: ancient and modern', *American Economic Review*, vol. LXIV, no. 2, pp. 307–16.

Hobbes, T. (1651) *Leviathan*.

Jennings, V. (2004) 'Addressing the economic bottom line', in A. Henriques and J. Richardson (eds) *The Triple Bottom Line – Does It All Add Up?*, Earthscan, London.

Jevons, W. (1866) *The Coal Question*, MacMillan and Co., London.

Jorna, R. (2006) *Sustainable Innovation*, Greenleaf Publishing, Sheffield, UK.

Jorna, R., van Engelen, J. and Hadders, H. (2004) *Duurzame Innovatie*, Koninklijke van Gorcum, Assen.

Kant, I. (1785) *Groundwork of the Metaphysic of Morals*, trans. T.K. Abbott, 2010, BN Publishing, Lexington, KY.

Karnani, A. (2010) 'The case against corporate social responsibility', *Wall Street Journal*, August 23, 2010, p. R1.

Locke, J. (1689) *Second Treatise on Government*.

McDonough, W. and Braungart, M. (1998) 'The next industrial revolution', *Atlantic Monthly*, vol. 282, no. 4, pp. 82–91.

McElroy, M. (1997) 'Paradigms lost and the myths we teach our children', *Green Teacher*, issue 53, pp. 6–10.

——(2000) 'Integrating complexity theory, knowledge management and organizational learning', *Journal of Knowledge Management*, vol. 4, no. 3, pp. 195–203.

——(2002) 'Social innovation capital', *Journal of Intellectual Capital*, vol. 3, no. 1, pp. 30–9.

——(2003) *The New Knowledge Management*, Butterworth-Heinemann, Burlington, MA.

——(2008) 'Social footprints – measuring the social sustainability performance of organizations', PhD thesis, University of Groningen, the Netherlands.

McElroy, M., Jorna, R. and van Engelen, J. (2006) 'Rethinking social capital theory: a knowledge management perspective', *Journal of Knowledge Management*, vol. 10, no. 5, pp. 124–36.

——(2007) 'Sustainability quotients and the social footprint', *Corporate Social Responsibility and Environmental Management*, vol. 15, no. 4, pp. 223–34.

McGillivray, M. and Clarke, M. (2006) *Understanding Human Well-Being*, United Nations University Press, Tokyo.

Malthus, T. (1998[1798]) *An Essay on the Principle of Population*, Prometheus Books, Amherst, NY.

Maslow, A. (1971) *The Farther Reaches of Human Nature*, Viking Press, New York.

Max-Neef, M. (1991) *Human Scale Development*, Apex Press, New York.

Meadows, D.H. (1998) *Indicators and Information Systems for Sustainable Development*, The Sustainability Institute, Hartland Four Corners, VT.

Meadows, D.H., Meadows, D.L. and Randers, J. (1992) *Beyond the Limits*, Chelsea Green Publishing, White River Junction, VT.

Meadows, D.H., Meadows, D.L., Randers, J. and Behrens W. (1972) *The Limits to Growth*, New American Library, New York.

Mill, J. (1923[1848]) *Principles of Political Economy, with Some of Their Applications to Social Philosophy*, Longmans, Green and Co., London.

Narayan, D., Chambers, R., Shah, M.K. and Petesch, P. (2000) *Voices of the Poor: Crying out for Change*, Oxford University Press for the World Bank, New York.

Nussbaum, M. (1988) 'Nature, function and capability', *Oxford Studies in Ancient Philosophy*, supplement 1, pp. 145–84.

——(1992) 'Human functioning and social justice', *Political Theory*, vol. 20, no. 2, pp. 202–46.

——(2000) *Women and Human Development: The Capabilities Approach*, Cambridge University Press, Cambridge.

Ostrom, E. and Ahn, T. (2003) *Foundations of Social Capital*, Edward Elgar Publishing, Cheltenham.

Owen, D. (2007) 'Assurance practice in sustainability reporting', in J. Unerman, J. Bebbington and B. O'Dwyer (eds) *Sustainability Accounting and Accountability*, Routledge, London.

Oxford University Press (2010) *Oxford Dictionary of Accounting*, Oxford University Press, New York.

Pearce, D. (1988) 'Economics, equity and sustainable development', *Futures: The Journal of Forecasting and Planning*, vol. 20, no. 6, pp. 595–602.

Pearce, D. and Turner, R. (1990) *Economics of Natural Resources and the Environment*, Johns Hopkins University Press, Baltimore, MD.

Porritt, J. (2005) *Capitalism as if the World Matters*, Earthscan, London.

——(2007) 'Foreword', in J. Unerman, J. Bebbington and B. O'Dwyer (eds) *Sustainability Accounting and Accountability*, Routledge, London.

Porter, M. and Kramer, M. (2006) 'Strategy and society: the link between competitive advantage and corporate social responsibility', *Harvard Business Review*, December 2006, pp. 78–92.

Rees, W. (1992) 'Ecological footprints and appropriated carrying capacity: what urban economics leaves out', *Environment and Urbanization*, vol. 4, no. 2, pp. 120–30.

——(2003) 'Understanding urban ecosystems: an ecological economics perspective', in A. Berkowitz, C. Nilon and K. Hollweg (eds) *Understanding Urban Ecosystems*, Springer-Verlag, New York.

Rousseau, J. (1762) *The Social Contract, or Principles of Political Right*.

Ruta, G. and Hamilton, K. (2007) 'The capital approach to sustainability', in G. Atkinson, S. Dietz and E. Neumayer (eds) *Handbook of Sustainable Development*, Edward Elgar Publishing Limited, Cheltenham.

Sayre, N. (2008) 'The genesis, history, and limits of carrying capacity', *Annals of the Association of American Geographers*, vol. 98, no. 1, pp. 120–34.

Schmidheiny, S. and World Business Council for Sustainable Development (WBCSD) (1992) *Changing Course*, MIT Press, Cambridge, MA.

Sen, A. (1984) *Resources, Values and Development*, Harvard University Press, Cambridge, MA.

——(1999) *Development as Freedom*, Anchor Books, New York.

——(2006) 'Conceptualizing and measuring poverty', in D. Grusky and R. Kanbur (eds) *Poverty and Inequality*, Stanford University Press, Stanford, CA.

Social Investment Forum (2010) *2010 Report on Socially Responsible Investing Trends in the United States*, http://www.socialinvest.org/resources/research/, accessed January 27, 2011.

Stern, D. (1997) 'The capital theory approach to sustainability: a critical appraisal', *Journal of Economic Issues*, vol. 31, no. 1, pp. 145–73.

Stiglitz, J., Sen, A. and Fitoussi, J. (2009) *Report by the Commission on the Measurement of Economic Performance and Social Progress*, http://www.stiglitz-sen-fitoussi.fr/documents/rapport_anglais.pdf, accessed September 28, 2010.

Thomson, I. (2007) 'Mapping the terrain of sustainability accounting', in J. Unerman, J. Bebbington and B. O'Dwyer (eds) *Sustainability Accounting and Accountability*, Routledge, London.

Unerman, J., Bebbington, J. and O'Dwyer, B. (2007) *Sustainability Accounting and Accountability*, Routledge, London.

United Nations World Water Assessment Programme (2006) *Water: A Shared Responsibility – The United Nations World Water Development Report 2*, UNESCO, Paris and Berghahn Books, New York.

Veenhoven, R. (2004) *World Happiness Database*, www.eur.nl/fsw/research/happiness, accessed September 28, 2010.

von Carlowitz, H.C. (1713) *Sylvicultura Oeconomica*, Johann Friedrich Brauns, Leipzig.

Wackernagel, M. and Rees, W. (1996) *Our Ecological Footprint – Reducing Human Impact on the Earth*, New Society Publishers, Gabriola Island, BC, Canada.

Wigley, T. (2000) 'Stabilization of CO_2 concentration scenarios', in T. Wigley and D. Schimel (eds) *The Carbon Cycle*, Cambridge University Press, Cambridge.

World Business Council for Sustainable Development (WBCSD) (1999) *Meeting Changing Expectations*, http://www.wbcsd.org/DocRoot/hbdf19Txhmk3kDxBQDWW/CSRmeeting.pdf, accessed March 22, 2011.

World Commission on Environment and Development (WCED) (1987) *Our Common Future*, Oxford University Press, Oxford.

World Council of Churches (1974), as quoted in S. Dresner (2002) *The Principles of Sustainability*, Earthscan, London.

World Resources Institute (WRI) (2005) *Navigating the Numbers – Greenhouse Gas Data and International Climate Policy*, WRI, Washington, DC.

INDEX

Note: Page numbers in italics indicate figures and tables. Page numbers followed by an "n" indicate notes.

AA1000 Accountability Principles Standard (Account-Ability), 161–63
AASHE (Association for the Advancement of Sustainability in Higher Education), 152–53
absolute metrics, 62–63
  see also context-based metrics (CBMs)
adaptive learning cycle, 97
Ahn, T., *Foundations of Social Capital*, 19
analog metrics, *119*, 119
  see also measurement
anthro capital
  carrying capacities of, 123
  defined, 35, 57
any-day behaviors, 15
areas of impact, 105–6, 176–81
assurance standards, 161

B Corporations, 49–50
Bakan, J., 47
Bebbington, J., 15–17, 147, 158
Behrens III, William, *The Limits to Growth*, 11–13
Ben & Jerry's, climate change mitigation metrics, 199–202, *200*, *201*
binary metrics, *119*, 119
  see also measurement
bottom lines, number of, 58–61, *60*
Boulding, Kenneth, 21–22

boundaries
  organizational, 103–4
  problem of, 156–57
Braungart, M., 79
Bright Exchange, 165
Brundtland Report, 14–15
built capital. *see* constructed capital
business strategy, and sustainability strategy, 47–54
business to business scorecards, 104

Cabot Creamery Cooperative
  2007 Water Sustainability Report, 214–19, *218*, *219*
  approach to sustainability, 169–75, *171*
  case study, 92–94, *94*
  credo, 175
  defining denominators for water use at, 126–29
  Destamminator, 128–29
  formulating duties and obligations at, 182–204
capital-based theory of sustainability. *see* theory of system
Capitalism as if the World Mattered (Porritt), 26–27
capitals, identified by Porritt, 27
capital/stakeholder basis of performance, *60*
Carlos, Heather A., 205–13

carrying capacity
  and human well-being, 36–39
  and sustainability context, 80–81
categorical imperative (CI), 155
cause metrics, 115, 175
cheese industry, duties and obligations
  (D/O) to, 202–4
Clarke, M., *Understanding Human Well-Being*,
  32
climate change mitigation metrics, 199–202,
  200, 201
commercial performance, 187
Commission on Sustainable Development
  (CSD), 34
Commission on the Measurement of
  Economic Performance and Social
  Progress report, 17–18
community, duties and obligations (D/O)
  to, 192–99
composite indicators, 34
consolidated sustainability scores, 133–34
constructed capital, defined, 35, 112
consumers, duties and obligations (D/O)
  to, 185–89
context-based index, 165
context-based metrics (CBMs), 61–66, *66*
  absolute metrics, 62–63
  and Cabot Creamery Cooperative, 173–75
  denominators in, *120*, 120–26, *121*
  developing, 114–20, *115, 116, 117, 118,*
    119
  numerators in, 130–31
  plotting and interpreting scores, 131–34,
    132
  relative metrics, 62–63
context-based sustainability (CBS)
  assurance standards, 161
  Cabot Creamery Cooperative, 169–71,
    171
  conclusions, 152–57
  and core business processes and cycles,
    46–55
  future of, 157–66
  scenarios of, *150*, 150–52, *151*
  summary of, 145–50
corporate social responsibility (CSR), 75
corporate sustainability management
  (CSM)
  boundary problem in, 156–57
  history of, 8–45
  third-party evaluators and evaluations of,
    161
Corporate Water Gauge, 127, 205–13
Costanza, Robert, 24–25

cross-company comparisons, measurement
  standards for, 70–74
CSM cycle
  methodology for practitioners, 94–99,
    96, 98
  practicing, 99–138, *113–121, 132, 134,*
    138
dairy industry, duties and obligations (D/O)
  to, 202–4

Daly, Herman
  Daly's rules, 27–29, 74–75
  Ecological Economics, 23–24
  influence of, 24–25
Daly's rules, 27–29, 74–75
Deegan, C., 143 n1
denominator-based sustainability
  measurement and reporting. *see* full-
  quotient-based sustainability
  measurement and reporting
Destamminator, 128–29
discretionary impacts, 99
  see also CSM cycle
double-loop CSM cycle, *98*
  see also CSM cycle
duties and obligations (D/O), at Cabot
  Creamery Cooperative, 182–204

Eccles, R., One Report, 135–36
eco-efficiency, 78–80, 129
Ecological Economics (Daly), 23–24
Ecological Footprint Method (EFM), 25–26,
  28, 66, 155
economic bottom lines, 55–58, *58, 113*
Economic Indicators, 56
Edmonds, James, 199
educational bottom lines, 57
efficiency, use of term, 78–80
Ekins, Paul, 24
  Four-Capital Model of Wealth Creation, 147
Elkington, John, and the triple bottom line
  (TBL), 26, 55–56
employees, duties and obligations (D/O)
  to, 188–92
environmental bottom lines, *114*
An Essay on the Principle of Population
  (Malthus), 9–10

FEE, 161
financial bottom lines, 55–58, *58*
Fisher, Irving, 20
Fitoussi, Jean-Paul, 17–18
Foundations of Social Capital (Ostrom and
  Ahn), 19

Four-Capital Model of Wealth Creation (Ekins), 147
full-quotient-based sustainability measurement and reporting, 223

GAAP for non-financial accounting, 160
Generally Accepted Accounting Principles (GAAP), 70–71
geographic information system (GIS), 223
geographic reach, 106
GHG emissions, 196
global community, duties and obligations (D/O) to, 196–99
Global Reporting Initiative (GRI)
  and assurance standards, 161
  and context-free sustainability, 75–82
  Economic Indicators, 56
  integrated reporting, 136
  launch of, 29
  Sustainability Reporting Guidelines, 158
government bottom lines, 57
Gray, R., 15–17, 147, 158
Greenfield, K., 47–48
Greenhouse Gas Protocol, 152–53

healthcare bottom lines, 57
Hicks, John, 20–21, 23
housing bottom lines, 57
human capital, 35, 112
Human Development Index (HDI), 34
human well-being, 32–34
  and carrying capacity, 36–39
  standards for, 125–26
  and sustainability context, *39*, 39–43
  Understanding Human Well-Being (McGillivray and Clarke), 32
  and vital capitals, 34–36, *36*

industry, duties and obligations (D/O) to, 202–4
integrated reporting, 135–36
intensity, measure of performance, 78–80, 129
inter-generational equity, 15
International Integrated Reporting Committee (IIRC), 136
interventions
  implementing, 137–38, *138*
  planning, 136–37

Jevons' Paradox, 79

Kant, Immanuel, 155
Kassoy, Andrew, 49–50

Kramer, Mark
  on boundary problem in CSM, 156–57
  on CSM and strategy, 47, 50, 53
  on CSM functions, 106
Krzus, M., One Report, 135–36

less sustainable performance, 66–67, *67*
  see also performance
life cycle assessments (LCAs), 68–70, 122
The Limits to Growth (Meadows et al.), 11–13
local community, duties and obligations (D/O) to, 192–93

Malthus, Thomas R., *An Essay on the Principle of Population*, 9–10
management, and strategy, 47–54
marginal improvements, 99
  see also CSM cycle
materiality, 108–9
McDonough, W., 79
McElroy, Mark W., 205–13
McGillivray, M., *Understanding Human Well-Being*, 32
Meadows, Dennis, *The Limits to Growth*, 11–13
Meadows, Donella, *The Limits to Growth*, 11–13
measurement
  and Cabot Creamery Cooperative, 173–75
  and CBS, 55–75, *58*, *60*, *66*, *67*
  frameworks for, 70–74
  full-quotient, 223
  of performance, 130–36, *132*, *134*
metrics, 173–75
Mill, John Stuart, *Principles of Political Economy with Some of Their Applications to Social Philosophy*, 10–11
Millennium Development Goals (MDGs), 34, 123
Milne, M., 15–17
more sustainable performance, 66–67, *67*
  see also performance
multi-bottom-lines, 58–61, *60*
  see also triple bottom line (TBL)

natural capital, 21, 34, 123
  and Cabot Creamery Cooperative, 170–71, *171*
  defined, 112
non-financial bottom lines. *see* triple bottom line (TBL)

non-financial capitals
  and Cabot Creamery Cooperative,
    172–73
  duties and obligations (D/O) to
    stakeholders, 111–14, *113*, *114*
non-financial performance, 32
normative impacts, 174
normative levels, 36–39
numerator-only reporting, 117–18, *118*
  see also reporting

objective indicators, 34
obligatory impacts, 99
  see also CSM cycle
One Report, 135–36
  see also reporting
organizational allocations, 39, 81
organizational performance. *see*
  performance
organizations, boundaries of, 103–4
Ostrom, E., *Foundations of Social Capital*,
  19
Owen, D., 161

Pearce, D., influence of, 24
people–planet–profit. *see* triple bottom line
  (TBL)
per capita equivalent (PCE), 62
  see also context-based metrics (CBMs)
per unit of production metrics, 63
  see also context-based metrics (CBMs)
performance
  capital/stakeholder basis of, *60*
  commercial performance, 187
  intensity, 129
  interpretation of, 32
  less sustainable, 66–67, *67*
  measurement and assessment of, 130–36,
    132, *134*
  more sustainable, 66–67, *67*
  non-financial, 32
  organizational, 32
  reporting, 134–36
  rules for, 74–75
  standards of, 9, 36–39, 110–30, *113–121*
  sustainability performance, 18, 66–67,
    67, 74–75
  sustainability scales for, 66–67, *67*
Porritt, Jonathan, *Capitalism as if the World
  Mattered*, 26–27
Porter, Michael
  on boundary problem in CSM, 156–57
  on CSM and strategy, 47, 50, 53
  on CSM functions, 106

present-day behaviors, 15
Prince's Accounting for Sustainability
  Project, 136
*Principles of Political Economy with Some of
  Their Applications to Social Philosophy*
  (Mill), 10–11
procurement, sustainable, 104
products, sustainability of, 67–70

quotient of quotients, 134
quotient-based sustainability measurement
  and reporting. *see* full-quotient-based
  sustainability measurement and
  reporting

Randers, Jorgen, *The Limits to Growth*,
  11–13
Rees, William, 25–26
regional community, duties and obligations
  (D/O) to, 194–96
relative metrics, 62–63
  see also context-based metrics (CBMs)
reporting
  and Cabot Creamery Cooperative,
    173–75
  and CBS, 55–75, *58*, *60*, *66*, *67*
  full-quotient, 223
  integrated reporting, 135–36
  numerator-only, 117–18, *118*
  performance, 134–36
responsible populations, 39
  and sustainability context, 81
Richels, Richard, 199

Safe Quality Food (SQF) program, 185
safety, duties and obligations (D/O) for,
  188–92
Sen, Amartya, 17–18
shareholder primacy, 47–54
shareholders, 32
social bottom lines, 57, *113*
social capital, 35, 112
Social Footprint Method, 66
social/geographic reach, 106
socially responsible investing (SRI), 164–65
socio-efficacy, 80
stakeholders
  and Cabot Creamery Cooperative,
    171–72
  duties and obligations to, 111–14, *113*,
    114
  engagement, 138–40
  identifying, 105–10
  well-being of, 176–81

standards of performance
    and carrying capacity, 36–39
    setting, 110–30, *113–121*
    vs. standards of accounting, 124
    Von Carlowitz on, 9
STARS (Sustainability Tracking
    Assessment and Rating System), 152–53
Stiglitz, Joseph, 17–18
stock exchanges, 165
strategies
    implementing, 137–38, *138*
    planning, 136–37
sub-bottom lines, 57, *58*
subjective schemes, 34
sufficient improvements, 99
    see also CSM cycle
supply chains, 104
sustainability
    business case for, 54–55
    defined, 37
    types of, 105
    Von Carlowitz use of term, 9
sustainability context
    determination of, 80–81
    GRI definition, 75–82
    and human well-being, *39*, 39–43
    Von Carlowitz's reliance on, 9
sustainability management, 38
sustainability performance
    resource-based view of, 18
    rules for, 74–75
    scales, 66–67, *67*
sustainability scores, consolidated, 133–34
sustainability strategy, and business strategy,
    47–54
sustainable development, defined, 14
sustainable procurement, 104

theory of system, 90–91, 94–99, *96*, *98*
    relevance of, 18–19
triple bottom line (TBL), 29–31, 125
    economic and financial bottom lines,
        55–58, *58*
    number of bottom lines, 58–61, *60*
True Sustainability Index®, 165
Turner, R., influence of, 24

ULE ISR 880 standard, 159
UN Commission on Sustainable
    Development (CSD), 34
UN Millennium Development Goals
    (MDGs), 34, 123
Understanding Human Well-Being
    (McGillivray and Clarke), 32
UNDP Human Development Index
    (HDI), 34
unsustainable behaviors, 15

vital capitals
    defined, 25
    and human well-being, 34–36, *36*
    stakeholder well-being, 176–81
    and the theory of system, 95–96, *96*
von Carlowitz, Hans Carl, 8–9, 29

Wackernagel, Mathis, 25–26
Walmart, 144 n3
water-related impacts at Cabot Creamery
    Cooperative, 126–29, 214–19, *218*, *219*
what if everybody did it ethic, 96, 155
Wigley, Tom, 199
World Business Council for Sustainable
    Development (WBCSD), 78–80
World Council of Churches, 13–14
WRE350 scenario, 199–202, *200*, *201*

[I]t is tempting, given all the caveats and challenges ... in every report on sustainable development indicators, to be daunted, to postpone the task, to wait for more thinking, more modeling, more agreement – to wait for perfection. While we are waiting for perfection, fisheries are collapsing, greenhouse gases are accumulating, species are disappearing, soils are eroding, forests are overcut, people are suffering. So it is important to get some preliminary indicators out there and into use, the best we can do at the moment. That way, as long as we are willing to evaluate and make corrections, we can start to learn, which is the only way we can ever achieve sustainable development.

Donella Meadows, 1998